"A must-read for all sea kayakers. . . original, practical, and comprehensive. It just might save your life!"

— **Eric Soares**, Commander of the Tsunami Rangers, co-author of *Extreme Sea Kayaking*

"John Lull must have more lives than a cat. He survived when his surf kayak snapped in half on a giant plunging wave at Pacifica, and again when a rock fall from a cliff obliterated his campsite on the rugged Oregon coast . His knack for survival is more than luck, though, and in Sea Kayaking: Safety & Rescue he shares his extensive knowledge of water, weather, and boats. What sets it apart from many other books on kayaking is that it's not just about avoiding hazards but also about how to deal with them."

— **Cathy Chute**, *Sea Kayaker Magazine*, December 2001

"I just bought your book Sea Kayaking: Safety & Rescue. I read pages 99 through 104, went out to the local river, and taught myself to roll in two short afternoons. Now I can roll, reenter and roll, and reenter and roll with paddlefloat assist. I attribute this success to the excellent way you explained the technique."

— **David Lengemann**, Coaster owner, New Jersey

"The step-by-step instructions and illustrations of different rescues are the best I've seen. Unlike many sea kayaking books that cater only to beginners, this one should continue to be useful to paddlers over the years as they try out new and more difficult things."

— **Sarah Ohmann**, Twin Cities Kayaking Association

"Lull's expertise and selfless commitment to paddling shine through in this book."

— **Keith Miller**, President, California Canoe & Kayak, Inc.

"The chapters on training and risk assessment are particularly helpful in developing the confidence, skills and judgment to begin to venture into more varied conditions at sea, and to do so safely."

— **John McCormack**, *KANAWA*, Winter 2001

"No matter what your skill, you will learn something here. Don't fuss over it, just go out and get it and read it."

— **Penny Wells**, *Bay Currents* (Bay Area Sea Kayakers' newsletter)

"This volume deserves an honored spot on the bookshelf of anyone who hefts a hull off a roof rack."

— **Paul McHugh**, *San Francisco Chronicle*

SEA KAYAKING
SAFETY & RESCUE

JOHN LULL

 WILDERNESS PRESS • BERKELEY

FIRST EDITION July 2001
Second printing September 2002

Photos and illustrations by author except where otherwise indicated
Page and cover design by Larry B. Van Dyke
Page composition by Archetype Typography

Front cover: *Stern Carry at Pillar Point, northern California coast,* © 2001 Michael Powers
Back cover: *Ebb tide at the Golden Gate,* © 2001 June Legler

Library of Congress Card Catalog Number 2001026962
ISBN 0-89997-274-8

Manufactured in the United States of America

Published by: **Wilderness Press**
                1200 5th Street
                Berkeley, CA 94710
                (800) 443-7227; FAX (510) 558-1696
                mail@wildernesspress.com
                www.wildernesspress.com

                Contact us for a free catalog.

 Printed on recycled paper, 20% post-consumer waste content

Library of Congress Cataloging-in-Publication Data

Lull, John, 1951-
    Sea kayaking safety & rescue / John Lull.—1st ed.
        p. cm.
    Includes bibliographical references and index.
    ISBN 0-89997-274-8
    1. Sea kayaking—Safety measures—Handbooks, manuals, etc. 2. Rescue work—Handbooks,
manuals, etc.   I. Title: Sea kayaking safety and rescue.   II. Title.

    GV788.5 . L85 2001
    797.1′224′0289—dc21

                                                                2001026962

CONTENTS

BE A SAFE KAYAKER

Kayaking is an activity that must be learned by doing. No book can be expected to replace on-water instruction, practice, and kayaking experience. This book provides guidance and important safety information, but the ultimate responsibility for safety lies with the reader and not with the author or publisher.

ACKNOWLEDGEMENTS

This book could not have been written without the help, support, and contributions of many individuals. I would like to thank, en masse, all the kayakers with whom I have shared adventures on the water over the past 20 years, including members of the San Francisco Bay Area Sea Kayakers. You are far too numerous to list here, but you all know who you are.

In particular, I thank Derek Hutchinson, who gave me my first official kayaking lesson; Frank Ducker, my first kayaking mentor; Penny Wells, John Jeppesen, John Dixon, and Andy Yun for so many great kayaking experiences during my formative years as a paddler; Bonnie Brill, whose entertaining mishaps provided fodder for this book; and, most of all, my domestic associate, June Legler, who had more kayaking adventures with me than she really wanted.

I am indebted to all of my fellow Tsunami Rangers, with whom I have learned most of what I know about the wilder aspects of sea kayaking. I especially thank the following Tsunami Rangers: Eric Soares and Jim Kakuk, super sea kayakers, who introduced me to the art of paddling ocean rock gardens; Dave Whalen who showed me just how much abuse a kevlar kayak can take; Debrah Volturno, my favorite kayaking co-instructor and one of the finest paddlers I know; Tim Sullivan for his cheer in the face of misadventure; Haruo Hasegawa and Bill Collins, who are always a pleasure to kayak with; and Michael Powers, who contributed most of the photographs for this book.

June Legler, Eric Soares, Jim Kakuk, Bo Barnes, Penny Wells, Grace Iannotti, and Kenny Howell also contributed excellent photographs. Debrah Volturno contributed photographs and illustrations.

I thank *San Francisco Chronicle* outdoor writer and expert kayaker Paul McHugh for writing the forward to this book; Keith Miller, President of California Canoe & Kayak (CCK), for helping me to refine my whitewater kayaking skills and for keeping me employed over the years as a professional paddler;

Kenny Howell, Sea Kayak Program Director at CCK, with whom I have worked and paddled for the past few years; Will Nordby and Andy Cominos for collaborating with me on two kayaking videos which provided a foundation for much of this book; Ralph Diaz, for insights on paddling in boat traffic; and the brilliant sea kayak designers Matt and Cam Broze, of Mariner Kayaks, who have always been generous with their advice.

Finally, I thank all the staff at Wilderness Press for their editing and design expertise, particularly Larry Van Dyke for his book design; Jannie Dresser, whose editing and organizational skills helped make this book readable; Tom Winnett for his concise editing; and Mike Jones, who approached me with the idea for this book.

FOREWORD

The John Lull I know is a very funny guy. A twinkle in his eye appears to be standard equipment, no matter what he's doing . . . blowing tenor sax in a blues band, or shredding glassy waves at his home break, Pillar Point, in his hard-railed Mega Rio surf kayak.

That makes it a bit startling to see that he's written such a sober book. Of course, that air of sobriety is derived from a great many sobering experiences. As Lull himself says, "I didn't learn much of this the easy way."

His two decades afloat began by taking a flimsy inflatable down a Class IV stretch of Northern California's Yuba River. This is a recipe for turning yourself into the creamy filling in a vinyl eclair. But he survived that fearsome introduction to paddle sports, and went on to achieve many other adventures in rivers, on bays and out upon the mother of all aquadynamic instructors: the Northern Pacific ocean. En route, he's achieved renown in the paddling community as one of the most skilled of a memorable group of coastal fun hogs, the Tsunami Rangers.

I've competed with Lull in open ocean sea kayak races and kayak surfing contests, and can report him as a formidable antagonist in both. He's strong and willing, and sports a boldness mildly restrained by wisdom.

I think my best line on this new book . . . the distillation of Lull's years in the cockpit . . . is that Lull has thrashed himself in strong winds, heavy current and huge waves so you won't have to. Until humankind develops the art of genetic tailoring to the point that we can award ourselves sets of gills on demand, risk and danger will be woven just as deeply into water sports as joy and beauty are. The trick is minimizing the former in order to heighten appreciation of the latter.

In helping folks familiarize themselves with this trick through the written word, Mr. Lull has no current peer. In crafting this volume, he's drawn not only on his extensive experience both as an adventuring kayaker and paddle sports instructor, but also his scientific background. He's got a master's degree in geology, and deployed that expertise in ten years of work with the U.S. Geological Survey in Menlo Park. That scientific discipline has bestowed upon him an ability to think analytically and write clearly.

He's applied those skills to reporting on state-of-the-art techniques for paddling safety, and all of us get to be the beneficiary. I myself have been flung about in rivers and seas since the mid-1970s, and I can assert that there are plenty of things in this book about which I had no clue prior to reading it. Things I heartily wish I had known prior to attempting clumsy self-rescues before getting washed onto a reef by heavy swells.

Of course, safety and rescue techniques just remain theory until they are learned and practiced, and I urge readers to take Lull's recommendation to do so seriously. It's far better to have a well-practiced expertise and not need it, than need it and not have it.

Paddle sports . . . especially sea kayaking . . . are growth industries not only in the U.S. but across the globe. The more people who learn and utilize good procedures, the fewer tragedies will occur to cast a pall over what can and should be a delightful if challenging activity.

I must report that there's a trend notable especially in the whitewater-running world, for paddlers to attempt daredevil runs and stunts with a minimum of training and experience, and nary a scrap of expertise in safety and rescue technique. This trend may hugely advance the process of natural selection, but it does nothing to enhance our sport. In such a milieu, Lull strikes a mighty blow for common sense.

It's my pleasure to write this foreword for a book that I feel is destined to become a modern classic in the paddle sports genre. This volume deserves an honored spot on the bookshelf of anyone who hefts a hull off a roof rack. Once its lessons are internalized, the reader should see a marked improvement in skills, judgment and (correspondingly) confidence. Lull's prose is lucid in the best sense of the word: It sheds a cascade of light upon its topic.

I only note . . . with considerable dismay on my part . . . that now it looks like I'll have to compete against Lull in the writing realm as well.

— Paul McHugh, Outdoors Editor,
San Francisco Chronicle

INTRODUCTION

Sea Kayaking Myths and Reality

Sea kayaking is often depicted as an idyllic excursion, usually on a mirror-calm, beach-fringed sea surrounded by lofty mountain peaks. In this Eden, the wind never blows, waves never form, tidal currents don't exist, and the sky is always blue. Paddlers drift along, taking a stroke now and then, but mostly resting their paddle across the cockpit as they gaze out at whale spouts or leaping dolphins. If you think I exaggerate, just look at any sea-kayaking calendar or trip brochure. Or walk into a kayak shop and mention your fear of whitewater and the Eskimo roll; in most cases, you'll be escorted immediately to the

A common image of sea kayaking. Although conditions can be as mild as shown here, this is a deceptive portrayal. The sea state can change rapidly from flat water to rough water, depending on wind, waves, and tide.

"touring" kayak section and told you won't even have to get your face wet in a sea kayak.

Curiously enough, this view of sea kayaking as a benign activity is recent. When I started sea kayaking in the mid-80s, venturing out to sea in such a tiny craft was considered a fairly serious adventure. The new calm-water perception of sea kayaking has likely attracted many more people to the sport. Unfortunately, it can also lead the unwary paddler into big trouble.

As is true of any myth, a kernel of reality lies in the rosy vision of idyllic paddling. On our planet, there are thousands of square miles of protected waterways where conditions can be exactly as described above. The problem is that the situation can change rapidly, even on protected waters. The Inland Passage of British Columbia and Southeast Alaska is a prime example. Most of the Inland Passage provides relatively easy, flat-water paddling. However, gale-force winds can arise with little warning, and the area is subject to strong tidal currents. In more exposed waters, such as San Francisco Bay and the Pacific Ocean, conditions can range from calm, flat water to

Reality check: Sea kayakers must be prepared to handle wind and waves. These conditions are typical in open water anywhere.

raging seas, sometimes on the same day. In the marine environment, change is the rule, not the exception. Therefore, to paddle safely, the kayaker must develop a realistic view of sea kayaking and become competent in a wide range of conditions.

Sea kayaking is an incredibly varied activity and is enjoyed in many different geographic settings. It is popular in widely diverse environments such as Florida, the Gulf Coast of Texas, the Atlantic seaboard, Alaska, Hawaii, the Pacific Northwest, the California coast, the Great Lakes, the British Isles, Japan, the coast of Australia, Greenland (where it probably originated), and in bays, lakes, and large rivers just about everywhere. I define sea kayaking in very comprehensive terms as *paddling any kayak (including surf kayaks and whitewater kayaks) anywhere in the marine environment, or paddling a sea kayak in any body of water.* This definition encompasses such diverse activities as kayak surfing, expedition paddling, calm-water excursions, storm-sea skiing, exploring sea caves and ocean rock gardens, surfing tide rips, island hopping, wildlife viewing, fishing, and simply cruising on the open sea.

Sea Kayaking Safety & Rescue focuses on the safety issues of sea kayaking. The book is especially relevant for those with a sense of adventure who want to go beyond the tamer aspects of sea kayaking and explore the sea in all its moods. A number of excellent sea-kayaking books are on the market, most of which either act as guidebooks or deal with basic technique. One book, *Sea Kayaker's Deep Trouble* by Matt Broze and George Gronseth, focuses on safety and outlines various tragedies and near-tragedies accompanied by a safety analysis for each. All of the instruction manuals and guidebooks have something to say about safety, of course, but most of them discuss safety in terms of hazard avoidance. This approach is especially good for the beginner, who needs to know what the hazards are and how best to avoid them.

In *Sea Kayaking Safety & Rescue* I take safety a step farther and discuss how to *deal* with hazards, not just *avoid* them. The best approach to safety at sea is to learn how to handle what the sea can throw at you; that way you are not caught off-guard or unprepared when conditions change suddenly during that long crossing or when that rogue wave hits you. Such an approach will not only increase your safety, but will also expand your paddling horizons and heighten your enjoyment on the water.

The best approach to safety at sea is to learn how to handle what the sea can throw at you.

A sea kayak is a wonderfully seaworthy craft, designed to handle everything from flat water to storm seas. The safety limitation is normally not the boat or the tempestuous seas; rather, it is the paddler. With the appropriate skills and experience, a sea kayaker can paddle safely in very wild water. In this book I outline the basic safety principles and safety equipment for kayaking in the marine environment (or in any large body of water). I also discuss the characteristics of specific kayaking domains and identify the skills a kayaker must have to navigate each domain successfully. I detail important rescue techniques that work in rough water, and discuss the Eskimo roll, towing methods, backup strategies, weather, safety in surf and rock gardens, and group dynamics. Finally, I examine how to assess risk and how to pursue a safe progression of training and practice.

Paddling a kayak is not especially difficult, but learning to deal with real conditions in a highly changeable environment takes time and requires much practice. If you rush your learning, it is all too easy to get into a situation beyond your skill level. By mastering all the basic kayaking skills, acquiring a complete set of backup skills, and gradually working up to more challenging paddling conditions, you will gain the judgment and expertise that will enhance your enjoyment of sea-kayaking activities and minimize risk. With these goals in mind, let's get on the water!

Using This Book

Sea Kayaking Safety & Rescue is an instructional manual and a reference book, covering safety issues in sea kayaking. Much of this information is not covered in the basic sea-kayaking books now available. I recommend you read the entire text to get a good overview of the subject matter, then return to specific chapters for more detailed study. The information here will become clearer as you gain kayaking experience. For example, after a few sessions in the surf, if you re-read the chapters dealing with surf kayaking, many of the concepts there will make more sense than they did on the first reading. As you learn the various rescues and other techniques, you can return to the book for review.

Almost everything I describe is based on direct experience. This book is not mere theory; techniques herein have been tested and found to work in a wide variety of conditions. After 20 years of kayaking in many different environments, from the ocean to inland waterways, I've gained a wealth of experience that I can share with you. I've paddled in many different group settings, including club trips, adventures with the Tsunami Rangers (a small, tightly-knit group of surf and open-coast kayakers), and many aimless wanderings on the sea with anyone who was willing and able to accompany me. After numerous incidents and a few close calls, I now have considerable respect for the sea and have tried to learn from every mistake I've made or witnessed. I've gained further insight into technical and safety issues through teaching and designing a variety of sea-kayaking classes for California Canoe and Kayak and the American Canoe Association.

To get the most out of the book, you should relate what you have read to your own kayaking experiences. Test the techniques as they are described and find out what works for you. If you apply the concepts in this book in a systematic fashion, you will improve your kayaking skills and minimize the risk. Consequently, you will increase your safety and enjoyment on the water.

Relate what you have read to your own kayaking experiences.

MICHAEL POWERS

Endurance and good physical condition is important for sea kayakers, especially when paddling out through surf, or into wind and current.

CHAPTER 1.
BUILDING A SAFETY FOUNDATION

Kayaking safety depends on a number of factors. This chapter explores some basic principles of safe paddling and the reduction of risk. Understanding these principles will help you evaluate your own skill level and decide what training to undertake. Then you can make intelligent decisions regarding where and when to paddle. Your safety requires more than sheer luck and avoidance of potential hazards. You must be prepared for adverse conditions. Though it is not unusual for a kayaker to get out on the water and dodge a bullet without even realizing it, you want to stack all the odds in your favor. Mastering each of the following principles will help you to do this.

Getting Into Shape

Kayaks are human-powered craft. For many, this is a real attraction because kayaking is a great way to get in shape and stay in shape. The best way to get in shape for paddling is to paddle, but it doesn't hurt to do some cross-training in other activities. Bicycling, hiking, and skiing are good forms of exercise that provide the aerobic conditioning you need for kayaking. Almost any kind of exercise is valuable. It is also important to stretch before and after paddling.

Endurance and the ability to paddle with power are important safety factors. You should learn to paddle efficiently, but in many situations substantial physical exertion is also required, as when you have to paddle through heavy weather or across a strong current; you might even need to tow someone else in such conditions. When punching out through a major surf zone, you may have to call on your reserve strength, and if you end up in the water swimming, you will certainly need to be in good shape.

Hopefully, you won't find yourself in any of these situations as a beginner. If you are new to

Be prepared for adverse conditions.

kayaking, take it easy at first. Paddling 2 or 3 miles on a calm day will be enough for your first few excursions. In time, you can work up to paddling greater distances in rougher weather.

Developing Skills

The more skilled you are at handling your kayak, the greater your capability to deal with wind, rough water, current, surf, and unexpected situations. Your skills can sometimes make up for bad decisions or poor judgment. One thing is certain: If you get into conditions well beyond your skill level, you are taking an unacceptable risk and will likely get into trouble. This happens commonly to novice kayakers when they venture out with little or no training.

Basic paddling skills can be placed into three main categories:

- Boat control (good stroke technique, balance, and edge control)

- Recovery skills (braces and the Eskimo roll)

- Rescue techniques

These basic skills form a foundation for the following more advanced skills:

- Handling wind and rough water

- Handling current and tide rips

- Surf zone techniques

- Navigation

These skills are very important because they allow you to paddle safely beyond calm water. More specific skills are needed for paddling ocean rock gardens and sea caves. In upcoming chapters I will discuss some direct applications of the various kayaking skills and demonstrate how they contribute to your safety.

If you put in the time and energy, most kayaking skills are relatively easy to master. You will need competent instruction. If you're lucky you can learn from a patient friend who has good kayaking and *teaching* abilities. Otherwise, seek reputable, professional instruction. You will also need time on the water to practice your skills. Ideally, paddle with more experienced kayakers who can act as good role models and mentors.

If you are new to kayaking, take it easy at first.

Learning to kayak is largely a kinesthetic experience. You need to train your muscles to feel the right movements. In this age of instant gratification, it is easy to get frustrated if you don't see immediate results. Allow yourself the time to learn.

Keith Miller, a first-rate kayaking instructor with many years in the paddle sports business, once told me that learning to kayak requires "CCR," or "Commitment, Concentration, and Relaxation." You need to start with a *commitment* to learning. Decide you will do what is necessary to master the skills. Stay with it and don't give up. *Concentration* is needed for skill development; to improve, you must focus on each task. This part actually isn't too difficult. Your mind won't wander when you're upside down and underwater trying to figure out how to roll, or when facing a wall of surf about to crash into you. Maintain this focus throughout your time on the water.

The most difficult part of CCR, at least initially, is staying *relaxed*. Stay loose and allow your muscles to feel what's going on. If you tense up, you'll have a difficult time learning to kayak. A relaxed paddling style is common to all good kayakers. If you apply CCR, you will learn, but no one can do it for

MICHAEL POWERS

Get competent instruction.

Refine your paddling skills by doing lots of kayaking.

Good judgment is always important when sea kayaking. In the situation pictured here, the paddler must use judgment and timing to choose a safe route through the waves and rocks.

The key is to gain experience without getting into serious trouble.

you. An instructor provides technique and feedback; *you* provide the CCR.

With good instruction, practice, and time on the water, your skill level will increase significantly. As a result, you'll have a lot more fun and can start paddling in more challenging conditions with a reasonable degree of safety.

Acquiring Good Judgment

The most important, yet hardest tool to acquire for safe kayaking is good judgment, but how do you develop it? Reg Lake, a pioneering whitewater and sea kayaker, put it this way: "You learn good judgment from experience; you gain experience by exercising poor judgment." This may sound like Catch-22, but it points to the close relationship between experience and judgment. Until you have some experience with different conditions, it is hard to make good decisions about where and when to paddle. The key is to gain experience without getting into serious trouble.

To some extent, your basic kayaking skills will help you resolve problems that result from making bad judgment calls. For example, an Eskimo roll might prevent a nasty swim in cold, rough water after you have misjudged your ability to handle a difficult surf zone. However, there is a limit to relying solely on skills, especially when they are not fully developed. Also, there are situations where the most finely honed skills won't help. The forces of nature are much more powerful than you or I. You must recognize what conditions you can handle and what conditions you can't.

Once you have some basic skills, find a way to push your limits and gain experience without taking major risks. Find a controlled setting where the consequences of failure are not serious. Ask a competent instructor to take you to a safe but challenging, environment where you can practice your newfound skills, one who can back you up if you have problems. Eventually, you'll want to venture out with a couple of trusted companions, *sans* instructor, to test your limits. Look for an area with an *easy bailout*; an area where you could get ashore quickly if you had to, or where you could drift or swim into a safe place. If you want to practice in the wind, look for an *onshore* wind (one that blows toward the shore).

When I started kayaking, instruction for sea kayaking was not readily available. My two partners and I inadvertently stumbled onto a safe method for practicing in wind and rough water. We found a point of land with sheltered water on one side, and a fairly strong onshore wind and choppy seas on the other. We really didn't know how the turbulent conditions would affect us in our kayaks, so we tentatively poked around the point into the wind and held position to see what would happen. When we found we were able to adapt to these conditions, we worked our way out a little farther, turned in different directions, and got a feel for the wind and waves. Whenever we got nervous, we simply retreated back into calm water to relax. After a couple of these practice sessions, we knew we could handle the conditions and began taking trips out into the open water well beyond the point. The process was a safe way to gain some experience. It also gave us a benchmark against which to judge similar conditions in the future; we knew the effect of a 20-knot wind and could estimate how we might fare in stronger wind.

You cannot gain good judgment and experience overnight; it takes time. Take an incremental approach by gradually working up to more challenging conditions. You will undoubtedly exercise some poor judgment along the way and thus gain new experience. Whenever something goes wrong, analyze why and how it happened. Figure out what you could have done to prevent the problem or to deal more effectively with its contingencies. Ultimately, your ability to make sound and safe decisions on the water will depend on how much you have learned from all your paddling experiences.

Whenever something goes wrong, analyze why and how it happened.

Mastering Seamanship

Seamanship extends beyond the basic ability to paddle and control your kayak to include an intimate knowledge of the sea, and an ability to operate safely there. An important component of achieving seamanship is having knowledge of the local weather, potential range in wave size, currents, and coastline features. Good seamanship really amounts to a complete integration of your kayaking skills, experience, and judgment with your knowledge of the marine environment.

You mostly learn seamanship from the sea itself. All that is required is that you *pay attention* when you're on the water and absorb what is happening around you. You can enhance the process by practicing your basic kayaking skills, learning how to read charts and tide tables, and by working on navigation skills. In time, you will dramatically increase your safety as you learn the lessons of the sea.

Managing Risk

Kayaking on the sea involves a certain amount of risk which is part of the attraction of sea kayaking. Risk adds spice to many activities. However, too much risk is simply unacceptable. Safe kayaking largely depends on the ability to assess the potential risks associated with various situations and keep them to a minimum. Your ability to manage risk will increase if you apply all the safety principles discussed in this chapter.

Risk management requires matching your skills and experience to sea conditions. An experienced and skilled kayaker may be assuming far less risk in storm seas than a first-time paddler with no training out on open water in moderate wind. Dealing with risk is a broad subject and will be covered in greater detail in Chapter 14.

Facing and Managing Fear

Fear can have a positive or a negative effect on your safety, depending on its intensity. A natural protective mechanism, minor fear or anxiety can raise your awareness and help keep you out of trouble. A higher degree of fear can lead to panic, which is likely to exacerbate existing problems and interfere with executing a solution. There are three general levels of fear.

Level 1: Lack of fear

Fearlessness can be dangerous if it is the result of complete ignorance about the risks involved in particular situations. This state of mind is analogous to having no pain receptors; you would sustain considerable injury picking up a hot skillet if you couldn't feel pain. Many paddlers have found themselves in serious trouble because they were unaware of potential hazards. A typical situation involves novice kayakers who launch in calm water and take off on a crossing, not realizing that conditions will be far different out in the main channel when the afternoon wind picks up. The probable result will be an immediate jump from Fear Level 1 to Fear Level 3 (see below) with potentially tragic consequences.

When lack of fear is based on experience, high skill level, and relatively benign conditions, there is no problem. Relax and enjoy the scenery. However, even skilled kayakers should be wary of complacency. Inattentiveness and overconfidence at sea can reduce your safety in certain circumstances, especially in areas with breaking waves.

Level 2: Minor fear or excitement

Excitement is usually accompanied by an adrenaline "rush" (what many paddlers live for) derived from a sense of danger and the knowledge that there is some risk. This state of mind can improve performance and safety as long as the risk hasn't been underestimated. A mild sense of fear can result in making safe decisions; it provides a warning, which, if heeded, will keep you from doing something foolish.

Level 3: Intense fear

High levels of fear usually lead to debilitating panic, poor decision-making, or inaction. Performance is hampered; the paddler may freeze up to the point of incapacitation. Overwhelming fear usually results from getting caught in unfamiliar conditions that tax the paddler's level of skill. If you find yourself in such a state, acknowledge the fear, try to relax, and assess your situation. Then make the best decision you can and *act*. By acting, you can usually reduce the fear and hopefully will work your way out of the situation. If you're dealing with another paddler in a state of panic, offer directions and encouragement in a calm manner. If the paddler is really incapacitated or can't keep from capsizing, you'll have to use a rafted tow (see "Towing," Chapter 9).

Obviously, it is best to avoid getting into any situation that will result in extreme fear. Be prepared for the conditions in which you'll be paddling. For your initial forays into new or unfamiliar conditions, choose a controlled setting, with easy bailouts nearby.

Adapting to Changing Conditions

The marine environment is subject to numerous variables, including weather, waves, tides, and

Even skilled kayakers should be wary of complacency.

currents, and these phenomena are always in flux. The sea constantly changes. In fact, major changes can occur in a matter of minutes. For example, most sea kayakers have experienced the sudden onslaught of a strong wind and the drastic changes that result. Tidal currents are reasonably predictable, but it is amazing how much the scene can change as a current builds. In ocean rock gardens and surf zones, the situation changes with every large wave set.

This dynamic behavior of the sea adds charm and interest to sea kayaking. But to paddle safely in such an environment, you need to be aware and capable of handling the full spectrum of conditions that can occur. During the learning process, be careful about where you paddle; make sure you have a bailout in case the situation gets too challenging. With time, your skills will increase, you'll gain a deeper understanding of the sea, and you can range farther and wider on your sea-kayaking journeys.

Gaining Self-Reliance

In marked contrast with rafting, where inexperienced paddlers can be carried as passengers through relatively difficult whitewater, sea kayaking demands self-reliance. In a kayak, you are the captain and crew; you must be able to pilot your own craft. No one can paddle your kayak for you.

This does not mean that you are as safe paddling solo as you are in the company of a group of competent paddlers. With a group, you have a few more options if something goes wrong. Assisted rescues are possible and—in a worst-case scenario—there is usually someone who can summon additional help. However, you should not rely on the group for your safety. In difficult conditions paddlers commonly get separated from one another. In rough, windy weather, your partners may be stretched to their own limits and unable to assist you. When this happens, you are essentially paddling solo and *must* be able to take care of yourself.

When embarking on a group trip, as opposed to a professionally-guided trip, where the guide has some responsibility for your safety, ask yourself if you could manage the paddle solo? If the answer is no, you need to reexamine the risks. The question is *could* you do it solo, not *would* you, a subtle but significant difference. Choosing not to paddle solo is not the same as being incapable of it. If you feel incapable of

No one can paddle your kayak for you.

doing a paddle without group support, you may be putting too big a burden on the group, and this can increase the risks for everyone.

How can you become self-reliant? The first step is to develop your kayaking skills, including self-rescues and the Eskimo roll (see "The Eskimo Roll," Chapter 7), under competent instruction. Gain experience by paddling in easy conditions first, gradually working up to more challenging ones. Self-reliance is achieved by mastering your kayaking skills as a whole, and by incorporating all the other basic safety principles into your repertoire. With all these tools in place, you can paddle safely in a wide range of conditions.

Self-reliance is achieved by mastering your kayaking skills as a whole, and by incorporating all the other basic safety principles into your repertoire.

California coastline.

CHAPTER 2.
SEA-KAYAKING DOMAINS

Understanding the environment in which you kayak is an important part of seamanship and risk management. If you don't anticipate conditions, it is very difficult to make any decisions regarding what is safe and what is hazardous. The fact that sea kayaks can be used in a wide variety of environments compounds this problem because it is all too easy to paddle into conditions beyond your skill level. I'll refer to the various paddling environments as "sea-kayaking domains."

There are at least six sea-kayaking domains including protected waterways, inland marine waterways, open water & open-water crossings, open ocean, surf zones, and ocean rock gardens. Although divisions between domains are somewhat arbitrary and overlap considerably, there are clear differences among them. For example, the open ocean and a backwater slough are very different environments. The last two domains, surf zone and ocean rock gardens, are clearly part of the ocean. However, they are treated as separate domains because they have unique characteristics that make them different from the open ocean.

A general understanding of the characteristics of each domain will allow you to make some inferences regarding the kayaking risks in each. Following each domain description is a "Skills Needed" section to help you determine which skills are important for your safety. You will gain a more complete knowledge of these domains after spending time paddling in them; first-hand experience is, of course, the best way to learn.

Protected Waterway

A protected waterway is a relatively small body of water that rarely develops waves larger than ripples or small wavelets. On the rare occasion when strong winds blow, it is easy to get ashore quickly. Lakes with less than a mile or two of *fetch* (the unim-

Protected waterway.

peded distance over the water that the wind can blow), rivers with slow-to-moderate current, inland sloughs, small estuaries, and protected harbors fit into this category, as do protected waters in small bays or inlets connected to larger, more exposed bodies of water.

Protected waters provide wonderful opportunities for exploration, wildlife viewing, fishing, and camping. They are also great places for beginning kayakers to work on basic skills in a reasonably safe environment.

Skills Needed

Only the most basic skills are needed to paddle in protected waters. However, it is a good idea to take at least one beginning sea-kayaking class covering strokes and rescues before paddling anywhere. Beginning classes are usually held in easy, flat water, giving you the opportunity to learn in a safe environment. You'll have a lot more fun if you know some basic strokes and can maneuver the kayak. It is also important to learn rescues; you are not safe out on the water in a kayak unless you know what to do if your craft capsizes.

Inland Marine Waterway

Inland marine waterway.

An inland marine waterway is a semi-protected embayment or other partly enclosed area along a coastline. Examples include fjords, most moderately-sized estuaries, parts of the Chilean coast, and the vast Inland Passage of British Columbia and Alaska. These areas are largely protected from ocean swell and surf, and during periods of calm weather can provide many miles of relatively easy paddling. However, conditions can change rapidly; it is best to prepare for strong wind, cold water, and tidal current. In some areas, currents can exceed 6 knots.

Skills Needed

To paddle safely in an inland marine waterway, you'll need good stroke technique for boat control in wind and choppy seas, well-practiced rescues (assisted and solo), navigation skills, and the ability to deal with current and with *tide rips* (areas of rough water, analogous to river rapids, where the current encounters underwater obstacles or accelerates around a headland). To deal with tidal currents, you need the skill to *ferry* across the current, to paddle upstream using eddies close to shore, and to cross an *eddyline* (a shear zone between the main current and an eddy). An Eskimo roll may not be essential, but you'll be much safer if you can roll.

Open Water and Open-Water Crossing

Open water denotes a relatively large body of water with a fetch of several miles or more. Examples include the Sea of Cortez in Mexico, the Great Lakes, and large estuaries such as San Francisco Bay. Wind is common in such areas, and the long fetch will result in the formation of relatively large seas (local wind waves). Seas can reach from 3 to 8 feet in height. Tidal current can also be a major factor.

Open-water crossing.

An *open-water crossing* (an area of water stretching out to an island or across a wide channel) of 3 miles or more has substantial exposure with no bailouts. The lack of bailouts is particularly important because the paddler must deal with whatever conditions arise during the crossing. You can pick a time for crossing when weather and tidal currents are favorable, but there is never any guarantee that the conditions won't deteriorate. Before attempting any long crossing, be sure you have the skills to handle wind and waves.

If you are a novice paddler or are unfamiliar with the area, forgo any major crossings and paddle along the shoreline instead (assuming there are beaches and other bailouts available). Postpone open-water crossings until you know you are prepared.

Skills Needed

You'll need the same skills that are required for inland waterways, but because of the greater exposure, you'll have to be comfortable in larger seas. Good balance, braces, and an Eskimo roll for backup will increase your safety considerably.

Open Ocean

When I discuss the open ocean, I refer mainly to the exposed coastal areas most familiar to me. My experience has been primarily on the Pacific Ocean along the coasts of northern California and southern Oregon. This region is known for its rugged shoreline, large waves, chilly water, and spectacular scenery. Some ocean coastlines have smaller surf and

Open ocean.

warmer water. Others have a more extreme, colder climate. Although most of the general principles regarding safe kayaking on the ocean are universal, you may need to amend the ideas in this discussion for regions that are significantly different from the coastlines of northern California and southern Oregon.

The open ocean has many of the same characteristics as the "Open Water and Open-Water Crossing" domain, but everything is on a larger scale. The wind can blow unimpeded for hundreds of miles, and seas can pile up to impressive heights, especially during a storm. Paddling in open water on the ocean in an area where landings are difficult or impossible is similar to making an open-water crossing: if you can't land, you have no bailouts, even though you may be close to shore.

Unlike in inland waterways, tidal current is not usually an issue in the open ocean, unless you are paddling near the mouth of an estuary or a large river, where the current will flow in (*flood*) or out (*ebb*) of the estuary, depending on the tide. Tidal currents can also form in straits between large islands. The *height* of the tide is important in regions of the ocean relatively near shore because water depth determines where waves break. For example, at low tide, waves will usually break farther offshore than at high tide.

The primary distinguishing characteristic of the open-ocean domain is the presence of *swell*. Swell forms when wind-driven waves move away from their source and travel across the ocean. These waves move at considerable speeds (from 15 to 20 knots or more) and vary greatly in height. Swell does not present much of a problem in deep water offshore; your kayak will simply move up and down as the waves pass by. However, when the waves encounter shallow water, they steepen and break. This can happen over a shelving beach, creating a surf zone, or in areas of shallow reefs and submerged rocks. It's possible to get caught by a breaking wave when paddling close to shore or around headlands if you don't stay alert, because different-sized waves break in different water depths (larger waves break in deeper water).

The ocean is subject to both seas and swell. It is important to understand the difference between these two. *Seas* are derived from local wind. If you are paddling in steep seas, either it will be windy where you are, or the wind will have subsided recently; seas don't last long once the wind has died. *Swell*, on the other hand, is a remnant of distant storms; waves move out of the storm center and travel many miles away from the winds that caused them. Swell features smooth waves with relatively long wavelength (distance from crest to crest), while seas are short, steep, choppy waves. In windy conditions on the ocean, seas are superimposed on the swell, creating a very dynamic situation. A typical marine-weather report will state the sizes of both the swell and the seas; you'll want to know both.

Given the variables of swell, seas, tide, and wind, you can expect conditions on the ocean to change considerably every day. This is especially important to keep in mind when on a multi-day excursion. Every year I spend about a week with my fellow Tsunami Rangers exploring the open coast. On none of these trips have we seen conditions remain stable for more than a day or two. In most cases, we have seen the wind, seas, and swell either increase or decrease dramatically over the course of a few days. To be safe, you must be ready for these changing conditions.

Skills Needed

To paddle safely in the ocean, you'll need good boat-handling skills, the ability to balance in rough water, a reliable Eskimo roll, and a command of reflexive braces, solo and assisted rescues, navigation skills, and basic kayak-surfing skills.

Learn most of these skills in more protected waters before venturing out on the open ocean. The best way to learn surfing skills is to get some initial instruction, and then practice in *small* surf, working up gradually to larger waves. I can't overstress the importance of surf-zone skills for ocean kayakers (see "Surf Zone," below). Competence in surf will prepare you for rough water at sea and will allow you to launch and land safely.

Surf Zone

As ocean swell approaches the coast and encounters shallow water, the waves begin to be affected by the sea floor. When the water depth is approximately twice the height of a wave, the wave begins to steepen. As they continue to move into shallower water, the waves steepen further and then break, releasing their energy. The resulting surf zone is one of the most dramatic and dynamic parts of the

Given the variables of swell, seas, tide, and wind, you can expect conditions on the ocean to change considerably every day.

Surf zone.

ocean. Kayakers who wish to paddle safely on the ocean need to learn how to deal with the surf environment.

Surf-zone characteristics vary considerably depending on wave size, sea-floor profile, wave type, tide height, swell direction, protection from offshore rocks and reefs, and weather. Larger wave sets alternate with smaller sets, and the overall wave size varies from day to day. Where waves approach a steep beach, they tend to break suddenly and explosively; these are called *plunging waves*. On gently sloping beaches, the waves break more gradually (*spilling waves*) and are easier to handle in a kayak. A beach that faces directly into the prevailing swell will obviously be more exposed to the wave energy than will a beach that faces away from the swell and is protected by headlands. You will eventually recognize different wave types and how to handle them through experience in the surf.

For ocean kayakers, the surf zone serves several purposes, operating as a playground, a gateway to the ocean, and a training ground.

- **A playground for the kayak surfer**

It is impossible to describe the sensation that comes from flying across the face of a wave in a kayak. You just have to experience it to understand why kayak surfing is such a compelling and addictive activity. But kayak surfing also has many practical applications for the sea kayaker. It is the single most important skill for the ocean kayaker. Having this skill will increase your safety and ability to handle rough water anywhere. Your surfing skill will come in very handy when you encounter rough seas or have to land on an exposed beach.

- **A gateway to the ocean for the coastal kayaker**

To paddle safely on the open coast, you'll need to know how to launch and land through the surf zone. Otherwise you'll have to rely on finding protected launching and landing sites, which may be many miles apart, seriously diminishing your bailout potential. Whenever you get close to shore or a reef, there is a good chance you'll encounter breaking waves. Your ability to read and handle such waves is crucial.

Landing in surf requires *surfing* and *wave-reading skills*. I've heard it said that sea kayakers don't really need to know how to surf; they just need to know how to launch and land. This is inaccurate—in many situations, to land effectively and safely, you need to surf in to shore. Trying to outrun waves that are moving at 15 knots is not very practical. There are situations where the surf zone is narrow and the *windows* (periods of flat water) between wave sets are long enough for you to sprint in, but they are rare. It is far more efficient, and safer, to use the wave energy and get a free ride to shore. As a bonus, it is also fun.

- **A training ground for developing rough-water skills**

There is no better place to learn how to handle rough water than the surf zone. A surf zone with small to moderate waves and a gently sloping beach meets the requirements of a controlled training situation; you can get ashore quickly and easily. It is far safer to learn how to handle rough water in the surf close to shore, than in storm seas two miles offshore.

In addition to the ocean paddler, surf training benefits the open-water kayaker. On my first kayaking trip in the Sea of Cortez, as a relative novice, I made a 3-mile crossing in rough seas. The experi-

The surf zone can be used as a playground for kayak surfers.

Sea kayakers on the open coast must be ready to cope with breaking waves. You can learn how in the surf zone.

ence was intimidating, and I was more than a little nervous being out there with my underdeveloped skills. I went back a year later, after getting some experience in the surf, and made the same crossing in even rougher conditions. This time it was fun and exhilarating; I felt confident and wasn't the least bit nervous. Spending time learning how to handle waves in the surf had made all the difference.

Surfing skill will also improve your boat control when running downwind. In this situation, the *following seas* (waves coming from behind) tend to lift your stern and push it forward. As your kayak slides down the face of the wave, it is easy to lose control, unless you know how to surf. If you can surf, a strong tailwind and steep following seas are a sheer pleasure, instead of a nightmare. You'll be a lot safer if you can control your kayak.

Skills Needed

Good boat-handling skills, balance, and bracing are important skills for the surf zone. As you spend time in the surf, all of these skills will improve. An Eskimo roll is essential to avoid the frustration and difficulties of repeatedly bailing out and swimming to shore. Finally, strong swimming ability is important as a backup to your roll.

Ocean rock garden on the northern California coast.

Ocean Rock Gardens

An ocean rock garden is formed by the forces of erosion and wave action on a steep, rocky shoreline. The waves sculpt the coastline by attacking zones of weakness, such as fractures and faults, and leave a network of passages through the rocks. The results of this sculpting include hidden coves, sea caves, arches, and sea stacks. A *sea stack* is a large rock that rises well above the waterline like a sentinel guarding the coast. An outer rocky reef studded with sea stacks absorbs wave energy, usually leaving some of the inner coves and passages calm and protected. However, higher tide and larger waves can transform an inner rock garden into a raging cauldron of whitewater.

In ocean rock gardens the interaction of breaking waves, surge, and rocks creates a very dynamic situation. Waves crash into and swirl around the rocks. On shallow, rocky reefs the waves break, forming a surf zone. In deeper areas, waves surge into narrow, constricted channels between rocks. This near-shore zone is an exciting place to paddle, but the hazards increase significantly with increasing wave size. The best time to paddle in rock gardens is when the swell is small.

The ability to navigate rock gardens safely will give you more options when paddling on the open coast. At first glance, a rock garden appears to be a confusing and dangerous welter of waves, rocks, and whitewater. But reasonably safe, navigable passages usually exist; it just takes time and experience to recognize them. Once you can do this, you can get ashore through the rocks and will have more bailouts available. You'll also have an incredible time exploring this unique environment.

Rock gardens present numerous opportunities to play in ocean whitewater. To do this safely requires lots of practice in easy conditions and enough experience to recognize the difference between a play spot and a danger zone. For more information on assessing conditions in rock gardens, see "Safety in Surf and Ocean Rock Gardens," Chapter 13.

Skills Needed

Boat control is extremely important; you need to be able to maneuver your kayak with precision in surging seas and narrow channels between rocks. Working on your strokes (especially draw strokes and other corrective strokes) and your boat lean will pay big dividends here. The ability to read and handle breaking waves, which can be learned in the surf zone, is also very important. Surfing skills are necessary for safe rock-garden paddling. A reliable Eskimo roll is essential, as rescues can be difficult in the rocks.

Once you understand the various domains, you can make intelligent decisions regarding where and when to paddle. As a beginner, stick to the easier, calm-water areas where you can start developing your skills in safety. Gradually work up to more challenging environments. Finally, always be aware that conditions can change quickly in any of the domains.

MICHAEL POWERS

It takes experience to navigate safely in ocean rock gardens.

Conditions can change quickly in any of the domains.

CHAPTER 3.
EQUIPMENT SELECTION AND USE

Equipment is important because your life may depend on it. You need to know what equipment to use for a given situation and be sure it is functional and in good repair. You also need to know how to use all your equipment, especially safety gear, including towlines, flares, and self-rescue devices, like the paddlefloat. Many kayakers take a basic sea-kayaking course, do one paddlefloat self-rescue in calm water, and then stow the paddlefloat away in the kayak, assuming it can be relied upon when necessary. This gives the paddlefloat too much credit — for an example of what can go wrong, see the story of a failed paddlefloat rescue in "Self-Rescues," Chapter 5. To avoid such a situation, test all equipment, and your ability to use it, in realistic conditions. You can count only on gear that you know how to use and have thoroughly tested in a variety of circumstances.

The Kayak and its Components

Your kayak is your lifeline. Actually, this is true for any boat out in open water; if you lose the boat, you could lose your life. The good news about a sea kayak is that a capsize is not (or should not be) a major problem. In this respect, the kayak has a real advantage over other types of boats. Even if you miss your roll and end up in the water, in most cases you can be back in the kayak within a couple of minutes, using an assisted rescue or self-rescue. This is one of the important safety features of a sea kayak, contributing to its *seaworthiness* (the ability to handle tempestuous waters).

Your kayak will remain seaworthy only if you keep it in good repair, with all of its components intact. The standard components are listed below, along with descriptions of various types of kayaks and the outfitting necessary for comfort and boat control.

Test all equipment, and your ability to use it, in realistic conditions.

Neoprene sprayskirt is fitted over the cockpit to keep water out of the boat.

Sprayskirt

The standard *closed-deck* sea kayak is kept watertight by virtue of a sprayskirt and sealed hatches. A *sprayskirt* is a piece of nylon or neoprene material that is worn around your waist; it serves the important function of sealing off the cockpit area. A *sit-on–top* kayak doesn't need a sprayskirt because it has a depression on deck to sit in; it is kept watertight with sealed hatches.

The main benefit of a watertight kayak is that it cannot be swamped in large seas because the water has no way to get in, assuming you keep the sprayskirt sealed. Without this feature, a kayak would be unsafe anywhere except in calm water. I read a story in *Sea Kayaker* magazine a few years ago about a rental operation in the Pacific Northwest that rented kayaks without sprayskirts because of a concern that the clients would get trapped in the boats! Consequently, two paddlers without sprayskirts ended up in serious trouble when their boats swamped and capsized in rough seas.

The sprayskirt should fit properly and be firmly attached so that it doesn't come loose in surf or during a roll. There is no danger of getting trapped in the cockpit because, of course, you will have thoroughly learned how to release the sprayskirt before going anywhere. The real potential for danger lies in wearing a loosely-fitted sprayskirt that pops off the kayak at the worst possible moment. I once watched a friend launch through a wide surf zone with three separate lines of breakers. He punched through the first two lines of smaller waves with no problem, but as he approached the largest breakers, a wave crashed on him and popped his inexpensive nylon sprayskirt. The boat immediately filled with water, and he went swimming. This wouldn't have been a big deal, except there were strong rip currents that kept recycling him back out to sea. By the time he finally made it in, with some assistance, he was cold and exhausted. He bought a high-quality neoprene sprayskirt the next day.

Flotation

Another important safety feature of a kayak is that it retains a certain amount of buoyancy, even after capsizing. This buoyancy can be achieved either with *bulkheads* (watertight walls fore and aft of the cockpit) or with airbags in *both* ends of the kayak.

Most modern sea kayaks come equipped with bulkheads, but airbags work well, provided they are kept fully inflated. Airbags must be large enough to fill the entire stern and bow sections and should be strapped in so they can't be pushed out of the boat after a capsize in surf or rough seas. On an expedition, the airbags can be deflated to make room for waterproof gear bags. The gear bags will function as flotation as long as they fill the empty space entirely. If not, the airbag can be inflated on top of the gear, thus holding it in place and filling excess space.

The importance of buoyancy cannot be overemphasized. A swamped kayak will sink without it. Flotation must be present in both ends of the boat or, if swamped, one end of the kayak will sink, leaving the bow or stern sticking straight up out of the water. This situation, known as "Cleopatra's Needle," makes rescue very awkward, if not impossible. Many of the so-called recreation kayaks do not have adequate flotation. Such boats are not safe unless fitted with bow and stern airbags. Unfortunately, these boats are usually sold without airbags; most paddlers who buy them don't realize the need for flotation.

Not long ago, I watched a paddler drift into a tide rip on San Francisco Bay and capsize. When I paddled over to offer assistance, I found him swimming without the kayak. The entire boat was "floating" just *below* the surface of the water! This was a recreation kayak with tiny foam blocks in each end, which only served to keep the boat from sinking to the bottom of the Bay. I had the hapless swimmer climb onto my stern deck and paddled him to shore. Two other kayakers heroically towed his swamped boat (which was basically a sea anchor) out of the tide rip. If the shore hadn't been close by, this could have been a disaster. If you want to sea kayak on open water, get a sea kayak. Don't try to cut corners with an imitation that is not seaworthy.

Sea sock

To increase buoyancy in a closed-cockpit sea kayak, you can add a *sea sock*, a nylon bag that fits inside the cockpit and attaches to the coaming. The bag is just large enough to fill the cockpit area forward to the footbraces, allowing you to sit inside it.

A sea sock considerably reduces the amount of water that can enter the kayak after releasing the sprayskirt and exiting the boat. This leaves the kayak relatively stable after self-rescue, even without

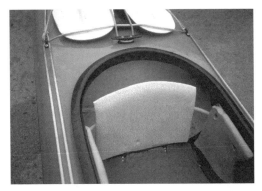

Rear bulkhead, just visible behind the seat. Also notice foam hip pads.

Airbag fills the stern to provide flotation in a kayak without bulkheads.

"Cleopatra's needle": A kayak without flotation will tend to sink.

pumping water out of the cockpit. The sea sock is not a necessity. However, it could prove useful when learning to surf or paddle in rock gardens, where capsizing and bailing out is a definite possibility, especially if your Eskimo roll is not reliable.

Hatches

Kayaks with bulkheads need hatches in order to allow access to the bow and the stern. These hatches must be well secured and watertight. The most reliable hatches I've seen are neoprene covers fixed in place over a coaming (similar to the way a sprayskirt fits over the cockpit coaming), combined with a hard cover to prevent implosion. The neoprene is flexible, watertight, and will not pop off; all these qualities are crucial to keep water out of the boat. Small VCP (heavy rubber) hatches are also very watertight, but are only about 8 inches in diameter. Larger VCP hatches can work, but will implode if not fitted tightly.

Boat designers have experimented with other hatch designs with mixed results. For example, pressure hatches with rubber gaskets are kept in place by a strap system that holds them down and compresses the gaskets for a watertight seal. Some of these work great; others are miserable failures. I've seen such hatches come loose in the surf and during rescues. Others just don't seal well, and the boat fills with water. Beware of these potentially dangerous design flaws. Be sure to thoroughly test any hatch system in realistic conditions such as the surf zone or other rough water.

A kayak with bulkheads needs hatches to gain access for gear storage.

Deck Lines

A sea kayak should be equipped with deck lines: ropes that run fore and aft along the deck. These lines are needed so that you can grab the kayak easily at any point and hang onto to it during a rescue. This is especially crucial if you capsize and bail out in moderate to strong wind. Without deck lines, you may have difficulty hanging onto the boat and it could be blown away.

Rudders and Skegs

Although not essential, a rudder or skeg can be used to help a kayak track (travel in a straight line), especially when travelling across the wind and downwind. Both situations can make boat handling difficult. Many kayaks tend to weathervane (turn into the wind) in a side wind. When traveling downwind, there is a tendency for a kayak to broach, or turn sideways to the waves. In these situations, if you have a rudder or skeg, you can deploy it to help hold the boat on course.

A rudder is mounted on the stern and controlled by using your foot pegs, which are connected by cables to the rudder. A skeg is usually mounted under the stern in a fixed position. The rudder or skeg can be lifted out of the water when not in use. Although a rudder is more common on sea kayaks, a skeg is probably more efficient because of its location under the stern, where it is constantly engaged. Because a rudder hangs off the end of the stern, it often lifts out of the water whenever the kayak is on a wave crest.

Rudders and skegs can be damaged, especially in surf; don't rely on them. Be sure to develop your paddling skills so that you can control your kayak without the aid of the rudder or skeg.

Choosing a Kayak

Your choice in a kayak has some bearing on safety. I've already pointed out the dangers of "recreation" kayaks without flotation; the intended use of such boats is limited to very calm water. Most sea kayaks, on the other hand, are versatile and seaworthy in a wide variety of conditions. A good paddler can do almost any kind of paddling in a sea kayak. Roger Schumann (a sea-kayak instructor and guide) paddled a sea kayak through the rapids of the Grand Canyon. Many paddlers use sea kayaks in the surf and in ocean rock gardens. However, some kayak designs are more versatile than others. You'll want to choose a boat that most closely fits your main paddling activities. Using the best boat for your purpose and for the conditions increases your margin of safety.

The standard sea kayak is designed primarily for cruising out on open water. For this purpose, a relatively long, straight-tracking boat is the best choice. This type of design sacrifices a certain amount of maneuverability, making it difficult to handle in surf and narrow channels among rocks. One option is to use a shorter sea kayak (from 13 to 14 feet in length), which combines the attributes of a standard sea kayak with those of a more maneuverable craft. This will give you a bit more versatility when

Standard sea kayaks (16–17 feet long).

paddling in areas with variable domains that include open water, surf, and rock gardens.

If your purpose is more specific, such as surfing, playing in the rocks, or exploring sea caves, you would be better off using a boat that is designed for the task at hand. For example, if your main goal is to surf, you'll want to use a kayak designed for surfing. Although almost any kayak will surf, a short, low-volume design, such as a whitewater or surf kayak, performs much better in these conditions than a long, straight-tracking sea kayak. You can surf in a sea kayak; it just takes more energy and work to handle the larger boat in surf. You'll also get more thrashed if caught in a big wave in the larger, higher-volume kayak.

A short sea kayak (mentioned above) is a good compromise if you want to explore the coast and do some surfing and inshore exploration along the way. I have spent a lot of time playing in rock gardens in a short sea kayak. More recently, however, I have used a whitewater kayak for this purpose, as long as there is no need to paddle any great distance in open water. I feel safer and have greater control in the whitewater boat in difficult hydraulics among the rocks, but the whitewater kayak is a miserable open-water cruiser. Which boat to use is largely a matter of paddling priorities.

Sit-on-Top Kayak

A sit-on-top kayak is often touted as a safer option to the closed-deck kayak. It is also sometimes described as a kayak for the beginner. Although there is some truth in both statements, they are more misleading and dangerous than truthful. Using a sit-on-top kayak does not mean you can get by with little or no training or knowledge. If you don't understand the environment where you are paddling and have not mastered basic paddling skills, you can get into just as much trouble with a sit-on-top as with any other craft.

The main advantage of a sit-on-top kayak is the ease of self-rescue. After capsizing, the boat will not swamp and can be easily remounted. This is especially useful in rock gardens and surf zones, where other forms of rescue can be difficult. It is also advantageous for divers, who need to be able to climb off and on the kayak with all their diving gear. However, as easy as remounting is, some technique is required to climb back on the boat efficiently, especially in

A short sea kayak (13.5 feet long) is especially useful in ocean rock gardens and surf.

DEBRAH VOLTURNO

Surf kayak.

MICHAEL POWERS

Whitewater kayaks are great for ocean rock gardens, as long as you don't have to cover much open water distance.

rough water (see "Self-Rescues," Chapter 5). In really serious storm-sea conditions, it may be impossible to remount.

Although self-rescue is relatively easy with a sit-on-top, it will blow away like a kite if you let go of it for even an instant on a windy day. If the wind is stronger than about 15 knots, you will not be able to swim fast enough to catch the kayak! This is of critical importance, especially to beginners who haven't formed the habit of hanging onto their boat when capsized. A friend of mine lost a sit-on-top kayak out on the ocean on a stormy day. Luckily we were close to shore and were able to get him ashore with only minor difficulty. The boat was never seen again.

The sit-on-top has two other potential disadvantages: (1) in cold water, the paddler is more exposed to hypothermia than in a closed-deck kayak, and (2) the paddler is not fitted as tightly to the boat as in a closed-deck kayak, resulting in less boat control and more difficulty executing an Eskimo roll. Both of these disadvantages can be mitigated with the right gear and outfitting. When paddling in cold water, a wetsuit or a drysuit should be worn to prevent hypothermia. Thigh straps and a seatbelt can be added to help with boat control. Most mass-produced sit-on-tops are not equipped with seatbelts. I assume there is a fear of entrapment, but it is no more valid than the fear of entrapment with a tightly-fitted sprayskirt. Safe use of a seatbelt requires a surefire release mechanism and the ability to use it. Without a seatbelt, the ability to roll and stay with the boat in surf and rough seas is seriously compromised.

Depending on design and outfitting, the sit-on-top can be used in the same way as any other type of kayak, and the same paddling skills are needed. Just because you can climb back on the boat after capsizing doesn't mean you don't need good stroke technique. If you want to paddle in surf or rough water, you'll also want to know how to roll; there is no fun in repeatedly capsizing and swimming after the boat.

Outfitting

Outfitting refers to customizing the cockpit area so that the kayak fits you properly. It is usually achieved by gluing foam blocks inside the cockpit, which can be shaped to fit and support your thighs, hips, and lower back. A boat that fits snugly will allow for greater boat control and a more reliable Eskimo roll. There will also be less chance of falling

JIM KAKUK

Sit-on-top kayaks have open, wash-deck seats, making them easy to remount in the water.

A boat that fits snugly will allow for greater boat control and a more reliable Eskimo roll.

out of the kayak if you capsize. These factors add up to greater safety.

To get an idea of how a kayak should fit, picture someone lifting you up under the armpits while you sit in your kayak. The boat should lift right off the floor with you, and there should be no movement between you and the boat. You must pinpoint the fine line between being jammed in and being too loose. This is just as important for sea kayaks as it is for river kayaks. I've noticed that most sea kayakers do not outfit their boats. If they had any idea how much energy they waste sloshing around in the boat and how much easier they could brace and roll with a better fit, they would immediately take care of the problem.

Every now and then I try out a new kayak that has not been outfitted. I'm always amazed at the loss of control when paddling a loose-fitting boat; it is also less comfortable. Paddling a kayak without outfitting is like hiking in loosely laced boots that are two sizes too large.

The important contact points in outfitting are as follows:

- **Feet:** Your feet should be firmly supported by the footbraces. This generally doesn't require any special outfitting; just be sure the footbraces are adjusted properly. The feet are used for leverage by pressing against the footbraces when paddling, bracing, or rolling the boat.

- **Thighs:** The thighs need to have good contact against the upper deck of the kayak. You can glue mini-cell foam supports inside the upper deck for this purpose. These are important for controlling boat lean and bracing.

- **Hips:** Your hips need to be in direct contact with the sides of the boat so that you don't shift from side to side. Most kayaks are roomy at the hips to accommodate a wide range of people. Glue in some foam to provide a reasonably tight fit (but not so tight that you can't slide your hips up and down to prevent potential back injury). I also like to glue in a thin pad of foam on the seat to provide friction so I don't slide around. Hip support will help transfer power directly toward moving the boat as you paddle. It will also hold you in the boat when performing an Eskimo roll.

- **Lower back:** Along with foot, thigh, and hip support, good support of your lower back helps provide leverage when paddling. A firm seat back will provide this support. However, your upper back should be free, to allow torso rotation. A high seat back is unnecessary and would hinder your ability to paddle efficiently. It would also interfere with boat entry and exit. As a general rule, the seat back should be no higher than the cockpit coaming (or the rear deck). Many sea kayaks have seat backs that are much too high. The solution is to cut the seat down to size or replace it with a back band.

Clothing

The primary purpose of kayaking clothing is to prevent *hypothermia* (a dangerous lowering of the body's core temperature) or, in the tropics, *hyperthermia* (overheating). To prevent hypothermia, it is necessary to dress for the water temperature. In cold water (less than about 70° F), a wetsuit, drysuit, or equivalent is needed. You must assume that immersion is possible and be prepared. In very hot climates with warm water, hypothermia is not an issue, but there is a danger of becoming overheated. To prevent this, wear light cotton clothing and a brimmed hat to keep the sun off your face and head.

Layering

Dressing in layers is probably the best way to control body temperature. Start with a base layer of synthetic thermal wear, such as lycra or capilene. Never wear cotton in a cool climate or cold water. Add layers as necessary for additional warmth and protection from the elements. On top of the synthetic wear, you can add a full wetsuit, a farmer-john wetsuit, or a drysuit. The full wetsuit is warm, but its neoprene sleeves somewhat restrict paddling. The farmer-john wetsuit is sleeveless and needs to be combined with a paddle jacket or a dry top. A drysuit will keep you dry and is therefore the warmest option, but it needs to be kept in good repair to prevent leaking. A drysuit is also bulky for swimming.

This well-dressed kayaker is wearing gear appropriate for paddling in cold water. Note the booties, wetsuit, sprayskirt, paddling jacket, personal flotation device (PFD), and helmet (for surf or rock gardens).

New garments made with polyurethane-coated fleece that are designed to take the place of wetsuits are now available. They are roughly equivalent to 2.5 mm of neoprene, and are much more comfortable than a wetsuit. I've found them to be warm and satisfactory in a variety of conditions. For cold water, they can be combined with capilene thermal wear and a paddle jacket.

A paddle jacket is used as an outer layer. It is always worn *over* the sprayskirt tube, to help keep water out of the kayak. A paddle jacket provides protection from the wind and helps keep you dry. Paddle jackets range from thin nylon shells to heavy-duty Gore-Tex drytops. You should use the right jacket for the conditions and ensure the jacket is of high quality. Be sure all seams are sealed to make the jacket relatively waterproof. Drytops are totally waterproof because they have latex seals at the wrists and neck. A good compromise is a jacket with latex seals at the wrists and an adjustable seal at the neck. Such a jacket won't be totally waterproof, but will be relatively dry because of the wrist seals.

Whatever clothing system you choose, be sure to test it thoroughly by swimming in the waters where you'll be paddling. You want to be able to swim fairly easily and, most importantly, to stay warm.

Footwear

Most paddlers wear some form of neoprene booties for footwear. Booties keep your feet warm and provide protection for your soles when they press against the footbraces. Rigid soles for walking on rocks or rough terrain when out of the kayak are beneficial. A wide variety of neoprene booties are available, some warmer than others; be sure to match them to the water temperature in which you'll be kayaking. Neoprene footwear is usually close fitting and fairly easy to swim in.

Some other types of footwear are worn when kayaking. In the Pacific Northwest, where wet, rainy conditions are the norm, many paddlers wear high-top rubber boots. These present a hazard when swimming if they fill up with water. However, some newer models are designed to prevent this problem. As always, test them before you need to rely on them.

In some situations, it is useful to have a pair of swim fins available. These cannot be worn inside a closed-deck kayak, but can be carried on deck. Fins

Whatever clothing system you choose, be sure to test it thoroughly by swimming in the waters where you'll be paddling.

allow you to swim more efficiently. If you have to swim through powerful surf or rescue someone who is having trouble in the surf, a pair of fins could make a big difference.

Personal Flotation Device

A *personal flotation device (PFD)* is a lifejacket that keeps you afloat when in the water. It helps keep your head above water in rough seas and allows you to rest, thereby saving your valuable energy for a rescue operation or a long swim. It definitely could save your life, and should be worn at all times when kayaking. The PFD is worn as the final layer, outside your paddle jacket. This order is important because the PFD will help keep the paddle jacket compressed during a swim and prevent the jacket from filling up with water if it leaks.

PFD design has evolved considerably in the past few years. The best PFDs for kayaking are relatively low-cut, with huge armholes to prevent interference with arm movement while paddling or swimming. These newer designs have gone a long way toward solving the main problem of older types: they allow you enough freedom to swim and dive beneath waves in the surf. They still have some buoyancy that you must fight, but with practice, you can swim reasonably well in a modern PFD. The ability to rest and stay afloat makes the trade-off between adequate buoyancy and swimming ease worthwhile. Be sure to buy the best PFD available!

Some controversy has surrounded the use of PFDs, especially in the surf zone, where the ability to dive beneath waves is important. It could be argued that a full wetsuit provides sufficient flotation and is a better choice for swimming. However, this is true only if you wear a *full* wetsuit, and have tested it for flotation; otherwise it is essential to wear a PFD.

Helmets and Headwear

A helmet is essential for sea-kayaking safety in surf zones and ocean rock gardens. It is also a good idea to wear one when practicing rescues in rough seas or tide rips. During such rescues, it is possible for the swimmer to collide with a kayak that is bouncing around in the waves. In general, whenever there is the remotest possibility of hitting your head, wear a helmet. An unconscious swimmer won't last long.

In surf and rock gardens there is always a chance of hitting your head on the bottom or on an obstruction, such as a rock or floating debris. In the surf zone, the main danger is colliding with another kayak or with your own kayak while swimming. It is sheer madness to paddle in rock gardens or sea caves without a helmet; you definitely want your head protected when you are tossed upside down in a shallow, rocky area. If there is any chance that you will be paddling through surf or in the rocks, bring a helmet. As a general rule, I always wear a helmet on the open coast.

In cold conditions, you should cover your head with a thermal layer. Much heat is lost through the head and neck. By wearing a hood you can stay warmer and reduce your chances of hypothermia considerably. Skullcaps can be worn with or without a helmet, and they are available in a variety of materials, ranging from neoprene to synthetic fleece. The addition of a skullcap will make surfing or rolling in cold water much more comfortable. These caps are also great to wear in rain and wind. If you're not wearing a helmet, you can choose from a wide range of hoods and fleece or wool caps. Don't underestimate the importance of keeping your head warm.

In hot climates, cover your head with a brimmed hat for protection from the sun. A chin strap can be used to keep the hat in place.

Gloves

Paddling gloves can be worn to keep your hands warm or to protect them when paddling in rocky areas, where you may end up pushing off rocks with your hands. The best gloves I've found for these purposes are made of thin neoprene with leather (or some other non-slip material) palms. These gloves allow good purchase on the paddle shaft. The problem with some gloves is that they are too slippery or too thick, making it difficult to grip the paddle. Look for thin, flexible gloves and try holding a paddle to ensure a good grip. You'll have to live with the fact that the gloves will wear out and have to be replaced once or twice a year, depending on how much you use them.

Pogies are another option for keeping your hands warm, especially in extreme cold. Pogies are sheaths of neoprene or nylon and fleece that fit over the paddle shaft. You place your hands inside them and grip the paddle directly. Although pogies will

It is sheer madness to paddle in rock gardens or sea caves without a helmet.

keep your hands even warmer than gloves, they will not provide any abrasion protection from rocks.

Safety Accessories

Safety accessories include items that are used to prevent problems, to help paddlers who are having problems, to assist with rescues, or to deal with any sort of emergency. These devices are backups to good judgment and kayaking skills; they should not be heavily relied upon. In other words, if you are constantly pulling out your paddlefloat to perform self-rescues, you'll get a lot of valuable practice, but this is a sign that you probably need to work on balance and bracing skills.

Paddlefloat

A *paddlefloat* is a bag that can be secured to the end of a paddle and inflated, and can then be used as an outrigger to stabilize the kayak while a paddler climbs back in. It can also be used to perform a reentry and roll. The paddlefloat should be carried where it is accessible but secure in rough seas. Many kayakers shove a paddlefloat under the deck rigging and assume it will stay there. If you want to carry it this way, be sure to clip it in so it can't be removed by a wave. Even better, keep it clipped in behind your seat, where you can still get at it easily when in the water. As I've already mentioned, the paddlefloat is useless unless you know how to use it. Be sure to get plenty of practice.

Paddlefloat and pump.

Pump

After doing any kind of self-rescue, your kayak will be partly swamped. Because a boat full of water is somewhat unstable, you'll need to remove the excess water. Unless your kayak is equipped with a foot-operated pump, you'll have to carry an easily accessible hand pump. Be sure the pump is attached to the kayak with a clip or tether.

A foot-operated pump is the best option because you can paddle and brace while pumping the water out, a real benefit if you are doing this in rough, windy conditions. Unfortunately most kayaks do not have a foot-operated pump and most paddlers, myself included, are not inclined to spend the time and effort to install one. However, if you find it difficult to balance your kayak while using a hand pump

Towline. Note the carabiner on one end (for clipping onto towed vessel) and shock cord (with rope coiled around it) at the other end.

in rough water, it would be wise to install a foot pump.

Towline

A *towline* is an often overlooked but essential safety device that should be carried by all sea kayakers. Even a solo paddler should carry one; you never know when you might come upon another boater who needs assistance. There are many different towing systems that work well (see "Towing," Chapter 9), but all systems need to meet some general specifications. A towline should be at least 30 feet long, to prevent collisions when towing downwind. The towline should have a shock absorber, which can be built in with a short length of shock cord. The towline should, of course, be readily accessible and easily deployed, even in strong wind and rough water.

Paddle Leash

When kayaking in strong wind, you might consider using a *paddle leash* to assure that you don't lose your paddle. A well-designed paddle leash will not interfere with paddling or rolling. One common style is a spiral rubber leash (similar to a telephone handset cord) with a quick-release mechanism. Another option is to tie the paddle to your wrist with a short piece of shock cord. If you do this, make sure there is a way to release the cord from your wrist quickly. Paddle leashes are for use in open water and should never be used in the surf zone where there is a serious risk of entanglement.

Spare Paddle

Carry a spare paddle in case you lose or break your main paddle. The spare is usually a breakdown paddle that can be lashed to your deck. Make sure the paddle is secure, yet easily released for use. A spare paddle is especially important on any wilderness outing or expedition.

Sea Anchor

A sea anchor is essentially an underwater "parachute," attached to an adjustable nylon cord up to approximately 100 feet long. The primary purpose of a sea anchor is to slow or stop downwind progress by dragging it off the bow of your kayak. By increasing the line length, you can create more drag. I have never used or carried a sea anchor. However, in

Spare paddle can be mounted on the stern deck where it is readily available.

situations where you might be blown offshore in a strong gale, the sea anchor could be an important safety device. It can also be used to help control and stabilize the kayak while drifting downwind in a storm. If you carry a sea anchor, it needs to be kept close at hand where it can be easily deployed.

Sling

A *sling* is a rope that can be used as a stirrup to aid a swimmer who is having trouble climbing back into the kayak. Ideally, it should be a separate rope or strap about 12 feet long, tied to form a loop. If you need a sling and aren't carrying one, a towline could be used for this purpose.

Rescue Tube

A *rescue tube* is a device commonly used by lifeguards. It consists of a piece of foam flotation, attached to a short line, which can be tossed to a swimmer in distress. The swimmer can then be helped ashore by the rescuer, using the attached line. The main value of a rescue tube is to give a panicked swimmer something to grab onto, which protects the rescuer from the victim's flailing arms. Although kayakers don't generally carry a rescue tube, this device might prove useful to those who anticipate paddling in large surf.

Weather Radio

A weather radio can be used to check conditions, especially wind velocities, and to get a weather forecast before heading out on the water. This information is valuable, even if you are going out for a day paddle. On an expedition, a weather radio will help you plan ahead. For example, without a weather radio, you could be camped in a calm cove with no way of knowing that the wind is blowing 30 knots out on the island where you are planning to go.

First-Aid Kit

A first-aid kit should be carried on any type of outdoor excursion, especially in wilderness areas. On day trips, kayakers should carry enough first-aid gear to at least deal with minor injuries. On longer expeditions, a more complete kit should be carried. The kit will vary somewhat, depending on where you are paddling and what types of injuries are likely. The most common injuries are cuts and abrasions, usually suffered when climbing around on shore. Keep the first-aid kit in a waterproof bag, and stow it close at hand.

As with all other gear, a first-aid kit will not be very useful unless you know how to use it. Wilderness first aid is beyond the scope of this book, but all paddlers should take at least a basic first-aid course and CPR training. Those who plan to undertake major expeditions should take a more comprehensive first-aid course.

Repair Kit

Most kayaks and kayaking accessories are sturdy and designed to take a tremendous amount of abuse. However, there is always a chance of damaging your boat or other equipment. Be sure to carry a repair kit to take care of potential damage. It is especially important to be able to repair your kayak, particularly on an expedition.

My repair kit consists mainly of a large roll of duct tape. This is somewhat of a cliché, but it is a fact that most typical boat damage can be adequately repaired with duct tape. Such repairs are temporary, but will do the job. Duct tape must be applied to a dry surface or it won't adhere. It also works better on fiberglass kayaks than on rotomolded plastic boats.

Using duct tape, I repaired the stern on my fiberglass kayak after smashing it on a rock ledge while running a large ocean cascade on the second day of a week-long excursion on the northern California coast. The repair held for several weeks after the excursion, allowing me to continue boating until I finally got around to applying a fiberglass patch.

Several other products are available for repairing fiberglass or kevlar kayaks. Marine-Tex is a heavy-duty structural epoxy that can be easily mixed and used to repair gouges and gel-coat damage. It takes several hours to cure. Check with your local marine store or kayak shop for this and similar products. On long expeditions it might be worth taking a small fiberglass repair kit. If you have a rotomolded kayak, you don't have too many options, other than duct tape, for repair in the field.

Other items in your repair kit will depend on the kayak and its fittings. You'll want to bring straps or ropes to fix seat backs and hatch covers. Aquaseal® is excellent for repairing holes in dry bags and flotation bags. If you have a rudder or a skeg on your kayak, be sure to carry extra hardware so you

My repair kit consists mainly of a large roll of duct tape.

can fix it if it gets bent or broken during surf landings or from other wear and tear.

Waterproof Flashlight

If you are paddling at night, or there is any chance you might do so, carry a waterproof flashlight. The light is mainly needed to signal your presence to other boaters and you are required by law to have one after dark. *Light sticks* (chemical-filled tubes that can be activated to give a glowing light for several hours) can be attached to your kayak or paddle; they don't destroy your night vision and are a great way to maintain contact among a group of paddlers.

A flashlight is useful when paddling in sea caves. Some caves are deep enough to be completely dark, once you paddle in a short distance. The best light for this purpose is a powerful dive light.

Signaling Devices

There are two main types of signaling used in kayaking. One is communication between paddlers. A whistle combined with paddle or hand signals can be used for this purpose. The other type of signal is used to attract outside assistance. It is generally a distress signal, and it is the primary use for the signaling devices described here.

Flares are commonly used as distress signals on the water. However, a flare will not be of any use unless someone sees it. The best procedure is to shoot a flare across the bow of another vessel. Of course this works only if there are other vessels in the area. In daylight, a smoke flare will last longer and be more visible than a rocket flare, while the bright flash of a rocket flare will be more visible at night. In a storm with high winds, you'll be extremely lucky if anyone spots any type of flare. Another problem with these devices is that they don't last forever. Most flares have an expiration date, after which they should be replaced. If you want really reliable flares, get the kind that are shot out of a "gun." The small hand-held flares are not very dependable. Flares should be kept in a waterproof container and stored in a pocket of your PFD or paddle jacket, in case you are separated from your kayak.

A marine VHF radio is invaluable in an emergency. In many cases, you can reach someone on the water with a radio call for help. You'll obviously have to know and be able to describe your location if you need to be rescued. The radio also gives you the option of summoning help when an emergency arises on shore.

If you don't have a radio or flares and need to summon help, you'll have to improvise. Any brightly colored object might be spotted, including your kayak. If you wave a colorful piece of clothing or a paddle blade, it just might get someone's attention.

Be sure to recognize flares, radio transmissions, and other distress signals for what they are: last-ditch, desperate calls for help when all else has failed. Such devices should never be relied on as primary backups. In this respect, I hesitate to call them safety devices. Safe paddling precludes the need for outside rescue. If you have to resort to shooting flares, all of your safety procedures have broken down, or were nonexistent in the first place. This doesn't mean you shouldn't carry flares or a radio; they might save your life. Just don't treat them as a substitute for poor judgment or lack of kayaking skills.

Chart and Compass

A marine chart provides you with a great deal of valuable information, including the location of shipping lanes, buoys, potential bailouts, shoals, rocks, and features useful for navigation. You can also use the chart to plot your course, determine distances, and keep track of your progress. All these factors are important to your safety. Unless you are paddling in a very familiar area, you should use a chart or a map to plan your trip and then bring it along to aid in navigating.

A compass is another useful navigational tool, essential on long crossings or when visibility is poor, as in fog. Marine compasses are easy to use and can be mounted on the front deck. The mounting can be permanent or removable. A standard orienteering compass will also work, but is a bit more difficult to read. The good thing about this latter type of compass is that you can carry it in a pocket, so that you always have it at hand.

Conclusion

Equipment is a basic component of risk management. Your primary equipment—your kayak and clothing—is essential to your safety on the water. This gear needs to be kept in good condition, and should be checked out before every trip. You don't want to

find out that one of your hatches has developed a serious leak when you're 3 miles from shore. Backup
safety equipment, such as signal devices, towlines,
and paddlefloats, should also be checked regularly
for damage. These items are rarely used, but when
you need them, someone's life could be on the line.

Get the best, highest-quality equipment you
can find. Never buy something just because it's cheap.
If you buy used equipment, check it out thoroughly.
You don't want to be out there with gear that is worn
out or in poor repair.

Finally, keep in mind that kayaking gear is
merely a tool. It gives you the means to explore areas
that are not accessible without specialized equipment.
Having the right equipment and knowing how to use
it is only one part of the formula for safety. It's pointless to fill your cockpit with flares, radios, and navigational equipment if you haven't mastered basic
kayaking skills.

**It's pointless to fill
your cockpit with
flares, radios,
and navigational
equipment if you
haven't mastered
basic kayaking skills.**

CHAPTER 4.
ASSISTED DEEP-WATER RESCUES

Capsizing is part of kayaking, especially during the initial learning stages. You won't capsize every time you get on the water. In fact, with a bit of experience you'll feel very stable in calm water, and after developing some bracing skills, you'll rarely, if ever, capsize in rough water. Your goal is to prevent capsizing. But you still have to be ready, and know what to do, in case you or someone in your group ends up in the water.

If you capsize and can't perform an Eskimo roll or fail to execute your roll, your only recourse, short of a bow rescue, is to exit the kayak and then reenter. Because a partly swamped kayak is highly unstable, simply climbing back in without assistance is difficult, especially in rough water. With the aid of another boater, the process of emptying water from the boat and reentering is relatively easy. Numerous assisted rescues have been designed for this purpose. They are all variations on one theme: Get the swimmer back in the kayak and get the water out of the kayak.

Most successful rescues are simple and efficient in wind and rough water. The more complex the rescue, the more likely it will fail. A lot of procedures that work in calm water will not work well in rough water. It is extremely important to practice and test any rescue in rough, windy conditions. Pay attention to details, such as where to put your paddle while conducting the rescue. Ignoring such details can create insurmountable difficulties in strong wind and rough seas. For example, if the swimmer lets go of the boat, even for a second, after capsizing in a 25-knot wind, the boat will blow away, making the rescue far more difficult.

You really only need one or two well-practiced rescues, with a few basic variations. After learning several different assisted rescues, I found myself using the *T-rescue* every time I had to perform a rescue out on open water. Over the years, I've rarely seen

Most successful rescues are simple and efficient.

anyone use any other type of assisted rescue, proba- bly because the T-rescue works so well! It is described below, with some minor variations. I also include a description of the *side-rescue* for situations where it is best to get the swimmer back in the boat first and then pump the water out. Because the T-rescue requires lifting the bow of the capsized kayak, the side-rescue is usually a better choice with a heavily loaded kayak.

Ideally, the swimmer is a key player during a rescue. It is just as important to learn how to help with your own rescue as it is to learn how to rescue someone else. The swimmer should never let go of the kayak, can help empty water, and must know how to climb back into the boat. However, it is also important for the rescuer to know how to deal with a panicked or incapacitated swimmer. I include information on dealing with such special circumstances in the final section of this chapter.

If you paddle a sit-on-top kayak, the ability to perform assisted rescues is as important for you as it is for closed-deck kayakers. If you are on the water with a closed-deck kayaker who ends up swimming, you'll want to be able to do a rescue. Even if you don't plan to paddle with closed-deck kayakers, you never know when you may encounter another kayaker in trouble. In extremely rough conditions, you or one of your partners might have trouble remounting the sit- on-top. You may need to adopt some of the assisted- rescue techniques described below.

Bow Rescue

The basic idea of the bow rescue is to stay in the boat after capsizing, bang your hull to gain atten- tion, and wave your arms above water so that your partner can present her bow to you. You then grab your partner's bow for leverage and right yourself. Of course, the bow rescue will only work if your partner is close by and can act quickly. Native arctic kayakers developed this rescue. They did not own drysuits and knew that swimming in such cold water generally meant death.

The bow rescue requires teamwork. If you have capsized and know your partner is nearby, do the following:

- **Step 1.** *(Photo 1)* Stay in the kayak, lean for- ward, tuck your paddle into one of your armpits, aligning it parallel to the kayak, and reach out of the water with *both* hands, one on each side of the hull. Bang loudly on the hull with your hands to gain attention, then wave both arms back and forth alongside the boat. Keep your hands out a few inches from the side of the kayak as you move them. Maintaining this distance will prevent getting a hand smashed against the hull in case your partner paddles in too aggressively.

- **Step 2.** *(Photos 2–4)* Relax and be patient. It will seem like forever, but it takes only a few seconds for your partner to get into position if she is close enough. Once you feel the bow of the other kayak, grab on with one hand and begin to pull yourself up. As you do this, reach around with the other hand and place it on the bow. Your partner's kayak should be perpendicular to yours. Next, right the boat using your hips and lower body, keeping your head and upper body in the water for as long as possible. Bring your head out *last*, after the boat is upright.

If you are the rescuer, do the following:

- **Step 1.** Paddle swiftly toward the capsized kayak, aiming your bow at one side of your partner's waving hand.

- **Step 2.** As you approach, just before slamming into the kayak, execute a strong reverse sweep stroke and pivot your bow toward and into your partner's waving hand. This takes good boat control and timing. Once the capsized boater has grabbed your bow, maintain your position while he rights his kayak.

The bow rescue has limited practical application because it will work only if the rescuer is close by and paying attention. However, it can work if you plan ahead, agreeing to use this rescue in case of a capsize. The bow rescue can also be used as a spotting technique for someone who is practicing the Eskimo roll. Doing so eliminates the need to bail out every time the roll is missed.

❶ – ❹ Photo sequence: Bow rescue.

PHOTO SEQUENCE: MICHAEL POWERS

Capsizing and the Wet Exit

Most beginners are more concerned with getting out of a capsized kayak than with getting back in. Even experienced paddlers can panic when they find themselves upside down, especially if they normally avoid capsizing and haven't learned to roll. The fact is, getting out of a kayak is the easy part. But problems can arise if you panic. So be sure to practice bailing out.

If you're a beginner using a closed-deck kayak, the first step is to make sure you know how to release the sprayskirt. Practice first on dry land. Check that the grab loop used to pull off the sprayskirt at the front of the cockpit is accessible, then practice releasing the sprayskirt. Lean forward and pull the grab loop forward and up to release it from the coaming. Do it several times with your eyes closed. Every time you replace the sprayskirt be sure to check that the grab loop is accessible, not tucked inside the cockpit. Once you are comfortable releasing the sprayskirt, move into the water to capsize and practice *wet exits* (exiting underwater).

Do several wet exits with a partner close by, until it becomes routine. Push out smoothly, while hanging onto both the kayak and your paddle. This is very easy; all it takes is a little practice. After capsizing, relax. Of course, the first time you capsize you won't feel very relaxed. That's why you need to wet-exit several times, until you get comfortable with the sensation. You must remember that you have plenty of time. Tuck forward, pull forward and up on the grab loop to release the sprayskirt, then gently push out of the cockpit. As you pull your legs out, grasp the cockpit coaming with one hand to maintain contact with the kayak. Remember: *tuck, pull, push, hang on.*

Whether you are a beginning or an advanced paddler, it pays to spend time working on a controlled, relaxed bailout procedure. Practice exiting your kayak in slow motion as smoothly as possible. This will help avoid injury and make it less likely that you'll lose contact with your kayak if you have to bail out in windy or stormy conditions. Letting go of your kayak in a strong wind is just about the worst mistake you can make; it could cost you your life! If you thrash and kick your way out of the boat, the wet exit will take longer than a more deliberate, controlled exit. You'll also burn a lot more oxygen, run out of breath sooner, and probably let go of the boat if you

Letting go of your kayak in a strong wind is just about the worst mistake you can make.

panic. Once you're out of the kayak, you'll have to get back in. The following rescues describe how to do this.

T-Rescue

The basic actions of the T-rescue involve lifting the bow of the capsized kayak up and across your deck to drain water, and then righting the kayak and holding it stable while the swimmer climbs back in. This works fine with kayaks that are not too heavily loaded with gear. With a gear-laden kayak, you might choose to use a side-rescue (described later in this chapter), eliminating the need to lift the capsized boat.

- **Step 1:** *(Photo 1)* After noticing that someone has capsized, the rescuer should first paddle up to the bow of the overturned kayak. Leave the kayak upside down. Tell the swimmer, who has by now performed a wet exit, to hang onto his boat and paddle. Place your paddle across your cockpit, tucked in against your stomach and under both arms. Using both hands, grab the other bow and position the other kayak so that it is perpendicular to your boat in the "T" configuration. The easiest way to do this is to swing your own boat around, using the bow of the other kayak as a pivot point; lean your boat toward the pivot point to help it turn. Have the swimmer work toward the stern of his boat *without letting go* of the boat. You may need to remind the swimmer not to let go of the boat.

- **Step 2:** *(Photos 1–2)* Place your hand nearest the other kayak on top of the overturned bow. This will provide stability as you lean toward the bow and reach underwater beneath the kayak with your other hand. Pull the bow up and over your cockpit, hanging on with both hands. As you lift, the swimmer can help by pushing down on the stern. Once the kayak is up on your deck, it acts as a giant outrigger and you will be extremely stable.

PHOTO SEQUENCE: MICHAEL POWERS

1 – 2 Photo sequence: T-rescue.

- **Step 3:** *(Photos 2–3)* Work the overturned kayak partway across your deck until the cockpit is well clear of the water. The swimmer should swim along and push from the stern. Most of the water in the kayak will drain out as the cockpit lifts clear (assuming the kayak has a stern bulkhead; for kayaks without bulkheads, see TX-Rescue, below). Lift the bow slightly to make sure all water has drained, then rotate the boat upright.

- **Step 4:** *(Photos 4–5)* Slide the kayak back into the water. As you do this, angle the stern toward your bow so that the kayaks end up with cockpits side-by-side, but facing in *opposite* directions. Otherwise you'll get in the way when the swimmer climbs back in. Now have the swimmer move to the cockpit while continually maintaining a hold on the boat.

- **Step 5:** *(Photos 6–7)* Take the swimmer's paddle and tuck it in next to yours under both arms. Grasp the cockpit coaming of the other kayak firmly with both hands, one on each side of the cockpit. You can lean toward the kayak as you do this; the other boat will offer plenty of support.

- **Step 6:** *(Photos 8–12)* Hold the kayak stable with both hands while the swimmer prepares to climb back in. The swimmer then holds onto the rear deck of his kayak with both hands, extends his arms, kicks his feet to the surface, and swims up on and across the deck just aft of the cockpit. It takes a bit of practice to do this smoothly. The trick is for the swimmer to keep his head down and feet up, just as one would do when swimming. This will eliminate the need to do an arm wrenching "pull-up" to mount the kayak, although you will have to use your arms to some extent. If absolutely necessary, the rescuer can help the swimmer remount by grabbing his PFD and hauling him up.

Once on deck, the swimmer should turn toward the stern of his kayak, push both feet

3 – **6** Photo sequence: T-rescue continued.

PHOTO SEQUENCE: MICHAEL POWERS

7 – **12** Photo sequence: T-rescue continued.

⓭ – ⓮ Photo sequence: T-rescue continued.

MICHAEL POWERS

If the swimmer is having trouble climbing aboard, the rescuer can lend a hand.

into the cockpit, rotate his upper body around, and pull his body into the seat. During this whole process, the swimmer should remain close to the kayak, maintaining a low center of gravity. This makes it easier for the rescuer to hold the boat steady. The rescuer needs to hang on tightly the whole time as the swimmer climbs in.

- **Step 7:** *(Photos 13–14)* Even after the swimmer is seated, the rescuer should not let go of the boat. First make sure the swimmer is all right, has reattached the sprayskirt, and is ready to go. Only then should the rescuer release the other kayak. The rescue is then complete. With practice, the entire rescue can be accomplished in less than 2 minutes.

Key Points

The T-rescue is one of the fastest and most efficient ways to get a swimmer back into a kayak. However, there are several key points to remember. Some of these points won't seem very important until you try doing the rescue in strong wind and rough seas.

- **Find the bow:** As the rescuer, you need to find and lift the *bow* of the capsized kayak so that the water drains out off the rear bulkhead (otherwise, the water will run toward the bow and won't drain from the cockpit). On most kayaks, the bow can be easily recognized by looking for the bolts that hold the footbraces in place, which are close to the bow.

- **Paddle placement:** Your paddle can get lost or be in the way if you don't place it under both arms, against your stomach, where it is out of the way but readily accessible. If you place the paddle under the deck lines, it can get in your way and be difficult to remove quickly. If the paddle is tethered to the kayak with a paddle leash, you can simply drop it in the water, out of the way.

- **Grasp the bow with both hands:** A common mistake many paddlers make is that they try to lift the bow with only one hand. This is not only difficult, but it also tends to throw you off balance. Lean toward the bow and lift it

with both hands; the hand closer to the capsized boat goes on top and your far hand
goes underneath. By tilting your boat toward
the overturned kayak, you can pull the bow
across your deck and lever it up with your
kayak. All of this is easier if the swimmer
weights down the stern while you lift the
bow.

- **Clear the cockpit:** After emptying water out
  of the kayak, make sure the cockpit is clear of
  the surface of the water before rotating the
  kayak upright. Otherwise, you can scoop up
  water with the cockpit as the boat is rotated,
  especially in choppy seas. The easiest way to
  get the cockpit clear of the water is to slide
  the kayak well up and across your deck. This
  is a good reason not to have a lot of gear
  cluttering up your front deck. Forget about
  scratching the kayaks—minor scratches
  don't matter. However, a heavily loaded
  kayak could cause structural damage; with a
  loaded kayak you may opt for the side-rescue, described below.

- **Face the kayaks in opposite directions:** It
  will be easier for the swimmer to climb back
  in if you aren't in the way. If you forget this
  step, and the boats end up facing the same
  way, go with it. The swimmer can still climb
  in, but needs to climb up directly across the
  cockpit instead of climbing on behind the
  cockpit.

- **Hold the cockpit firmly on *both* sides while
  the swimmer climbs in:** The rescuer must
  hold the kayak steady. Don't be afraid to lean
  over toward the boat while hanging on. You
  can stabilize yourself by hanging onto the
  other kayak.

- **The swimmer must be able to climb back
  on deck:** This skill is often overlooked, but it
  is very important and must be learned. It is
  possible to muscle yourself up by partly submerging, then doing a swift pull-up onto the
  deck. However, this requires considerable
  upper-body strength and is more difficult
  than swimming up and across the kayak
  deck, as described under Step 6 above. The
  real trick to swimming onto the deck is to be

**By tilting your
boat toward the
overturned kayak,
you can pull the bow
across your deck and
lever it up with your
kayak.**

DEBRAH VOLTURNO

PHOTO SEQUENCE: MICHAEL POWERS

(Top left) Rafted T-rescue. Two rescuers can raft together for increased stability during a rescue.

1 – **6** Photo sequence: TX-rescue.

sure that you kick your feet near the surface of the water. You should be able to swim right up and across both your deck and the deck of the rescuer's kayak with only minor assistance from your arms. Practice this until you can do it easily. There is a way to aid climbing on deck, but it is more time-consuming and requires the use of a rope or a strap (see "Using a Sling," below).

• **The rescuer must hang on until the rescue is complete:** Don't let go until the rescued paddler has reattached the sprayskirt and is ready to go. I've seen a paddler immediately capsize again after being rescued because the rescuer let go too soon. The rescue had to be performed all over again, and the swimmer was very cold by the time it was over. Be sure to check with the rescued paddler before letting go.

Variation 1: Rafted T-Rescue

In rough conditions, a second kayaker can raft up next to the primary rescuer to help out. Of course, this option requires at least three paddlers in the group, including the swimmer. This rescue is performed exactly as above, except the second paddler is positioned alongside the rescue kayak on the far side from the capsized kayak. The second paddler holds onto and helps stabilize the rescue kayak. If necessary, the second paddler can reach across and help haul up and empty the capsized boat or help get the swimmer aboard.

Variation 2: TX-Rescue *(Photos 1–6)*

If the capsized kayak has air bags for flotation instead of bulkheads (whitewater kayaks, surf kayaks, and some sea kayaks lack bulkheads), you cannot drain the water out completely by simply lifting the bow. Rather, the boat must be positioned so that water can be drained from both bow and stern.

Perform the TX-rescue exactly as the standard T-rescue with one exception: After pulling the bow across your cockpit (Step 3 above), continue to slide the kayak across until you can "see-saw" the boat back and forth to empty all the water. You'll have to rock the boat only once or twice to accomplish this. The swimmer can help by pushing up on the stern or by grabbing the bow and pulling down. Then right

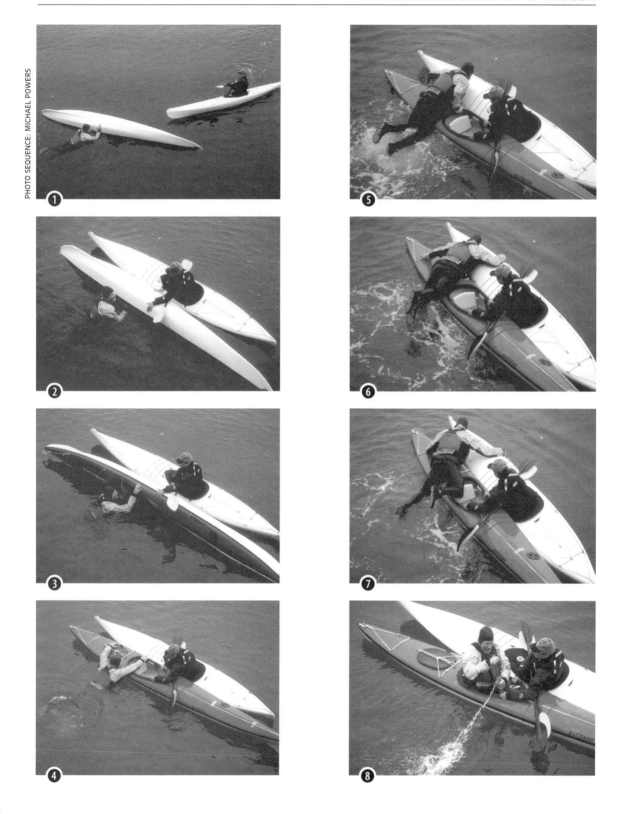

the kayak, slide it back in the water, and finish the rescue in the same way as the T-rescue.

Side-Rescue

The side-rescue is similar to the T-rescue, except that the water is pumped out of the kayak (using a hand pump or foot pump) after the swimmer climbs back in. This rescue is a good choice if you are dealing with a heavily-loaded kayak and don't want to lift the bow, or if the swimmer is not adequately dressed for the water temperature.

Both paddlers can pump to remove water quickly.

- **Step 1.** *(Photos 1–2)* Paddle alongside the capsized kayak. Position yourself so that the two boats face in opposite directions and the swimmer is on the far side of the overturned kayak. Think about this configuration as you paddle to the rescue so you don't waste time repositioning. As always, make sure the swimmer hangs onto the kayak.

- **Step 2.** *(Photo 3)* Flip the kayak upright quickly, scooping as little water as possible. Either the swimmer or the rescuer can do this.

- **Step 3.** *(Photos 4–7)* Stabilize the kayak by hanging onto both sides of the cockpit and proceed as in Steps 5 and 6 of the T-rescue.

- **Step 4.** *(Photo 8)* Once the swimmer is seated, hold the boat stable while the swimmer pumps excess water out of the kayak cockpit, using either a hand pump or a foot pump. When using a hand pump in rough water, the sprayskirt can be mostly sealed with the pump jammed in along the side. The process can be speeded up if both paddlers use hand pumps. Don't let go until the pumping has been completed.

Discussion

The side-rescue has two advantages over the T-rescue: (1) the swimmer spends less time in the water and (2) there is no need to lift the swamped kayak onto the rescuer's deck. The one disadvantage

❶ – ❽ Photo sequence, previous page: Side-rescue.

is the time and energy spent pumping water out. This takes at least several minutes.

So which rescue should you use? I suggest learning and practicing both the T-rescue (including the TX variation) and the side-rescue until you can do them quickly and easily. Allow the circumstances to dictate which rescue you choose. On day trips with empty or lightly-loaded kayaks, the T-rescue is usually the best choice because it is faster and more efficient; it doesn't require pumping water. Use the side-rescue if dealing with a heavily-loaded kayak or if the water is extremely cold and you need to get the swimmer out immediately.

Both of these rescues work well in rough water, and neither of them is difficult to perform, if you have practiced. I've read at least one kayaking book in which the author made it sound like sea kayaking was the easiest thing in the world to learn, except for the rescues. The fact is, it is much easier to learn and perform a rescue than it is to perfect most paddling strokes. You can get by without perfect stroke technique, up to a point. But rescues have to work! The best ones are those that are simple and easy, because they have to work when you really need them, usually in the worst conditions.

Rescues with Double Kayaks

The main problem encountered while rescuing a *double kayak* (one that accommodates two kayakers in two separate cockpits) is dealing with the large amount of water taken on by such a high-volume kayak. Before beginning any rescue with a double kayak, you may need to partly lift, rock, and rotate the capsized boat, with the aid of the two swimmers, in order to remove some of the water. One solution to this problem is to use a sea sock in each cockpit of the double kayak. This will reduce the amount of water that can enter the boat during a capsize.

Once excess water has been cleared out, the T-rescue can be used with a double kayak that is not loaded down with gear. If the boat is too heavy, use a side-rescue instead. Both paddlers in a double kayak should be equipped with pumps to speed up the job of pumping out water. A single rescuer can stabilize a double kayak fairly easily. Hold onto the bow cockpit, with the kayaks facing in opposite directions, while the stern paddler climbs in, followed by the bow paddler. This is even easier if the rescuers are in a double kayak; the rescuers can stabilize the boat by hanging onto both cockpits while the swimmers climb in.

Special Circumstances

Be prepared to alter your rescue techniques to deal with specific problems. It is impossible to foresee every potential problem, but you should be prepared to deal with every situation, especially those listed below. While these situations may not be common, they can happen and are best avoided by continually practicing safety procedures, such as hanging onto your kayak.

All-In Rescue

Assisted rescues assume that at least one paddler is still upright. But what happens if the entire group ends up in the water? With everyone in the water, at least one paddler will have to get back into a boat before proceeding with a T- or a side-rescue. The best way to handle an "all in" situation is for each paddler to immediately begin a self-rescue. The first paddler to successfully complete a self-rescue can then help the others using assisted rescue technique.

The traditional "all-in rescue," described in some kayaking texts, involves getting at least two of the group together, emptying one kayak by pushing it over the other kayak, then having one swimmer hang onto the emptied kayak while the other swimmer climbs in. Finally, the rescued kayaker proceeds to rescue the other members of the group. This technique is based on the important assumption that the boaters are close enough to get together while in the water. If the paddlers are spread out in wind and rough seas, it probably won't work and it will be faster and more efficient to use self-rescues (described in the next chapter).

Using a Sling

A strap or rope sling can be used to assist a swimmer who is having trouble getting out of the water and onto the kayak. A 12-foot length of floating nylon rope is ideal for this purpose. Tie the ends of the rope together to form a loop. With a paddle across the deck of the swimmer's boat, place the loop over one end of the paddle shaft and drop the rope down between the two kayaks. The swimmer then reaches under his kayak, pulls the rope beneath the hull, and

Alter your rescue techniques to deal with specific problems.

A rope sling can be rigged to provide a stirrup.

loops it around the other end of the paddle on the outboard side of the kayak. This will form a stirrup, allowing the swimmer to step up onto the deck of the kayak. Increasing the number of loops around the paddle shaft will raise the height of the stirrup, if necessary.

There is a disadvantage in having to deploy a rope to get the swimmer back aboard: anytime you have to rely on a device or make the rescue more complicated, risk is increased. However, this may be the only way to complete a rescue and it's best to be prepared for it. This is especially true for instructors and guides who are paddling with novice kayakers. However, all kayakers should learn how to climb on deck without having to resort to a sling.

Runaway Kayak

Losing a kayak in the wind out on the open sea is a potentially disastrous situation that must be dealt with swiftly and decisively. In a strong wind (approximately 20 knots or more), it is impossible to swim fast enough to catch a kayak as it blows away. When the wind is blowing against a current, the event becomes even more serious. In this situation, the kayak will fly away with the wind, while the swimmer is carried in the opposite direction with the current.

If the swimmer you are rescuing gets separated from his kayak in the wind, you have to act immediately. The more time that elapses, the farther the separation gets between swimmer and kayak. Don't let the boat get away! You have a few options, depending on the situation.

Option 1: Stop the downwind progress of the runaway kayak. This is probably the best option, but you must act quickly. Immediately paddle to the downwind side of the boat to hold it in place while the separated paddler swims over. To accomplish this, position your kayak downwind and next to the capsized boat, reach across to the upwind side with your paddle and use a powerful sculling draw stroke to stop or slow the downwind movement of both kayaks. If you do this quickly, when the separation between swimmer and kayak is not too great, the swimmer should be able to catch up to you. Of course, the swimmer must *swim*, not bob around like a helpless victim. If the swimmer is not doing anything, tell him to get moving right away. If the swimmer still does not respond, or can't catch up to the kayak, you will have to use one of the options listed below. Ideally, in this case, you'll get help from a second rescuer.

A second rescuer, if present, can paddle over to the swimmer and lend assistance. The second rescuer should have the swimmer climb up on the rear deck of her kayak, then paddle over to the primary rescuer holding the runaway kayak. If the swimmer can't climb up onto the second rescuer's kayak, have him grab the stern and then tow him over. This is difficult because the swimmer is essentially a sea anchor, but you can make slow progress, especially if the swimmer kicks along.

Option 2: Tow the runaway kayak over to the swimmer. Turn the capsized boat upright (it'll tow with less resistance if upright), hook up a short line, and tow the kayak back to the swimmer. The main problem is the extra time required to right the boat and hook up a line. This works best if you have a line ready to deploy instantly. You'll also have to unhook and stow the rope after completing the rescue.

If the kayak has traveled a considerable distance from the swimmer, towing may be the best option. Hopefully, you won't lose sight of the swimmer in the process. If another paddler is present, one of you can go for the kayak while the other stays with the swimmer.

Option 3. Carry the swimmer on your stern deck to the kayak: Have the swimmer climb onto your rear deck and lie prone, staying low and facing forward. He can dangle his legs in the water to help stabilize your kayak. Then paddle after the runaway kayak. Don't use this method unless you have good bracing skills and a solid roll, otherwise you may end up in the water too. You'll have to brace while the swimmer climbs aboard, and your kayak will be somewhat unstable with someone riding on the stern deck.

This is a marginal solution because after taking the time for the swimmer to climb aboard you may not be able to paddle fast enough to catch the runaway kayak. By simply having the swimmer grab your stern you can save some time but this usually won't work. You make very slow progress pulling someone who is in the water.

The one advantage to the stern-carry option is that you don't lose contact with the swimmer. It might be a reasonable choice if you are close enough

Use a draw stroke to stop downwind progress of a runaway kayak.

DEBRAH VOLTURNO

Stern deck carry.

MICHAEL POWERS

to shore that you can carry the swimmer to safety should you fail to catch up to the runaway kayak.

Familiarize yourself with all the runaway-kayak options through practice. If you can find a safe area with onshore wind, you can try these scenarios in a realistic way. Practice and master using a sculling draw stroke to push another kayak sideways. Also, practice carrying another paddler on your stern deck. This important technique can be used in other rescue situations. Hopefully, you'll never have to deal with a runaway kayak in strong wind. Losing a kayak is much less likely if you and your paddling partners all learn to hang onto the kayak when bailing out. Just remember that you still need to be ready to act swiftly in case it happens.

All this emphasis on chasing down a kayak may sound strange to whitewater kayakers. In a river, rescuing the swimmer always takes precedence over the kayak and other gear. But the situation is different in sea kayaking. On a river, in most cases it is relatively easy to get a swimmer ashore, after which the kayak can be retrieved. Out at sea, 2 or 3 miles from shore, the kayak takes on a much greater importance. At best, it would be very difficult to paddle 3 miles in wind and rough water with another paddler draped over your stern. In some cases, it would not be possible. In cold water the swimmer would probably be suffering from hypothermia by the time you reached shore. Out at sea, swimmer and kayak need to be reunited to avoid serious consequences.

Panicked Swimmer

Capsizing at sea can be a traumatic experience, especially if the water is rough and the paddler is inexperienced. If the swimmer is a novice and panicked or dazed, or you don't really know his skill level, the best policy is to assume you will get no help from him. The first step is to make sure the swimmer hangs onto the kayak as you set up to do the rescue. Give loud, firm, clear commands.

I like to place an inexperienced or panicked swimmer at my bow, where I can keep an eye on him and communicate easily. The best way to do this is to paddle up alongside the capsized kayak on the same side as the swimmer. This way you present your bow to the swimmer as you grab hold of his kayak. Tell the swimmer to grab your bow, lie back, and wrap his legs around it. This sounds strange, but it is very

A panicked or inexperienced paddler can hang onto the bow of rescuer's kayak.

MICHAEL POWERS

stable and comfortable for the swimmer. If the swimmer doesn't understand, just make sure he hangs onto your bow. Now proceed with a T-rescue or side-rescue, as outlined above. The only real difference is that the swimmer won't be assisting you as you lift and drain the kayak (T-rescue) or flip the boat upright (side-rescue). Then assist the swimmer, if necessary, in climbing back on deck and into the cockpit.

Incapacitated Swimmer: The Scoop Rescue

An unconscious or injured swimmer will not be able to climb back into the kayak without your help. This situation is uncommon, but I know of a few cases where a paddler with a dislocated shoulder had to be rescued. The scoop rescue is one way to get an incapacitated swimmer back into the kayak.

Paddle up alongside the capsized boat on the side opposite the swimmer. It is best to have the boats facing opposite directions, as with other assisted rescues, but this is not absolutely necessary. Reach across and grab the swimmer with one hand. With the other hand, rotate the capsized kayak up and onto its side, with the cockpit facing out toward the swimmer, away from your kayak. Let water spill in through the cockpit, so that the boat sits lower in the water. This will make it easier to shove the swimmer into the boat.

Once the boat is sitting low enough, start pushing the swimmer into the cockpit toward the bow, feet first. If the swimmer has a dislocated shoulder, she might be able to help using her good arm and legs. If the swimmer is unconscious or unresponsive due to hypothermia, roll her on her back so she is not face down in the water. Continue to feed the swimmer into the kayak as far as possible. Then rotate the kayak upright, pump out the water, and get ashore as quickly as possible.

This rescue is easier to perform with a second paddler rafted up next to the primary rescuer, as in the rafted T-rescue. The second paddler can stabilize the kayaks and help pull the swimmer into the kayak. Once the rescue is complete, you'll probably be faced with using a rafted tow (see "Towing," Chapter 9) to get the incapacitated swimmer ashore. This requires at least two paddlers, one to hold onto the injured

PHOTO SEQUENCE: MICHAEL POWERS

❶ – ❹ Photo sequence: Scoop rescue.

5 – 6 Photo sequence: Scoop rescue continued.

paddler and one to do the towing. When you are alone with an injured paddler, the situation is more difficult. Hopefully, the injured kayaker will be able to keep the boat upright while you tow. If not, use a "push-tow" (see "Towing," Chapter 9), with the victim facing you and hanging onto your bow as you push the other kayak along. If all else fails, hang on and signal for outside assistance.

Conclusion

An assisted rescue is your primary backup after bailing out. I've described the T- and side-rescues in detail because these techniques have been proven to work well in a wide variety of conditions. However, there is always room for innovation. If you discover a technique that works well for you, use it. Just make sure it works in wind and rough water.

The single most important factor in learning rescues is to practice them. If confronted with having to make a real rescue in 25-knot winds and 8-foot seas, you don't want to waste time trying to remember what to do. If you have practiced these rescues, you'll respond almost automatically, and the situation will not get out of hand.

A few years ago, I went for a paddle on Tomales Bay in Northern California with a couple of friends. The wind was gusting up to 30 knots, so we took just a short cruise along the shoreline. While eating lunch on the beach, we noticed a couple of kayakers out on the water. At first, we thought they were practicing a rescue. But after watching them struggle for several minutes, it was clear that they were not. So I reluctantly abandoned my lunch and paddled out to see if they needed help. When I arrived, I found a man in the water clinging to his kayak, while his girlfriend paddled alongside him. They were both being blown down the axis of the bay, not toward shore. I got the swimmer back in his kayak using a T-rescue, then escorted the couple ashore. They had rented the kayaks and were not prepared for the windy conditions. When I asked them if they knew how to do a rescue, they explained that they had "learned how" in a beginning class, but couldn't remember what to do. This is a classic case of what happens if you don't follow up with practice.

This tale also illustrates that knowing how to perform a rescue effectively can mean the difference between a minor incident and a tragedy. Even in a

30-knot wind, I had no real difficulty rescuing this paddler. If I hadn't known the rescue well, the situation would have been far more serious. So don't take rescues lightly; learn them and practice them.

The single most important factor in learning rescues is to practice them.

CHAPTER 5.
SELF-RESCUES

The ability to perform a self-rescue is an essential safety skill for all sea kayakers. An assisted rescue is obviously not an option if you end up in the water while paddling solo. You'll have to get back into the kayak on your own. Even when paddling with a group, you can become separated and end up by yourself, especially in a strong wind. Another possibility is that everyone ends up in the water (an "all-in" situation).

Self-rescues vary depending on whether you are paddling a sit-on-top or a closed-deck kayak. It is relatively easy to perform a self-rescue with a sit-on-top kayak because the boat doesn't take on water. However, there is some technique involved. Remounting a narrow surf ski (high-performance racing sit-on-top) requires considerable practice, especially in rough water. With a closed-deck kayak, the basic challenge is to reenter the boat and pump out the water. A partly swamped kayak is unstable; it is difficult to climb back into the cockpit without some way to stabilize the boat. The best solution is to climb in underwater and roll up (the *reentry roll*). Of course this will work only if you can perform an Eskimo roll. Another option is to climb in while stabilizing the kayak, using the paddle with flotation on one blade as an outrigger (the *paddlefloat rescue*). However, due to it's greater complexity, the paddlefloat rescue is not as practical in wind and rough water as a reentry roll.

Self-sufficiency is essential for sea kayaking safety. If you can't rescue yourself, and are relying on someone else to rescue you in challenging situations, you are severely limiting your ability to be self-sufficient and increasing your vulnerability to risk. Therefore, you need to master a reliable self-rescue. Several effective self-rescues are described below. They must be practiced thoroughly before you can rely on them.

Self-sufficiency is essential for sea kayaking safety.

PHOTO SEQUENCE: MICHAEL POWERS

Self-Rescue for Sit-On-Top Kayaks

The main advantage of a sit-on-top kayak is the ease of self-rescue. You'll want to perfect your technique so that you can use it in rough water. Practice in a safe location until you can remount the boat easily, every time.

- **Step 1.** If you have a seatbelt, be sure you know how to use the release mechanism before you get on the water. When you capsize, release the seatbelt to bail out (unless, of course, you are going to roll). Hang onto both the kayak and the paddle, and keep holding on after bailing out. This is extremely important, especially if you are out at sea on a windy day.

- **Step 2.** *(Photos 1–2)* Flip the boat upright and position yourself next to the seat. Kick your feet out behind you and swim up so you are across the seat on your stomach.

- **Step 3.** *(Photo 3)* Rotate around and place your rear end on the seat in a sidesaddle position.

- **Step 4.** *(Photo 4)* Turn to face the bow of the kayak and pull your feet out of the water and into the footbraces. Reattach the seatbelt and thighbraces if you have them.

This simple rescue will become almost automatic with practice. The two things to remember are to keep your center of gravity low as you climb up, and to place your feet in last.

With a narrow surf-ski type of sit-on-top, you may have to alter the procedure slightly due to the kayak's instability. After swimming across the seat onto your stomach, stay low and rotate your body, headfirst, toward the bow. Then swing your legs down on either side of the craft as you sit up. Straddle the boat in order to stabilize. Then carefully pull your feet out of the water and into the footbraces.

1 – **4** Photo sequence: Self rescue with a sit-on-top kayak.

Paddlefloat Rescue

Until you know how to do a reentry roll, your best chance for self-rescue in a closed-cockpit kayak is to use a paddlefloat. You inflate the float and place it on the paddle blade thus allowing your paddle to be used as an outrigger; this stabilizes the kayak while you climb back in. The paddlefloat can also be used to perform a paddlefloat reentry roll.

In its present general form, the paddlefloat rescue was originally worked out by Matt and Cam Broze of Mariner Kayaks. Will Nordby, a prominent northern California kayaker, designed the inflatable bag used in the paddlefloat rescue. This rescue can be performed with a number of different variations. In the description below, I outline a method that works well in a wide range of conditions.

- **Step 1.** *(Photo 1)* After capsizing and bailing out, be sure to hang onto both your paddle and your kayak. Position yourself in the water next to the cockpit and leave the boat upside down so that it doesn't take on more water. Locate and unclip your paddlefloat.

- **Step 2.** *(Photos 2–4)* Lie on your back and slide one leg up into the cockpit toward the bow of your kayak, which remains upside down. This will allow you to hang onto the kayak while keeping both hands free. Slip the paddlefloat over one blade of your paddle and secure it, with either a drawstring or a clip, so it can't come loose.

- **Step 3.** *(Photo 5)* You will now be lying comfortably on your back with one leg in the kayak. Relax and inflate the paddlefloat. Take your time and be sure to inflate it fully so it won't slide off the paddle.

- **Step 4.** *(Photos 6–7)* Pull your leg out of the cockpit, reach under and grasp the cockpit coaming with both hands, one on each side of the cockpit. Then, quickly flip the boat upright, rotating it toward you. This will scoop up the least amount of water. While you do this, keep your paddle under both arms, between you and the kayak to prevent

❶ – ❹ Photo sequence: Paddlefloat rescue.

PHOTO SEQUENCE: MICHAEL POWERS

⑤

⑥

⑦

⑧

PHOTO SEQUENCE: MICHAEL POWERS

the paddle from flipping up in the air as you right the boat.

- **Step 5.** *(Photo 8)* Slide the paddle blade opposite the paddlefloat beneath the straps or deck lines which are rigged directly behind the cockpit for this purpose (if you don't have this rigging, see "Variation," below). The paddle will now be perpendicular to the kayak, forming an outrigger with the paddlefloat out in the water.

- **Step 6.** *(Photos 9–10)* Starting from aft of the paddle, kick your feet out and swim up across the stern deck on your stomach, just as you would with an assisted rescue. Then, hook your foot closest to the paddle over the paddle shaft. Alternatively, you could hook your foot up on the shaft to help lift yourself out of the water. Once on deck, stay low to the boat and keep your weight shifted slightly toward the paddlefloat.

- **Step 7.** *(Photos 11–12)* Turn your body, head-first, toward the stern. As you do this, hook your other leg over the paddle shaft, then swing the leg closest to the cockpit into the kayak. It is important to keep at least one limb on the paddle shaft at all times. At this point, you are lying prone on the rear deck of the kayak with your head toward the stern and one leg in the cockpit.

- **Step 8.** *(Photo 13)* Reach down with the hand nearest the paddle shaft (on the paddlefloat side) and place it on the shaft, then swing your other leg into the cockpit. Stay low, hugging the kayak, still keeping some weight out toward the paddlefloat. Relax—you're almost in.

- **Step 9.** *(Photo 14)* Now for the trickiest part: Staying as low as possible, begin rotating your body toward the paddlefloat. As you do this reach with your free hand (the one not on the shaft) toward the paddlefloat until you can grasp the paddle shaft. Then, and only then, release the other hand so you can

⑤ – ⑧ Photo sequence: Paddlefloat rescue continued.

PHOTO SEQUENCE: MICHAEL POWERS

9 – **15** Photo sequence: Paddlefloat rescue
continued.

MICHAEL POWERS

The paddle can also be placed across your lap while pumping, where it is available for bracing, if necessary.

Know how to use the equipment. . . . Relax!

continue to rotate around to face up and slide forward into the seat. As you do this, it is very important to keep your weight shifted toward the paddlefloat; otherwise you'll probably tip over.

* **Step 10.** *(Photo 15)* Once seated, either leave the paddlefloat outrigger in place to help stabilize the boat while you pump the water out, or pull the paddle out and place it across your lap, where you can grab it to brace yourself. One advantage of having the paddle in your lap is you can use it to roll back up if you tip over while pumping. In rough seas, reattach the sprayskirt (before pumping) to keep water from washing in. If you are using a hand pump, shove it down inside the cockpit coaming with the sprayskirt sealed around it. After pumping the water out, stow the pump and paddlefloat so you can resume paddling. If you have a foot pump, you can stow the paddlefloat immediately and pump while paddling.

Practice is the vital ingredient in learning the paddlefloat rescue. If the process described above sounds complicated, don't be discouraged. There are many points to remember. With practice, you will perform the paddlefloat rescue smoothly and efficiently. Without practicing this rescue in a variety of conditions, the paddlefloat will do you no good.

To show what can go wrong, I'll describe my first rough-water attempt at a paddlefloat rescue during a practice session under the Golden Gate Bridge on a windy summer afternoon. Having done the rescue successfully the first time I tried it in calm water, I was fairly confident, so I flipped over, exited the kayak, and grabbed the paddlefloat. That was the last thing I did right.

I placed the float on one end of my paddle, clenched the valve in my teeth to open it and, in my excitement, pulled the valve right out of its housing. *Lesson one: Know how to use the equipment. Lesson two: Relax!* I didn't drop the valve in the water and, with some struggle, was able to get the valve seated back where it belonged. I proceeded to inflate the paddlefloat, but stopped short of inflating it fully. I rigged the paddle-shaft outrigger and began to climb in.

As I pulled myself up on the boat, the outrigger suddenly sank and the boat flipped back over. I turned to watch the paddlefloat blow away across the surface of the bay like an errant balloon. *Lesson three: Inflate the float completely and attach it firmly to the paddle with a drawstring or clip.* Having lost a key piece of equipment, my paddlefloat rescue was over. Luckily, this was a practice session and I was able to get back into my kayak with an assisted rescue. My whole attitude toward learning rescues changed after this experience. I worked on solving the problems I had discovered, and resolved to always test everything in real conditions. You'll never have to flail about in the cold waters of the San Francisco Bay if you follow the steps outlined above carefully and get plenty of practice.

Deck Rigging for Paddlefloat Outrigger

You'll need to use the proper deck rigging to hold the paddlefloat outrigger in place, so that it can't move up and down or side to side. Some kayaks come equipped with deck-mounted rope or shock cord for this purpose. If you use shock cord, make sure it is sturdy and well tightened, so that the paddle will be fixed in place. I prefer to use rope or strapping because it doesn't stretch much. Make sure you can release the paddle easily. This is usually accomplished by pulling the paddle straight out, away from the kayak, with the blade flat to the deck.

Variation

If you are using a kayak without rigging for the paddlefloat (like some rental kayaks), you'll have to hold the paddle in place while climbing back in. Do this by holding the paddle shaft firmly against the coaming, behind the cockpit, and hooking your thumb around the paddle shaft while grasping the inside of the coaming with your fingers. As you climb into the kayak, you must maintain the perpendicular orientation of the paddle shaft to the kayak at all times.

The main disadvantage to not having the outrigger affixed is that it is more difficult to climb in, holding the paddle shaft in place and thereby maintaining the outrigger throughout the process. However, this variation is worth practicing even if you do have rigging, because it gives you another option.

Make sure you can easily remove the paddle from the deck rigging.

MICHAEL POWERS

If you don't attach the paddle to the deck, you can hold it in place against the rear coaming with one hand.

MICHAEL POWERS

Important Points to Remember

While climbing back in the kayak, the two most important things to keep in mind are to *stay low* and hug the kayak, and to *keep some weight on the outrigger.* You need to keep the center of gravity low for stability. To assure that you keep your weight shifted toward the paddlefloat, have at least *one limb on the paddle shaft* as you climb on and rotate into the seat. This means you don't remove a hand or foot from the shaft until you have replaced it with your other hand or foot.

In Step 6 of the paddlefloat rescue, I described mounting the kayak aft of the paddle which is slightly easier than climbing up in front of the shaft, especially if the outrigger is not affixed. However, some find it as easy to climb in from in front of the shaft, closer to the cockpit. See what works for you; try it both ways until you find the better method.

How you stow the paddlefloat and pump is important. You don't want to capsize and bail out, only to discover that your paddlefloat has washed off the deck and been lost, or that your pump is stowed away in one of the hatches. The most common error many paddlers make is to simply stow the pump and paddlefloat under the shock cord on deck. This works fine in flat water, where you probably won't need these items. If you capsize in rough water, they could easily be swept off the deck—just when you need them. Either stow the pump and paddlefloat under deck lines and attach them with a clip, or clip the paddlefloat in behind your seat where it can be reached when you're in the water and stow the pump under the front deck where you can grab it easily, once back in the boat. Since I don't like having things cluttering up the deck, I do the latter. The main thing is to clip them in and have them readily accessible.

The best place to stow a hand pump is under the front deck where it can be reached easily and won't get lost. Mount 2 loops of shock cord under the deck to hold the pump in place.

Paddlefloat Reentry Roll

The paddlefloat can also be used to assist with a reentry roll. The paddlefloat reentry roll is performed by entering the boat underwater, then rolling up using the buoyancy of the float as an aid. It requires no balancing act while climbing on top of the kayak and is therefore a good rough-water rescue, especially when the standard paddlefloat rescue would be difficult or impossible. No matter how rough the water is, you'll be able to get back in the kayak with a paddlefloat reentry roll, a good backup when other methods fail. It is also relatively easy to learn even if you can't do an Eskimo roll yet.

- **Step 1.** *(Photo 1)* After bailing out, maintain contact with both your kayak and your paddle, as usual. Retrieve the paddlefloat. Hook one leg well into the cockpit, and inflate the paddlefloat on the end of the paddle, exactly as in Steps 1–3 of the standard paddlefloat rescue. For the reentry roll, be sure to set up on the *upwind* side of the kayak; this will make it easier to roll up. But don't let the boat get away from you.

- **Step 2.** *(Photo 2)* Extend the paddle blade with the paddlefloat attached away from the kayak. Place the other blade flat on the inverted hull directly over the seat. The paddle is now oriented perpendicular to the kayak.

- **Step 3.** *(Photo 3)* Twist onto your side and slide both feet well into the cockpit toward the bow. You may have to tilt the boat slightly onto its side while pushing your feet in. Grasp the paddle shaft (still in position as described in step 2, above) with both hands, holding it perpendicular to the kayak, keeping the near blade flat against the hull of the boat.

- **Step 4.** *(Photos 3–4)* Take a deep breath, prepare to submerge, and release your outboard hand (the one closest to the paddlefloat) from the paddle shaft. As you submerge, rotate upside down, swing your free hand around under the boat, and grasp the cockpit coaming on the opposite side. Now pull yourself firmly into the seat. Find the footbraces and brace your knees and thighs against the deck. *Make sure you have good contact with the footbraces and are completely in the kayak.*

- **Step 5.** *(Photos 5–8)* Once seated in the kayak, release the coaming, reach up and grasp the paddle shaft again with both hands. Then lever yourself upright with a smooth hipsnap. *Keep your head down* as you roll up; pull

❶ – ❹ Photo sequence: Paddlefloat reentry roll.

PHOTO SEQUENCE: JUNE LEGLER

your head out last. Once you are up, pump the water out as in a standard paddlefloat rescue.

Variation

One variation of this rescue is to hold the paddle alongside and parallel to the kayak, with the paddlefloat toward the bow, as you pull yourself into the cockpit. After getting seated underwater, swing the paddle out to the 90° position and roll up. This variation is easier for those who know how to roll.

Tips

Failure to execute the paddlefloat reentry roll can usually be attributed to one of the following mistakes.

- **Rushing the process and starting to roll before being firmly seated in the kayak with both feet on the footbraces.** Make sure you are well braced in the boat before starting the roll. You've got plenty of time to do this. Most people can hold their breath for at least 20 to 30 seconds. It only takes about 3 seconds to get seated in the boat if you relax and don't panic.

- **Pulling your head up before the roll is complete.** *(Photos 5–6)* Keep your head close to but just beneath the surface as you roll the boat. The paddlefloat provides tremendous support, but don't work against it by pulling your head up out of the water.

- **Trying to roll on the downwind side in a strong wind.** Set up so you roll on the upwind side. Roll up into the wind. This might sound counterintuitive, but since the boat is being pushed downwind, it is much easier to roll up on the trailing edge (upwind side).

This rescue is amazingly easy, once you get it. It is also a relatively foolproof method of getting back into a kayak in wind and rough seas. Be sure to practice it until you can do it efficiently.

5 – **8** Photo sequence: Paddlefloat reentry roll continued.

Paddlefloat rescues provide a means of self-rescue if they are mastered and practiced in realistic conditions although there is no getting around the fact that these rescues are time-consuming. Inflating the paddlefloat and pumping water out of the boat are the main reasons for the relatively slow pace of the process, and there is no way to speed this up. Relax and conserve as much energy as possible while completing these chores. Paddlefloat rescues are backups to other paddling skills, including balance, bracing, and the Eskimo roll. You may never need to resort to a paddlefloat rescue if you have mastered these other skills. Nevertheless, always carry a paddlefloat and know how to use it, just in case.

Paddlefloat rescues are backups to other paddling skills.

Reentry Roll

The reentry roll (*sans* paddlefloat) is an excellent self-rescue technique. It takes less time than a paddlefloat rescue because there is no need to deploy and inflate a float. Because it requires no special devices and can be performed quickly in almost any conditions, the reentry roll should be your primary self-rescue.

Obviously, you need a good Eskimo roll to perform this rescue. You may be asking yourself why a paddler with a good Eskimo roll would end up in the water in the first place. Even the best roll can fail. If you are caught by surprise and capsize when out of breath, you may rush the roll and fail to complete it. If your sprayskirt pops off and you fall partway out of the kayak, you may have to bail. It's also possible for a large breaking wave to hold you under until you simply run out of breath and have no time to roll back up. This is unusual, but it happened to me once. If you have a reliable roll, you'll rarely end up in the water. Yet, consider it a possibility and be prepared by mastering the reentry roll.

Perform the reentry roll as follows:

- **Step 1.** Position yourself facing the capsized boat next to the cockpit, on the upwind side. Place the paddle alongside and parallel to the boat against the near side of the cockpit. If you are setting up for a *right-side* roll, hold the paddle against the coaming with your *left* hand. Do this by placing your hand palm down, shoving your fingers under the coaming lip, while wrapping your thumb around the paddle shaft and the inside of the

coaming. You now have a firm grip on the near side of the cockpit with the paddle in position.

- **Step 2.** *(Photos 1–2)* Face the bow, lie back, and shove your feet forward into the cockpit, keeping your head above water. As you do this, rotate slightly away from the boat onto your side to prepare for the complete entry.

- **Step 3.** *(Photo 3)* Relax, then take a deep breath and submerge, rotating your body and shoving farther into the kayak. Reach around with your free hand, grab the other side of the cockpit, and pull yourself firmly into the seat (just as in the paddlefloat reentry roll). Find the footbraces and brace your knees and thighs firmly against the deck. Make sure you have good contact with the footbraces and are completely seated. This sounds like a lot to do, but it only takes a few seconds; *you have plenty of time.*

- **Step 4.** *(Photos 4–7)* Now that you are seated, release the coaming and grasp the paddle with both hands. Quickly slide your forward hand up to check the blade angle; the blade needs to be horizontal. Set up carefully and roll. Then pump out the water.

Tips

Failure to execute this rescue can result from any of the same mistakes that can occur during the paddlefloat reentry roll, especially trying to roll before getting firmly seated in the kayak, with both feet planted on the footbraces. There are two other potential problems that can occur during the reentry roll:

- **Failing to orient the paddle blade correctly.** It is important to make sure the forward paddle blade is horizontal. The potential for incorrect orientation occurs because the blade tends to rotate out of position while you are climbing into the cockpit. I struggled with this for some time before finding the solution. All you have to do is slide your hand forward to grab and orient the blade. This takes a fraction of a second, yet it has a major influence on the success of your roll.

1 – **3** Photo sequence: Reentry roll.

- **A swamped kayak is difficult to roll.** A swamped boat feels different than an empty kayak when rolling. With all that water sloshing around, the kayak is harder to roll, and it rolls up more slowly, throwing off your timing. You'll need a strong hip-snap and good technique. It's important to make the roll on your first attempt, because each successive attempt scoops more water into the boat. Using an extended-paddle roll can increase your success rate. If you miss your roll and the kayak gets swamped, you may have to resort to a paddlefloat roll. It is possible to reduce swamping by reattaching the sprayskirt while under water, but this uses up valuable time, giving you only one shot at rolling. Another way to help prevent the problem of swamping is to use a sea sock.

Reentry Roll Variations

An alternate to the *side entry* method of entering the cockpit as described in Steps 2 and 3 above is the *somersault* method. To use this technique, *face the stern* of the kayak, then submerge and grasp the cockpit on both sides, holding the paddle against the coaming on one side, parallel to the kayak. With your head directly beneath the cockpit, do an underwater somersault and swing your legs up and into the cockpit. Finally, pull yourself firmly into the seat and roll up.

I prefer the side entry to the somersault method for three reasons: (1) using the side entry, you climb most of the way into the kayak before submerging your head; (2) it can be difficult to submerge and somersault underwater when wearing a PFD; and (3) the somersault method can be disorienting. However, if you find this technique works well for you, by all means use it!

An *extended-paddle roll* (also known as a *Pawlata roll*) can increase your chances of completing a successful roll on your first attempt. This roll is performed like a *sweep roll* (a roll in which the paddle is used like a sweeping brace), except that the paddle is held in a fully extended position, giving a great deal of leverage which makes it easier to roll a swamped

PHOTO SEQUENCE: MICHAEL POWERS

kayak. The blade orientation problem is also resolved in the extended-paddle roll due to the fact that the rear blade is held in a vertical position (with a feathered paddle).

The extended-paddle roll is frowned on by some kayaking "purists," because it requires you to shift hand position and to over rely on the paddle. Nevertheless, it is a powerful and reliable roll, an excellent choice when rolling a swamped kayak. It is also a great backup if your regular roll fails. I've gotten out of some serious situations using the extended-paddle roll.

Once you roll up, you may or may not want to pump the water out immediately, depending on the situation. In most cases, you want to remove water immediately because it destabilizes the kayak. However, if you are in a dangerous location, such as a sea cave with breaking waves or a major surf zone, quickly reattach the sprayskirt (if you have time) and paddle to a location where you can pump the water out more safely. With a foot pump, you can pump while you paddle. The kayak will be unstable until most of the water is pumped out, so be ready to brace or roll again.

The reentry roll may sound like a complicated maneuver but it can be done efficiently. It takes less than 15 seconds to perform, not including the time necessary for pumping water out. The trick, as always, is to practice the maneuver until it becomes effortless. Start out by practicing it in a heated pool or warm water, then practice it in increasingly varied and challenging conditions. The advantage of the reentry roll as a self-rescue is that it gets you back in the boat quickly. You still have to pump, but at least you are out of the water.

The advantage of the reentry roll as a self-rescue is that it gets you back in the boat quickly.

Scramble Rescue

The scramble rescue is another technique for climbing back into a closed-cockpit kayak. While it is definitely worth learning, I don't consider the scramble rescue to be reliable in rough water. If you can pull it off, use it, but don't completely depend on it. The best reason for learning the scramble is that it enables you to climb into and out of your kayak in relatively calm water where you can't really land on shore, for instance in some rock gardens and areas with steep cliffs. It also lets you launch your kayak from the

PHOTO SEQUENCE: JUNE LEGLER

water in rock gardens as an alternative to a seal launch (with a seal launch, you enter the kayak and slide off the rocks into the water). Perform the scramble rescue as follows:

- **Step 1.** *(Photos 1–2)* With the kayak upright, face the cockpit. Swim up and across the cockpit on your stomach.

- **Step 2.** *(Photo 3)* Rotate your body so that your head is toward the bow, keeping your center of gravity low as you hug the boat. *(Photo 4)* Sit up with your legs straddling the boat and push your rear end down into the cockpit. This is a remarkably stable position. *(Photo 5)* Finally, pull your legs into the cockpit, sit down onto the seat, and reattach the sprayskirt. Pump out the water, if the boat is partly swamped.

Balance is required while pulling in your legs; it may help to lean back slightly for increased stability (or even to scull with the paddle). If you have long legs, you may have

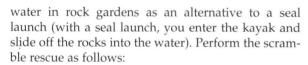

❶ – ❺ Photo sequence: Scramble rescue.

to sit up just behind the cockpit in order to get your legs in; this takes more balance.

Variation

Bo Barnes (former sea kayaking program director at Outdoors Unlimited, University of California, San Francisco) showed me the following variation on the scramble rescue. You may find it more efficient and easier to learn than the technique described above.

- **Step 1.** (*Photos 1–2*) Face the cockpit and swim up across it so that your stomach lies over the far side of the coaming. Picture a taco: you are the taco shell folded over your kayak (the filling).

- **Step 2.** (*Photo 3*) Quickly rotate your entire body around to a face-up position and drop your rear end into the cockpit. Do this in one smooth motion. You are now sitting roughly sidesaddle in the seat. (*Photo 4*) Swing one leg forward and across to the other side of the kayak so you are straddling it as in step 2 above. Now pull your legs into the cockpit and reattach the sprayskirt.

With practice the scramble rescue (either variation) can be accomplished in a few seconds. This reentry technique is very effective in relatively calm water. It can be done with a partially swamped boat in fairly rough water but will be more difficult in such conditions. The reentry roll is more reliable in rough water, although in tight places (such as narrow caves or shallow rocky areas) climbing back into an upright boat may be more practical than reentering upside down and rolling.

If you want to exit your kayak in the water without tipping over, release the sprayskirt and pull up out of the seat just far enough to get one leg out. Then pull the other leg out into a sidesaddle position and slide into the water. You can reenter using either scramble method described above.

❶ – **❹** Photo sequence: Scramble rescue variation.

Self-Rescue for Double Kayaks

Climbing back into a double kayak is relatively easy because double kayaks are more stable than most singles. However, a rescue is complicated by the fact that a double kayak takes on a tremendous amount of water. You and your partner may have to push up the bow or rock the boat to evacuate excess water before righting the boat. The best solution is to use a sea sock in each cockpit.

After capsizing do the following:

- **Step 1.** Hang onto the kayak and prepare to right it. If the boat is severely swamped, try rotating and rocking it while it is upside down. One swimmer should be positioned at the bow, the other at the stern. Then flip the boat upright quickly, trying not to scoop too much water.

- **Step 2.** Both paddlers should move to the stern cockpit, one on each side. While the stern paddler climbs in by swimming up and across the deck, just aft of the cockpit, the other paddler stabilizes the boat by hanging on to both sides of the coaming near the front of the cockpit.

- **Step 3.** Once the stern paddler is seated, the bow paddler moves to the bow cockpit and climbs in while the stern paddler supports the boat using a *sculling brace* (performed by sculling the power face of the paddle blade back and forth across the surface of the water, like spreading peanut butter). It is best to scull and lean slightly toward the *upwind* side, but be prepared to brace on either side, as necessary.

- **Step 4.** Both paddlers can pump to remove the water quickly. If conditions are extremely rough, one paddler can pump water while the other sculls for support.

Practice climbing in and out of the double kayak until you can do it easily. Because most doubles have a wide beam, this is not too difficult. If necessary, a paddlefloat or a sling can be employed in rougher conditions.

A double kayak takes on a tremendous amount of water.

Conclusion

Self-rescues are extremely valuable for attaining confidence and self-reliance in your seagoing adventures. They are essential backup tools that you can use without having to rely on someone else to rescue you. As with all kayaking techniques, these rescues must be practiced before you can use them effectively in real conditions. Even after you have learned them well, be sure to review them periodically. It's easy to lose your edge over time. Hopefully, you won't need to use self-rescues very often. Once you know how to roll, learn the reentry roll and make it your primary self-rescue.

Self-rescues are extremely valuable for attaining confidence and self-reliance in your seagoing adventures.

CHAPTER 6.
RESCUES IN SURF AND OCEAN ROCK GARDENS

Surf zones and ocean rock gardens are coastal areas exposed to breaking waves. Capsizing is more likely in these rougher waters and rescues become more difficult. An Eskimo roll is essential for safety, especially for paddlers in closed-cockpit kayaks. However, even a bombproof roll will not guarantee that you will stay out of the water. Some waves are powerful enough to rip you out of your kayak. If you get jammed between rocks, you may not be able to roll and will need to bail. Therefore, rescues are essential backups and you should take the time to master the skills to use them.

Many of the rescues that work well in open water are not practical in surf or rock gardens. Where waves are breaking, either a rescue has to be swift or the kayaker will need to swim or be towed to a safer location before reentering the boat. The main problem is that kayaks get tossed about in the waves, endangering everyone involved in the rescue. You need to pay special attention whenever performing a rescue in the vicinity of breaking waves.

A fast self-rescue, such as a reentry roll or sit-on-top rescue, is a good choice unless there is an easy swim to a safe location. The assisted rescues and paddlefloat rescues described in previous chapters are generally too time-consuming to be used in the midst of breaking waves. Other options are described below.

Swimming

Knowing when, how, and where to swim is a key issue for the surf kayaker and ocean rock garden paddler. Swimming to shore is not usually an option on open seas, but in surf and rock gardens, swimming is often the best, or *only* rescue option. You may be able to swim to shore, or you might need to swim with your kayak out of the breakers to an area where you can complete either a self-rescue or an assisted rescue.

In the Surf Zone

If you capsize and bail out in the surf, in most cases the best choice is to swim to shore. It may not be possible to hang onto your kayak, especially in large surf. If you lose the boat, don't worry; it will usually wash in. The important thing is to prevent injury: be sure not to get between the kayak and shore. Always try to stay on the seaward side of the boat so that it doesn't hit you. As you swim in, body-surf the waves to speed you toward shore and save energy.

To prepare to swim in surf, spend some time practicing body-surfing techniques. Find a safe, gently-sloping beach with small waves. Dress appropriately depending upon the water temperature, then wade in and practice diving under waves. Swim with the waves and ride them in toward shore. As you get comfortable, work up to swimming in larger waves. You'll want to practice swimming in your paddling gear (pfd, helmet, etc.) to make sure you aren't wearing anything that can seriously interfere with your

Practice swimming in surf and rock gardens, but don't forget to wear a helmet.

FIGURE 1. Rip Currents

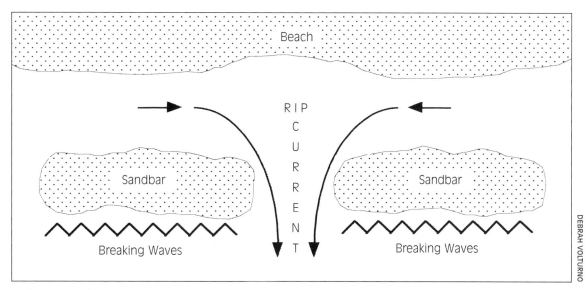

Rip currents form when waves break on a submerged sandbar and water piles up inside the bar. The excess water then returns seaward, carving a channel in the bar and forming a continuous outgoing current. Feeder currents form inside the bar, flowing laterally along the beach.

ability to swim. Once you start kayaking in the surf, you'll inevitably get additional swimming experience, especially if you haven't perfected your roll!

Body-surfing experience is essential if you ever end up swimming in a wide surf zone with large waves. A long swim in surf can exhaust you, so conserve as much strength as possible by using the wave energy to help you reach the beach. If you capsize far from shore in a wide surf zone, it will help if you don't immediately bail out. The kayak will be pushed toward shore by the force of the wave and you can take advantage of the free ride by staying in the kayak. To protect your body, tuck forward into the roll set-up position. Then either roll or wait a few seconds before exiting the boat. This will get you closer to shore and most of the wave energy will dissipate before you bail.

If you discover you are not making progress toward shore—or are struggling to make progress toward the shore—you might be swimming against a *rip current*. A rip current forms off a beach where waves break on an underwater sand bar. As the waves break over the bar, water piles up inside the bar and returns seaward, carving a channel in the bar and creating a current that moves *away* from the shore. The net result of this wave and current action along the beachfront is the growth of a series of sand bars where waves break, separated by channels with rip currents. The water is deeper in the rip channels so the waves there tend to soften and surge rather than break. The absence of breaking waves is one clue to the location of a rip. Also watch for foam lines and choppy water extending out to sea.

If you are caught in a rip current, use this tactic: Swim parallel to shore towards an area where you see breaking waves. This usually indicates a sandbar rather than a channel. Once in the breakers, body-surf toward shore. Just in-shore of the sandbar, you might encounter deeper water and a current that is moving laterally, parallel to the beach. This feeder current supplies water to the outgoing rip current. You'll have to swim fast and hard across this lateral trough in order to reach shore and avoid being recycled back into the rip.

It is best to avoid kayaking in large surf and areas with rip currents until you have developed a reliable roll. The roll will reduce your chances of having to swim. Even so, if you capsize in a large, powerful wave, you might get pulled out of the cockpit before you get a chance to roll. *Always be prepared to swim.*

In Ocean Rock Gardens

In ocean rock gardens you are usually swimming *with* your kayak to a safe place where your can reenter the boat. If you're lucky, the surge will carry you and the kayak out of the danger zone, into calmer water. If this does not happen, swim out, pushing or pulling your kayak as you proceed. You may have to wait for things to calm down, during a window in the wave sets. When an opportunity occurs, don't waste time! Swim out quickly before the next wave set arrives.

Be prepared to contend with large wave sets and the powerful surges that accompany them. As the waves roar in, the safest thing to do is dive down and grab hold of the rock, clamping on like a limpet. Be aware that your kayak is getting tossed around on the surface; don't let it hit you. After the waves pass, resurface, grab your boat if possible, and swim to the closest protected location. This protected area may be on shore, the shoreward side of a large rock, a nearby

MICHAEL POWERS

Swim your kayak to a safe place, where you can reenter the boat or perform a rescue.

cove, or out in deeper water. The main thing is to get where you can reenter the kayak. Inspect the kayak for damage before carrying on. If the boat is taking on water, land and repair it, if possible.

In a worst-case scenario, you may have to abandon the boat and swim to shore. If there is no safe place to climb ashore, you'll have to get help from a companion who can use a stern carry to transport you to safety.

Practice swimming in rock gardens to get comfortable with this environment. Start in areas with gentle surge and small waves. You may find that it is considerably easier and less intimidating to swim than to paddle your kayak in these chaotic waters.

Assisted Rescues

In the surf zone, an assisted rescue is not necessary unless the swim to shore is too far or difficult. If you must rescue a swimmer in distress, you'll either have to get him to shore or back into the kayak.

Sometimes it is possible to tow both swimmer and kayak out of the surf and into deeper water, where a T-rescue can be performed. This will only work near the outer margin of the surf zone where deep water is nearby. Have the swimmer hold onto your stern with one hand, the boat with the other. He should kick along while you paddle out between wave sets. You'll have to paddle hard; progress will be slow. Resist the temptation to use a tow line. In the surf, ropes introduce the possibility of entanglement, a serious danger .

If you can't tow the swimmer back out through the surf, or if he has lost contact with his kayak, use a stern deck carry. Have him climb onto your stern deck and lie prone (on his stomach). Then paddle and surf into shore. The stray kayak should wash in on its own.

If you are on shore and decide to swim out to rescue someone, first try to determine what the problem is so you don't get yourself in trouble. Look for dangerous rip currents or other hazards. Once you ascertain the risk and perceive it is safe to perform the rescue, put on swim fins if you have them (see below). Swim out and approach the swimmer with caution. Be sure he is not panicked and don't let him grab you! After calming him down if necessary, use a lifesaving carry to bring him in: come up from behind and wrap one arm around his chest, under his arm. Swim in

Using a lifesaving carry to help a swimmer in distress.

MICHAEL POWERS

using backstrokes with your other arm. Be sure to keep his head above water.

Swim fins are an important safety device for swimming in the surf. While you cannot wear them in a kayak, you can keep them close at hand and put them on if you end up in the water. If you have to perform a swimming rescue, fins will make the job easier and safer.

I learned the value of fins from Andy Taylor of *Force Ten* (a team of storm sea kayakers in Elk, California, founded by the late Steve Sinclair). Andy had joined our band of Tsunami Rangers in 1998 for a week of paddling on the Oregon coast. We launched through large surf into a fearsome sea, churned up by 25-knot winds with gusts to 35 knots. We had already scouted out a potential campsite several miles to the south. However, our view from the road, several hundred feet above the shore and a quarter mile away, allowed only a glimpse of a beach that appeared to be partially protected from the huge surf. We all had our fingers crossed as we surfed downwind in steep seas toward our destination.

Andy and I arrived first and surfed in, one at a time, to the only possible landing at one end of a crescent beach, somewhat protected by a rocky point to the north. To the south, the beach gave way to a huge jumble of house-size jagged rocks which were being pounded by powerful 10-foot waves. After landing, Andy and I stood on the beach and watched the rest of our group approach the surf zone. Eric judiciously waited for a large wave set to pass but Michael cruised past him without paying attention to the waves (his first mistake). A large wave caught him and Michael was tossed end over end. He failed to roll (mistake number two), and finally bailed out. We expected him to swim in, but he appeared to be hanging onto his capsized kayak, drifting swiftly to the south toward the larger surf and the rocks. Meanwhile Eric and the rest of the group surfed in without incident. Now we had to decide what to do about Michael's predicament.

Most of us hiked south onto the rocks where we would be well-positioned to pick up the pieces when Michael and his kayak finally washed ashore. Andy ran to his kayak, donned swim fins, and began to swim out. He quickly reached Michael and managed to swim about two hundred meters back against the wind and through the surf, pulling Michael and his kayak along. They came in close to shore just north of the dangerous rock pile where the rest of us waded out to help bring Michael and his kayak up on the beach. This rescue would have been far more difficult if Andy had not had his fins.

In the surf, an assisted rescue should primarily be considered a backup to self-rescue. Assuming Michael couldn't swim in with his kayak, he still had a couple of options for a self-rescue: 1) Perform a reentry roll, then paddle in, or, 2) abandon the boat and try to swim in. Because he didn't do either, he had to be rescued.

In ocean rock gardens, the type of assisted rescue depends on circumstances. A T-rescue can be effective where there is no danger of being hit by a breaking wave or being pushed into a dangerous area by surge or current. Otherwise the swimmer and his kayak have to be extracted from the danger zone. This can be accomplished with a stern tow, stern carry, or a throw rope, depending on the situation.

Stern Tow

A stern tow, with the swimmer hanging onto your stern and swimming along, works well for a short-distance rescue. The stern tow is mainly an assist to the swimmer, who must kick and swim along, rather than hang on as dead weight. This is a simple and efficient way to pull the swimmer out of a *churn* (area of surging whitewater) or the mouth of a cave. If possible, the swimmer should hang onto her kayak with her free hand. Otherwise, the boat can be retrieved separately, using a short tow line, if it doesn't wash out on its own.

Stern Carry

If you aren't making headway with a stern tow, or the swimmer has to be transported a considerable distance (50 yards or more), use a stern carry. Have the swimmer climb onto your stern, then paddle to safety. Once the swimmer is safe, retrieve the capsized kayak by pushing or towing it out of the churn.

Throw Rope

If the swimmer cannot be retrieved safely by kayak, use a throw rope. Paddle close enough to make an accurate throw, then toss the bag, using an underhand or side-arm throw. The rope should be attached to your kayak with a jam cleat or other

MICHAEL POWERS

Practice tossing a throw rope to gain accuracy.

quick-release mechanism. I have a throw rope attached with a short length of shock cord, looped around a cleat just aft of the cockpit. Once the swimmer has a grip on the line, you can tow him to safety. He should try to hold onto his kayak while being towed. If the kayak is turned upright, it will move more efficiently.

Whenever performing a rescue, always consider your own safety. The first rule of rescue is to never put yourself into serious danger while trying to rescue someone else. The end result could be a worse situation than you started out with. In some cases the only reasonable rescue is a self-rescue. The swimmer must swim out of the danger zone or perform some type of self-rescue without any outside help. This is especially true in areas with breaking waves, where the use of tow lines is dangerous.

The first rule of rescue is to never put yourself into serious danger while trying to rescue someone else.

Self-Rescues

Never assume that someone will rescue you. This is a particularly poor assumption in surf and rock gardens where conditions may be too intimidating or dangerous for your partners to rescue you. If you end up swimming in surf or in a rock garden, don't drift around waiting for assistance: take steps immediately to rescue yourself.

If you end up out of your kayak in the surf zone, self-rescue is usually the best choice. After exiting the kayak, swim to shore, as described above. If you are faced with a long swim, another option is to perform a reentry roll. Wait for a window in the wave action, then reenter and roll. Set up to roll on the seaward side of the boat, so you are rolling up into any waves that may approach. Once in the kayak, either surf in or paddle offshore out of the surf zone; pump the water out of your boat before making another attempt to land. With a sit-on-top kayak, simply climb back on, assuming the boat hasn't gotten away from you.

Performing a self-rescue in a rock garden or a sea cave usually involves swimming with your kayak to a safe location where you can reenter the boat. If swimming out of a cave, use the outgoing surge to help make progress toward the mouth of the cave. Hang onto the rock whenever a wave surges in so that you are not pushed back into the cave. As you work your way out, push or pull your kayak along, but don't let the boat hit you. If a large wave set crashes in, dive under the waves. Once out of the cave, reenter the kayak with a reentry roll or a scramble rescue. You might even be able to use a paddlefloat rescue if there is not much wave action.

If the cave has a larger deep-water chamber, you might be better off swimming back into it where you can reenter your kayak. Most wave action is concentrated in narrow or shallow parts of the cave; if you can work your way to deeper water, it should be possible to reenter the kayak, then paddle out. *Every situation is different.*

If you are swimming in a rock garden area, swim to deeper water where the waves aren't breaking or into a protected area behind a large rock, where you can reenter your kayak. Depending on the conditions, use a reentry roll, scramble, or paddlefloat rescue. Another possibility is to swim ashore or onto a relatively flat *wash-rock* (an emergent rock with water surging partway over it). To swim onto a wash-rock, use a *swimming seal landing*: swim with the surge up onto the rock, then grab on as the water recedes. Either push your boat up first (making sure to get it high enough on the rock so it stays in place), or hang on and pull it along with you. Then you can do a *seal*

Most wave action is concentrated in narrow or shallow parts of the cave.

launch: empty water out of the kayak and climb in, wait for a surging wave, and paddle off the rock on the cushion of surging water.

Expect the Unexpected

Good kayaking skills and judgment should assure that you don't end up in many rescue situations. However, in surf and ocean rock gardens something can go wrong when you least expect it. I've missed my "bombproof roll" and ended up swimming in the surf on more than one occasion, just when I thought everything was going fine. When paddling in rock gardens I've been caught several times by a large wave that I was not expecting. In one case, I was paddling out of a sea cave when a wave roared in, capsized me, and pushed me under a rock overhang. Now I found myself upside down, in the dark, trapped under a rock! I had to wait for several seconds before the surge pushed me free and I was able to roll back up. I should have been prepared for this because a year earlier I had to use a stern tow to extract a friend out of the same cave, after he capsized, was pushed under the very same rock ledge, and ended up swimming.

Whenever paddling in surf or ocean rock gardens, be prepared for rescue situations. Swimming ability is critical. If you end up in the water, it is often necessary to swim out of whitewater, surge, or breaking waves before reentering the kayak. Swimming and other rescues should be treated as *backups* to more primary skills, including good judgment, wave reading ability, boat control, bracing, and the Eskimo roll. These skills are all essential for paddling in surf and rock gardens. Practicing and mastering them will greatly reduce the odds of having to perform a rescue in potentially difficult conditions.

Finally, if you find yourself involved in numerous rescue operations in surf and rock gardens, consider the fact that you or your companions need more work on basic kayaking skills and the ability to read and handle waves. You are probably paddling in areas well beyond your skill level. The goal is to avoid having to do any rescues.

The goal is to avoid having to do any rescues.

CHAPTER 7.
THE ESKIMO ROLL

Nearly every sea kayaking tragedy I have ever heard about would not have happened if those involved could have performed an Eskimo roll. The roll is a basic skill that will contribute significantly to your safety. Learning the roll will provide other benefits. It will give you the confidence to increase your overall boating skills and allow you to gain paddling experience in a wide range of conditions.

Rolling technique is described in numerous kayaking publications but the best way to learn it is with competent instruction, followed by lots of practice. Below are reasons to roll, and tips on how to go about learning, then troubleshooting the roll. I'll also discuss how to develop a reliable *combat roll:* a roll that works in the real world of waves, current, surf, wind, and cold water.

The roll is a basic skill that will contribute significantly to your safety.

Ten Reasons to Roll

There are numerous reasons sea kayakers should learn to perform an Eskimo roll. I've highlighted the most important ones below. So far, no one has been able to give me a reason *not* to learn how to roll.

1. The roll could save your life.

2. The roll takes only about 3 seconds to perform and eliminates the need for rescue.

3. Essentially a brace, the roll will improve other bracing strokes, thus reducing the risk of capsize. I have yet to see anyone with a really effective brace who cannot roll.

4. In situations where rescue is difficult or nearly impossible (storm seas, surf, some areas in ocean rock gardens), the roll might be your last recourse before taking a nasty swim—or worse.

5. The ability to roll will boost your confidence tremendously, allowing you to relax in rough

conditions. *A relaxed paddling style is the key to skillful kayaking.*

6.   The confidence and extra safety margin provided by your ability to roll will enable you to push your limits and paddle in more challenging conditions. You will be better able to handle unexpected conditions—and they are the rule rather than the exception in sea kayaking.

7.   Unless you can roll, you will have an extremely difficult time learning to handle surf—an essential skill for paddling the open coast.

8.   Part of what makes a kayak seaworthy is the fact that it can be rolled. You'll want to take advantage of this fact.

9.   If you ever want to paddle solo, the ability to roll will increase your safety margin.

10. Rolling is a great way to cool off.

To summarize, the Eskimo roll provides a quick and efficient capsize recovery to avoid a rescue situation or a dangerous swim. In addition, the safety cushion and the confidence you will gain by learning to roll will allow development of new paddling skills, especially those most useful for challenging conditions. Simply put, the Eskimo roll is an essential foundation skill for any seagoing kayaker.

Ability to roll has always been considered a necessity for whitewater *river* kayakers. It is no less important for *sea* kayakers. In fact, it may be even more important for sea kayakers, especially those who paddle in wind and rough water where swimming to shore is hardly an option. In a river, you can usually swim to shore, even if you lose your boat and paddle.

Learning to Roll

Once you understand the value of the Eskimo roll, you will want to begin learning the technique. I describe how to perform a *sweep roll* below, and there are excellent descriptions of rolling technique available in books and on video (see "Resources," at the end of the book). If you find analytical descriptions useful, you might want to review some of this literature. Ultimately you have to learn the roll by getting on the water and practicing it.

Commitment and Attitude

Anyone can learn to roll; all it takes is a strong desire to learn and the willingness to act on it. Remember "CCR" (Commitment, Concentration, Relaxation)? All three attributes are necessary to learn to roll, though commitment comes first. If you start with a conscious and firm commitment to do whatever it takes to master the roll, and get some instruction, you will succeed.

My commitment was sparked by my first experience with kayak surfing. I spent the day getting pummeled in the waves, swimming in cold water, and hauling a swamped sea kayak ashore to dump out the water, over and over again. In spite of the ordeal, I managed to get enough rides to discover and appreciate the absolutely indescribable sensation of flying on a wave, even if every ride ended in mayhem. Several times throughout the day, I noticed a fellow student who was doing no better, except for one detail: he knew how to roll. Every time he capsized, he simply rolled back up and paddled out for more! Needless to say, this left a lasting impression. I went home the following day, eager to learn how to surf and knowing that I *needed* to learn how to roll. My next step was to take a roll class, followed by weekly pool sessions until I could execute a decent roll. With this attitude, the whole process of learning to roll was relatively easy and enjoyable.

The first step is to decide you are going to master the Eskimo roll. Don't get impatient or discouraged if you encounter some difficulty during the learning process, just persevere. No one can learn to roll in one quick session. Even those who manage to roll up during their first lesson will need practice to gain a reliable roll. It is very common during the initial learning stages to perform several excellent rolls one week, then lose the ability entirely the following week. But if you bring a real commitment to the task, you will eventually develop a bombproof roll.

Instruction and Practice

Once you have the commitment, find a competent instructor. Most kayak shops and schools hold roll sessions on a regular basis and provide instruction. If you start on your own, without a qualified instructor, your practice will likely incorporate and reinforce mistakes. A good instructor will catch the mistakes and teach you how to correct them.

No one can learn to roll in one quick session.

The only way to learn is to set up a regular practice schedule and stick to it.

It doesn't matter what type of roll you learn as long as it works. Some paddlers favor a *sweep roll*, others prefer the *c-to-c roll*. Both work fine in a sea kayak, but you may have to experiment to see which type you prefer. An instructor can help you determine this. Every type of roll works on the same basic principles so if you learn one, you can learn others later on. Start by learning one type of roll that you can perform with complete confidence at any time.

Most sea kayaks with adequate outfitting can be rolled almost as easily as a whitewater kayak. However, when first learning to roll, it is probably better to use a whitewater kayak if you have the option. The smaller kayak is a bit easier to learn in. Once you develop a good roll, it should be simple to transfer the skill to a sea kayak, as long as you have fully assimilated the roll technique. If you have trouble making the transition, it means your roll still needs work. Also, be sure you have a snug fit in the sea kayak.

After taking a couple of lessons with an instructor, *practice*. Many paddlers make the mistake of taking one roll class, then waiting two or three months before trying again. Or they attend one roll session, get discouraged, and give up. The only way to learn is to set up a regular practice schedule and stick to it. Ideally, you want to attend a roll session at least once a week for several weeks, until you can roll with confidence.

Once you acquire a pool roll, practice it in real conditions as soon as possible. Have a partner spot you on the water, ready to perform an Eskimo bow rescue (see "Assisted Rescues," Chapter 4) in case you miss your roll. After several practice sessions, both in the pool and on the water, you should be performing most of your rolls successfully. If you are still having trouble, you are doing something wrong and need to correct the mistake before it becomes an ingrained habit (see "Troubleshooting," below). Ask for feedback from a knowledgeable paddler or an instructor. By observing your attempts at rolling, an instructor can usually spot any problems easily.

When you can roll every time from a *setup position* (where you set up for the roll before capsizing—see below), start practicing from a *non-setup* position. Just tip over without any preparation, then set up underwater and roll. Challenge yourself to roll after capsizing with the paddle in one hand or while paddling forward. Have a partner tip you over without warning while you keep your eyes closed, then roll. Also, try rolling at different speeds, especially in slow motion. These exercises will prepare you for rolling after an unplanned capsize. Before you know it, you'll be rolling up without even thinking about it.

Performing a Sweep Roll

For those who haven't yet learned to roll, I'll describe the *sweep roll* (also known as the *screw roll*), a very effective roll for sea kayaks. The following description is for a right-hand roll; if you want to roll on the left side, substitute left for right.

- **Step 1.** *(Photo 1)* Set up by leaning well forward (bend at the waist) and toward the left side of the kayak. If you are limber enough, "kiss the deck." Hold the paddle with both hands along the *left* side of and parallel to the kayak, with your right hand forward and the power face of the forward blade facing upward. You'll have to rotate your right wrist downward slightly to get the power face in this position. Doing all this puts you in the *setup position*. Now capsize either right or left.

- **Step 2.** *(Photos 2–3)* Maintain the setup position after capsizing, then push the entire paddle up and out of the water. Make sure the forward blade is horizontal (flat to the surface of the water), then begin to sweep the forward blade out and *away* from the bow. The blade should slice cleanly along the surface of the water with little or no resistance. Move your whole upper torso with the paddle; don't rely solely on your arms.

- **Step 3.** *(Photo 4)* As you move the paddle out toward a position perpendicular to the kayak and untwist your torso, the boat will begin rolling up. Drive your right knee against the upper deck of the kayak (the "hip snap") to help right the boat. Keep your head in the water and lean back as you complete the hip snap.

❶ – ❹ Photo sequence: Performing a sweep roll.

PHOTO SEQUENCE: JUNE LEGLER

PHOTO SEQUENCE: JUNE LEGLER

⑤ Photo sequence: Performing a sweep roll continued.

Your head acts as a counterweight, so keep it down in the water as you roll up.

- **Step 4.** *(Photo 5)* Follow through by continuing to sweep the paddle toward the stern. The kayak will roll upright with your head leaving the water last. You will be leaning back against the stern deck.

An alternative to leaning onto the stern deck is to let your upper torso shift from a left-leaning position (during the setup) to a right-leaning position as you roll the kayak upright. In other words, you'll be leaning to the right side, or even forward, instead of back while completing the roll. Your upper body acts as a counterbalance. This will work as long as you keep your head down when you roll up.

Troubleshooting

Most rolls that fail, do so for one or more of the following reasons:

- **Poor setup:** If you don't set up properly, with your body tucked forward and the paddle positioned correctly, the roll is doomed from the start.

- **Rushing the process:** This is closely related to a poor setup. After capsizing it is important to take the time to set up properly, then perform the roll in a precise and relaxed fashion.

- **Incorrect orientation of the paddle blade:** The working paddle blade needs to be oriented in a horizontal position so it can slice near or just below the surface. You should feel little or no resistance while moving the paddle—this is a key point.

- **Lifting your head out of the water:** This is the most common mistake, and usually the last one to be corrected. As the kayak rolls up, many kayakers have a strong tendency to pull their head out in order to get a breath. However, this will only push the boat back over. Your head acts as a counterweight, so keep it down in the water as you roll up. Your head should be the last part of your body to exit the water.

The above mistakes tend to recur, even after you have mastered the roll. If you start missing rolls, look for one of these mistakes and correct it.

The Combat Roll

It is very important that your roll work in wind, surf, tide rips, storm seas, ocean rock gardens, and any other rough water situation. After all, these are the conditions in which you are most likely to capsize. The difference between a pool roll and a *combat roll* (a roll that works in real conditions) is primarily psychological. The technique is the same, but the shock of an unexpected capsize in cold, rough water can make rolling seem more difficult. Other problems can also arise. Strong wind or current can make it difficult to roll on one side or the other. In large surf, you may have to wait a few seconds before rolling. With experience you can overcome these problems.

Overcoming Psychological Impediments

The best way to overcome the trauma of an unexpected capsize out at sea or in the surf zone is to get used to it. You need to practice capsizing and rolling in such waters until these experiences are routine. Start by rolling close to shore in a lake or bay, with a partner close by. When you are comfortable rolling in calm water, roll farther from shore and in choppy water. Work up to rolling in wind and in rougher conditions. Always make sure you have an easy bailout or someone to rescue you if your roll fails during these practice sessions.

You can often incorporate roll practice into your kayaking trips. Do a few rolls every time you go out on the water. Look for different conditions to practice in, such as tide rips. The surf zone is a relatively safe place to work on rough-water rolling technique: if you miss the roll in surf, you can swim to shore. Surf also provides a realistic rough water environment; it is inevitable that you will get tossed around by the waves. After you gain confidence rolling in surf, your roll should work just about anywhere. Be sure to pick an easy surf zone with small waves and no rip currents to practice in.

Your roll should work just about anywhere.

Combat Roll Tips

After any capsize, tuck forward immediately into the roll setup position with your upper body close to the front deck of your kayak. This is a very protected position and an important part of making a successful roll. Also, be sure to relax while underwater: you will burn less oxygen and can hold your breath longer, thus allowing you to pause and get

Be sure to relax while underwater: you will burn less oxygen and can hold your breath longer.

oriented before rolling. Saving your breath will allow you to make a repeat attempt if you miss your roll, switching sides, if necessary (see "Rolling on Both Sides," below). Whenever you capsize, try to tune into what is going on; after tucking forward, find the surface with your paddle and align it parallel to the kayak. Hold your upper torso close to the kayak, near the water surface. This will orient you as the boat gets pushed around by waves. It will also insure a good start on the roll.

Surf can help or hinder your roll, depending on the orientation of your kayak. If you tip over sideways to a breaking wave, rolling up on the wave side will be easy, whereas it will be nearly impossible to roll on the shoreward side. If you time it right and don't get disoriented, you can use this to your advantage. The trick is to "go with the capsize." If you capsize in a breaking wave, you are probably rolling over toward shore. Continue to roll all the way around and you'll be coming up on the wave side (known as *windowshading*). This is an easy roll if you have the presence of mind to pull it off. You can practice by purposely capsizing and rolling with a wave.

If you capsize in the surf and become disoriented, the best thing to do is tuck into your setup position and wait a few seconds for things to calm down, then roll up. Usually the wave will release you in two to three seconds (although it might *seem* a lot longer), allowing you to roll on either side. However, in some cases, a large violent wave can hold you under for twenty seconds or longer. When you realize you are going over, take a final breath, then relax to conserve oxygen. This will take experience, but keep reminding yourself to relax.

If you capsize and get pushed into very shallow water, it might not be possible to get your paddle set into the roll position. In some cases, you may not even be able to reach the grab loop to release your sprayskirt. The solution is simple: just push off the bottom with your hands and right the kayak. You will still need to keep your head down and use a hip snap to right the boat, just like you do when rolling with the paddle in hand. You might even be able to push off the bottom using the paddle. In a *combat* situation, whatever gets you upright and keeps you in the kayak is just fine.

Ideally, you want to accomplish the roll on your first attempt. This will save your breath, get you back on the surface where you can see what's going on, and get you paddling again. In surf and ocean rock gardens, it may be important to roll up quickly and paddle to a safer location. However, if you miss the roll on your first attempt, set up and try again. On the second attempt, pay close attention to your technique and do the best roll you can. Keep trying as long as possible; you should be able to get a quick breath even if you don't complete a roll. You might want to switch sides, in case the wind or the hydraulics are interfering with your ability to roll.

In some cases, you won't have time to attempt a second roll. If you capsize, miss your roll, and know you are about to be raked across a shallow reef or pushed into a rock pile, bail out and dive below the waves. You might not even have time for the first roll attempt; this is a judgment call. If you find yourself in such a situation, you've probably already made at least one serious error in judgment. Now you'll have to do whatever it takes to recover. Either swim out or reenter the kayak, depending on the situation.

Rolling On Both Sides

Once you have learned to roll on one side, start learning to roll on the other. This is not too difficult, because you have a backup; whenever you miss a roll on the "off" side, you can roll up on your "good" side. Eventually, you'll be able to roll easily on either side, an important skill for situations where you need to switch sides in order to roll successfully.

In open water, strong wind (20+ knots) is the most likely culprit impacting your ability to roll. If you capsize when broadside to the wind, it will be difficult or impossible to roll on the *downwind* side of your kayak, depending on the wind's strength. The overturned kayak is being pushed downwind across the surface of the water. When you try to roll, the leading edge of the moving kayak will catch water, pushing the kayak back over (this is analogous to trying to roll on the upstream side of a river, when caught in a hole). The solution is to switch sides and roll on the *upwind* side, or trailing edge. A roll on the upwind side will be easy to execute because the relative movement of the kayak with the water's surface is working in your favor and the trailing edge (on the upwind side) wants to plane upward.

If you capsize in a tide rip, it will be difficult to roll on the upstream side; in this situation, the water is moving under the kayak, while the leading

In a combat situation, whatever gets you upright and keeps you in the kayak is just fine.

edge of the boat is facing upstream. If there is no wind, you'll probably be able to roll on either side once you are moving at the same speed as the current. However, wind can complicate the situation. I once capsized while surfing in a strong tide rip near Alcatraz Island in San Francisco Bay. The 25-knot wind was blowing *against* the current. When I tried to roll, nothing happened. I didn't even get up far enough for a breath of air. So I carefully set up again and did the best roll I could— it didn't come close to succeeding. I felt as though some monster from the deep were holding my kayak upside down with an iron grip. Finally, nearly out of breath, I decided to switch sides and make one last desperate roll attempt. The boat immediately popped up, even though this roll was rushed and sloppy. It turned out I was initially trying to roll on the *upstream* and *downwind* side of the kayak. This was a double whammy: the wind was holding my kayak hard against the current, making it absolutely impossible to roll on the upstream side, but ridiculously easy to roll on the downstream (and upwind) side.

After a capsize in wind or current, or both, how do you know which side is downstream or upwind? You probably won't know. Set up on one side and try to roll; if that doesn't work, roll on the other. The key is to be aware of the need to switch sides immediately if your roll fails after capsizing in wind or current. You should incorporate this into your practice sessions. Roll up partway on one side, then capsize and roll up on the other. This will prepare you for the real situation.

An ocean rock garden can present another situation where you need to be ready to roll on either side. A rock or cliff may prevent you from rolling on one side or the other. Debrah Volturno, a prominent kayak instructor, Tsunami Ranger, and member of the U.S. Surf Kayak Team, found herself in this situation while paddling at Point Bonita, in the Pacific Ocean outside the Golden Gate. A powerful surging wave pushed and rolled her over against a wash rock. When the rock prevented her from setting up to roll on her favorite side, she had to switch sides and roll up on her "off" side. Debrah later told me she learned that day the value of knowing how to roll on both sides.

Switch sides immediately if your roll fails after capsizing in wind or current.

The Extended Paddle Roll

The real goal of combat rolling is to right yourself any way you can after a capsize in order to avoid going for a swim. The *extended paddle roll* (also known as the *Pawlata roll*) can be your backup, if your usual method fails. A variation on the sweep roll, the extended paddle roll uses the entire length of the paddle for support. This serves as a powerful aid to rolling upright even when your technique isn't perfect or you are fighting other impediments to the roll (swamped kayak, fatigue, disorientation, etc.).

The extended paddle roll is performed just like a sweep roll, except you set up by sliding the paddle forward and grasping the back blade in one hand, with the "sweeping" hand on the shaft. With a feathered paddle, the back blade is held in a vertical position, placing the sweeping blade in a horizontal position. Once you get used to the longer leverage of the extended paddle, you'll find that this roll is easy and effective.

The main problem with an extended paddle roll is that you have to shift your grip on the paddle. When you roll up, you won't be in a ready position and will have to shift back to a normal grip on the paddle before going anywhere. However, this is a superior alternative to bailing out and performing a rescue, as long as you avoid using the extended paddle roll as a crutch. Instead, keep it as a backup to your primary roll.

I have used the extended paddle roll to get out of serious situations, when my normal roll failed me. In one case, after exercising poor judgment, I used this roll to prevent a swim in huge breaking waves, up against a steep cliff, with no escape route (see "Safety in Surf and Ocean Rock Gardens," Chapter 13). If I had bailed out, my boat would have swamped and probably been dashed to pieces, and I would not have been able to get ashore. I've also used the extended paddle roll when performing a reentry roll with a swamped kayak; the extra leverage is useful when rolling a boat filled with water.

Mastering the Eskimo Roll

I can remember very clearly the first time I used my roll to get out of real trouble. I was on a trip with some friends from the San Francisco Bay Area Sea Kayakers, exploring the rock garden south of Point Arena in northern California. While paddling

BO BARNES

The extended paddle roll.

My successful roll turned what would have been a major ordeal into a minor incident that no one even noticed.

back to our launch site, Bonnie Brill, Michael Powers, and I decided to take a short cut down a long passage eroded through the sandstone terrace. After proceeding some distance, it became obvious that the passage culminated in a dead end. So I headed out toward the open sea though a narrow slot while Michael was busy taking a picture of Bonnie that would later appear in "Sea Kayaker Calendar."

I surveyed the scene from the mouth of the slot and observed waves crashing on the cliffs to either side. I knew I would have to time it well to make it out past the breakers. Unfortunately, as I paddled out, my timing was off. Just as I thought I was clear, a huge wave reared up in front of me. At that moment I was both terrified by the sheer power of the wave and stunned by the beauty of the translucent jade-colored sheet of water, back-lit by the setting sun. The next moment I was tumbling backwards, enmeshed in tons of whitewater. At this point, I felt that my choice was to roll up or die. As soon as the wave released me, I rolled and paddled out as fast as I could. Then I watched Michael and Bonnie leisurely paddle out the same slot during a window in the wave action, unaware of my adventure only moments before. My successful roll turned what would have been a major ordeal into a minor incident that no one even noticed.

Mastering the Eskimo roll will prove a significant milestone as you build your kayaking skills. Its real beauty lies in its usefulness in preventing minor problems from escalating into serious trouble. Most sea-kayaking tragedies and near-tragedies develop from a simple error in judgment or a moment of inattention, followed by a descending spiral of mistakes. Major problems can be prevented through the execution of a successful Eskimo roll, thus ending the downward spiral before it gets out of control. Although a well-practiced rescue can be very effective, any rescue will take a lot more time and energy than this simple, elegant technique.

CHAPTER 8.
BACKUP STRATEGIES

The kayaking skills and rescues discussed so far provide lines of defense, or backups, against potential dangers inherent in most sea-kayaking activities. The first line of defense is good judgment and basic paddling skills. Braces, rolls, rescues, and signaling devices all function as backups. As a general rule, the greater number of *reliable* backups you have mastered, the safer you are. A backup is not reliable unless it can be used in a wide range of conditions with dependable results. In other words, an Eskimo roll that works only in a swimming pool cannot be considered a functional backup in the real world of kayaking on the sea.

The prudent paddler will have as many backups in place as possible, and will work to strengthen all kayaking skills to prevent minor mistakes from escalating into major problems.

Four Levels of Defense

Lines of defense for the sea kayaker can be divided into four levels, with subsequent levels functioning as backups.

Level 1: Judgment and Primary Skills

- Knowledge and experience
- Seamanship
- Boat control (propulsion and maneuvering strokes)
- Balance and edge control (boat lean)

Level 2: Recovery Skills

- Brace strokes (capsize prevention)
- Eskimo roll (capsize recovery)

Level 3: Rescues

- Assisted rescues
- Self-rescues

Level 4: Outside Assistance

- Flares
- Radio
- Other signaling devices

Level 1 skills are your main line of defense. With experience, good judgment, and a mastery of overall paddling skills, you will rarely need to use your backups. However, even if you have excellent Level 1 skills, you must be ready to rescue another paddler who may not have such well-developed skills. If you paddle in surf or breaking waves, there is a good chance you'll need *Level 2* backups (bracing and rolling). Any time you push your limits or encounter a new situation, you'll want all your backups to be ready and available.

There is a major jump between Levels 2 and 3. Level 2 involves capsize prevention (a brace stroke) or recovery (a roll). In either case, you are still in the kayak. *Level 3* backups are needed when you are out of the kayak, in the water. This is where real problems can begin. When immersed in cold water, hypothermia is possible. If you become separated from the kayak, you could be in serious trouble. Any in-water rescue takes more time and energy than a brace or a roll. The goal is to stay within Levels 1 and 2 as much as possible, yet be ready and able to perform an efficient assisted rescue or self-rescue.

Boat Lean: Balance, Edge Control, and Bracing

Balance is an important Level 1 skill; it will prevent the need to constantly brace or roll when paddling in rough water. The key to balance is relaxation and *boat lean*, which is the ability to hold the kayak on edge. Boat lean allows you to *heel* (tilt) the kayak to either side without capsizing or losing your balance. This is also a key component of any brace stroke. Boat lean has other applications, including carving turns and side-surfing.

To learn a controlled boat lean, sit in your kayak on the water and rock it side to side, using your lower body. Try not to move your upper torso; keep it upright and stable, over the center of gravity, while you rock the boat using your hips, knees, and thighs. Once you are comfortable with this, tilt the kayak to one side and hold it there. Do this by shifting your weight to one side as you lift the opposite knee. Don't lean out over the water with your upper body; keep it centered over the kayak. Because the configuration of your upper body is centered over the kayak, with the boat heeled to the side, this position is sometimes called the "J-lean;" when viewed from behind or in front, depending on which way the boat is leaning, your body forms a "J." Practice holding the J-lean while paddling forward and backward.

With the boat lean, you can keep your kayak balanced in rough seas and surf. Lean the kayak slightly *into* the waves for stability. In surf, if you are sideways to a breaking wave, lean the boat into the wave and maintain the boat lean until the wave releases you or has lost its energy.

Boat lean will help you control the edges of the kayak hull, which will in turn allow greater boat control and balance. You can use this edge control to sharpen your turns or correct your course. It is especially useful when paddling downwind in steep following seas. A sea kayak will carve a turn on its

KEN HOWELL

High-brace position with boat lean. A balanced boat lean has many applications and is one of the most important skills for kayaking.

JUNE LEGLER

Low-brace position.

outside edge; lean the boat *away* from the direction you want to turn. Initiate the turn using a *sweep stroke* (sweep the paddle blade out and away from the kayak bow) while leaning the boat *toward* the sweeping blade. The boat will turn away from the lean direction. With practice, you'll be able to control your direction simply by leaning the kayak.

Boat lean is also used when bracing to stop a potential capsize (a Level 2 skill). I'll describe a brace on the right side. Start by heeling the kayak as described above, leaning the boat to your right. Hold your paddle horizontal with the right blade over the water on the side toward which the boat is leaned. For a *high brace*, the power face of the blade is facing down, flat to the surface of the water. The paddle should be held *below* chest level, with your elbows tucked in close to your sides to protect your shoulder from potential injury during the brace. For a *low brace*, the back of the blade is facing down and your elbows are positioned above the paddle shaft. Using either a high or a low brace position, lean the boat farther to the right, until it begins to capsize. Just as the paddle blade hits the water, drive your right knee upward against the deck, while your head and upper torso shift to the right. This will return the kayak to an upright position. Your paddle shaft should remain nearly horizontal to the water throughout the brace.

Balance, edge control, and bracing are all powerful tools that will increase your safety considerably in rough water. They help prevent capsize and allow greater boat control. Once you have learned these skills, you may never need Level 3 backups, except to rescue other paddlers.

Backups in Action

To demonstrate how the four defensive levels function, I'll describe some scenarios with paddlers of different skill levels. Although based on realistic situations, the scenarios and characters are fictional in these examples.

Scenario 1: Ignorance is bliss, until something goes wrong

Paddler Profile: Herb is a total beginner. He has never taken a class, but has paddled once before on calm water with a friend. His friend showed him how to hold the paddle and sit in the boat, then took him on a very short cruise. This is the sum total of Herb's kayaking experience.

Herb has talked his girlfriend, Annabel, into renting kayaks on a local bay. Annabel has never paddled before, but Herb assures her that it is safe and easy. At the rental shop, he tells a little white lie about having taken a kayak class. But this doesn't bother his conscience; after all, his friend showed him how to paddle. Herb is given a sleek, closed-deck sea kayak. He doesn't know what the yellow bag (a paddlefloat) is for, but doesn't really want to ask. Annabel is given a sit-on-top kayak because she has not had any instruction. She is told she won't "get trapped" and can just climb back on if she falls off.

On the beach, Herb shows Annabel everything his friend taught him. Five minutes later they are on their way across the water, paddling toward a distant island that appears to be about one mile away. Actually, the island is three miles away, but Herb doesn't know that. For the next half hour, everything seems to be going just fine. The freshening breeze feels good to both Herb and Annabel although they are struggling to keep their boats going in a straight line.

The first sign of trouble arrives with little warning. Suddenly the waves are getting bigger, with whitecaps springing up everywhere, and the breeze has turned into a strong enough wind to cause serious problems in boat control and stability. The island doesn't look much closer, even though the shoreline behind them appears to be a long way back. Both paddlers decide they should turn around and head back.

By alternating forward and reverse strokes, Annabel manages to get turned around, but Herb can't get his boat to go where he wants. Suddenly, for no comprehensible reason, Herb is upside down, underwater. The icy-cold drenching is a shock, but he manages to shove out of the kayak and grab hold of the deck lines. After yelling to Annabel, he rights the boat and attempts to climb back in. This only results in a somersault back into the water. Annabel finally paddles over to Herb and his overturned kayak. As she reaches out to try and help, she too capsizes.

By now the wind has increased to 25 knots and the situation is getting out of hand. Things go from bad to worse when Annabel realizes her sit-on-top kayak is skittering away with the wind and waves. She tries swimming after it, but the boat is

The first sign of trouble arrives with little warning.

traveling too fast. Both Herb and Annabel are getting cold and scared. They have run out of options. Luckily, they are spotted by an observant fisherman, who picks them up in his skiff and takes them ashore. Herb and Annabel escape with a mild case of hypothermia.

Analysis

This would have been a routine paddle for kayakers with some experience and moderate paddling skills. However, Herb and Annabel had none. They might have gotten away with a short cruise close to shore, but instead they used poor judgment by paddling straight out across the channel toward a distant island. Defensive Level 1 (judgment and primary skills) was extremely weak for Herb and Annabel. Levels 2 and 3 (bracing, rolls, rescues) were not even an option.

The only backup available to Herb and Annabel was Level 4: outside assistance. In their case, this backup wasn't really a backup because it depended solely on luck. They had no flares or other signaling devices and they depended entirely on the observation skills of boaters who happened to be in the area. Herb and Annabel took an unacceptable risk and were lucky to survive.

It is important to learn some basic kayaking strokes and rescues before paddling anywhere. Only with additional practice should you paddle far into open water. If Herb and Annabel had practiced rescues in a beginning kayaking class, they might have been able to execute a T-rescue to get Herb back into his kayak.

It is important to learn some basic kayaking strokes and rescues before paddling anywhere.

Scenario 2: A little knowledge can be helpful

Paddler Profile: Bob has been kayaking for a year. He took a couple of classes and has rented kayaks and practiced rescues on several occasions. He even took an Eskimo roll class and has been to a couple of pool sessions, but isn't able to complete his roll every time. He recently bought his own sea kayak.

Although Bob usually paddles with friends from a local kayak club, when he gets an unexpected day off from work, he decides to take his new boat on a solo trip out on San Francisco Bay. Conditions are calm when he launches and he knows the area fairly well. His confidence is bolstered after an easy and uneventful trip over to Angel Island.

While eating his lunch on the island, Bob notices the afternoon wind has picked up and the bay looks choppy. He's not really worried, although he has had little experience paddling in strong wind. Once on the water, Bob realizes the wind is getting stronger and paddling is more difficult than he anticipated. The boat keeps turning into the wind. Finally he decides to use the rudder. Just as he reaches back to release the line to deploy the rudder, a strong gust of wind capsizes him.

Bob isn't panicked. He tries to roll twice, but finally bails when his breath runs out. Now in the water, Bob hangs onto the boat and pulls out his paddlefloat. After inflating the float, he sets up the outrigger and climbs onto the deck of his kayak. Just as he twists around to get into the seat, the boat capsizes. When he tries again, the same thing happens. Bob has never tried this rescue in such rough conditions and just can't seem to keep his balance after climbing up. After two more unsuccessful attempts, he's beginning to get tired, uneasy, and despite his wetsuit, cold.

Finally, Bob decides to try the paddlefloat reentry roll. He has practiced it a couple of times and he figures it may be his last chance to get back in the kayak. He takes his time, slides into the cockpit, and executes the paddlefloat roll with no problem. It turns out to be much easier than he expected. Bob quickly pumps the water out while stabilizing the boat with the paddlefloat. He then reattaches the sprayskirt and completes his journey with no further problems.

Based on his experience, Bob decides he should practice his roll and the paddlefloat rescue. He also is determined to develop a solid reentry roll *without* the paddlefloat.

Analysis

Bob's primary mistake was a two-part error in judgment. He slightly overestimated his paddling skills and by going solo he eliminated the possibility of an assisted rescue. In addition, he was careless when deploying the rudder, causing the capsize. However, unlike Herb and Annabel, Bob at least had some potential backup techniques, four to be exact: the Eskimo roll, reentry roll, paddlefloat rescue, and paddlefloat reentry roll. The first backup failed, Bob didn't try the second one, the third one failed, but the fourth one worked. Although his Level 2 backups were marginal and he hadn't mastered all Level 3 backups, he was persistent and able to use his final Level 3 backup, the paddlefloat reentry roll.

Scenario 3: The Unforeseen Wave

Paddler Profile: Melanie is an experienced sea kayaker who has been paddling for several years. She has good boating skills, including an effective brace and a solid Eskimo roll. Melanie has also done some kayak surfing, but has not spent a great deal of time in the surf. Her wave-reading skills are not fully developed.

She joins some friends to do an open-ocean paddle on the northern California coast. Everyone in the group has paddled on the ocean before, but Melanie is the most experienced kayaker. The group launches through small surf with no problem and heads down the coast. The day is brilliant with sunshine and the group is soon mesmerized by the light dancing across the waves.

After rounding a major headland, Melanie can't resist a slot in the rocks that leads into a beautiful cove surrounded by steep cliffs. Without further ado, she heads in, while the rest of the group judiciously paddles out and around the rocks. The slot narrows into a long passageway, but the water appears calm as Melanie cruises through on the surge.

Just as she nears the end of the passage, Melanie watches in horror as the water suddenly sucks backwards. She knows what this means and realizes there is no time to do anything but brace for the impact. She turns her head just in time to see a huge wall of whitewater barreling toward her. In the next instant she and her kayak are tumbling upside down into the cove. Five long seconds later, Melanie rolls up to find herself bouncing up and down in a churning cauldron of waves. The quiet cove has been transformed into a raging beast. Melanie realizes she can ride it out if she just stays in the deeper water of the cove. After a few more waves wash through, the water calms and Melanie quickly paddles back out through the slot. She finally rejoins her wide-eyed friends, who had thought they might never see her again.

Analysis

Melanie made an error in judgment by heading into the rocks without first watching several wave sets to see what would happen in the slot when a

The quiet cove has been transformed into a raging beast.

large wave washed through. Due to her limited experience paddling in ocean rock gardens, she paddled right in, assuming the water would remain calm. However, because she had a reliable set of backups in place, she came out of the experience unscathed.

Although her brace failed her, Melanie was able to execute a roll, which eliminated the need to exit the kayak and resort to Level 3 backups. If she had failed to roll or been pulled out of the kayak, Melanie probably could have performed a reentry roll, but her swamped kayak might have been damaged in the rocks. This was a situation where the ability to use Level 2 backups was essential.

All three of the above scenarios started with a failure in judgment, mostly resulting from a lack of experience. In each case, a minor error resulted in a capsize. Level 1 skills failed in all three cases. In the first scenario, Level 2 & 3 backups were not available, so the capsize immediately became a serious problem. In the second and third scenarios, backups were used to prevent the situations from leading to major trouble. Having mastered reliable backups can make the difference between a minor incident and a tragedy.

Rescue Hierarchy

Once you reach the point where there is a swimmer in the water, it is important to choose the best rescue that will prevent descending to level 4 (outside assistance). Which rescue you choose is highly dependent on the situation. There is no one rescue that will work in every situation. Whenever faced with the need to perform a rescue, you must act decisively and efficiently. If your first-choice rescue is not working or fails, alter your methods or move on to another type of rescue without hesitation.

Below are some examples of possible rescues to be used in various situations. The rescues are listed in order of preference, depending on the scenario. The first-choice rescue should be the one that can be performed most easily and efficiently. Remember: these are only suggestions. Every rescue situation is unique and demands that you remain flexible and willing to improvise to make the rescue work. The rescues listed are those most likely to work in the given situation. In some unusual cases, a rescue not listed could be the first choice; for example, a T-rescue can sometimes be used in the surf zone, if conditions allow. All rescues

After Things Go Wrong: Analyze Your Mistakes

Anytime something goes wrong during a kayaking trip, you should thoroughly analyze the situation and determine exactly what mistakes you, or others, made. Then figure out how to correct those mistakes so they don't happen again. Do this for minor incidents (e.g., the group got separated) and "near misses," as well as for major incidents (e.g., you needed a Coast Guard rescue). Any serious incident usually indicates a major failure in your backup system. Mistakes generally fall into one or more of the following categories:

- **Inadequate information or knowledge** (e.g. ignorance about tidal currents)

- **Miscommunication, or lack of communication, between paddlers** (e.g. signals not used, when needed)

- **Poor decision making** (e.g. deciding to continue in stormy conditions when a bailout is available)

- **Failure to execute a specific skill or technique; inadequate skills for the conditions** (e.g., failure to perform a rescue efficiently)

Search the above categories for any mistakes that may have led to the incident. Also look for failures in your backup system. Finally, look for the *key mistake* that precipitated the problem. Usually you can find one error that started the event, followed by a series of mistakes that intensified the problem. Share your lessons with others, especially those you paddle with regularly. That way everyone can benefit. The biggest mistake you can make is to not recognize your mistakes.

below are for closed-cockpit kayaks, except where otherwise indicated.

Open Water:

In a group:

1. T-rescue.

2. Side-rescue (might be first choice in very cold water or with heavily loaded kayaks).

3. T- or side-rescue with sling.

4. Scoop rescue (incapacitated paddler).

Solo:

1. Reentry roll.

2. Paddlefloat rescue.

3. Paddlefloat reentry roll.

In Surf Zone (beach break):

1. Swim to shore.

2. Reentry roll.

3. Tow out of surf, then perform T-rescue or side-rescue.

4. Retrieve swimmer using a stern deck carry.

5. Lifesaving rescue: Swim out to rescue swimmer in distress.

Note: Options 3, 4, and 5 obviously aren't available in a solo situation. Towing in surf means the swimmer hangs onto the rescuer's kayak (no tow line).

Surf (offshore point break):

1. Reentry roll.

2. T-rescue or side-rescue (may require towing away from area of breaking waves).

3. Paddlefloat rescue (may first have to swim out of area of breaking waves).

4. Swim to shore (if possible).

In Ocean Rock Gardens:

1. Reentry roll.

2. T-rescue or side-rescue (may first require towing out of breaking waves).

3. Paddlefloat rescue (after swimming to safe area, if necessary).

4. Swim to shore if possible (may be first choice if shore is very close).

Sit-On-Top Kayak Anywhere:

1. Climb back on (sit-on-top rescue)—usually the first choice with a sit-on-top in any conditions, as long as the boat hasn't gotten away.

2. Climb on with assistance from another kayaker.

3. Swim to shore (if possible); probably necessary only if the boat is lost.

The rescue hierarchy depends entirely on specific situations. In open water, well offshore, the first priority is to get back in the kayak. Assisted rescues, the reentry roll, and paddlefloat rescues can be used in open water. In the surf, usually the first-choice rescue is to swim ashore. However, the reentry roll might take precedence over swimming if you capsize well offshore in a wide surf zone. If you capsize and bail out while surfing a *point break* (waves that wrap around a point of rock and break) at a considerable distance from shore, swimming ashore might be your last choice. In many cases, the area inshore of a point break will be protected enough to perform a T-rescue or a paddlefloat rescue. In rock gardens, it is usually best to rescue yourself, using a reentry roll. However, there are often calm areas in the rocks where any type of rescue will work fine. In general, the first choice for self-rescue is a reentry roll; it is far more efficient than a paddlefloat rescue.

You should not follow the above rescue hierarchies slavishly, without reference to what is happening at the time of the rescue. Base your action on your particular situation and use the rescue most likely to succeed.

Rescue Limitations

All rescues have limitations. In severe circumstances, such as a major storm with gale-force winds, the Eskimo roll might be your final backup, short of outside help. In such conditions, assisted rescues and paddlefloat rescues will be difficult or even impossible. A reentry roll leaves you with the task of reattaching the sprayskirt and pumping water out of the kayak. In storm seas, Level 1 & 2 skills are extremely important because they keep you out of the water and in the boat. Rescues are good backups in most cases, but they are not infallible.

Thankfully, I've never been involved in a situation where it was impossible for a kayaker to get back into the boat after capsizing out at sea. If it did happen, the best recourse might be to stay with the swimmer and signal for outside assistance, using a radio or flares. Or the group could split up, with some paddlers heading for shore to summon help and others staying with the victim.

Keep Your Backups in Good Working Order

If you never make a mistake, have perfect judgment, superior boating skill, and never get into conditions beyond your skill level, you probably won't need any backups. Otherwise, your backup system is the only thing that stands between safe, enjoyable kayaking and disaster.

Rescues are good backups in most cases, but they are not infallible.

CHAPTER 9.

TOWING

All sea kayakers should be prepared to tow, by carrying a towline and knowing how to use it. Don't be tempted to try and get by with only one or two tow lines in a large group of paddlers; in order to deal with paddlers who have become exhausted or incapacitated, you may need several lines.

Once when I was helping conduct an instructor training session on San Francisco Bay, only half the group had towlines (and these were kayak instructors!). As it turned out, we had just enough. While crossing from Angel Island to Sausalito, a distance of approximately 2 miles, we encountered a strong headwind that came roaring down off the hills. This wind was stronger than usual, and as it increased in strength about half the group began falling back, making no headway. One paddler kept getting blown off course. Half of us hooked up towlines to those who were having trouble. For the next two hours we fought into the wind making very slow progress. We eventually made it across. Interestingly, no one who needed a tow had a towline. If one more person had needed help, we would have been in trouble.

DEBRAH VOLTURNO

There are several situations where towing is necessary. Some of the more likely ones include:

- *Exhaustion*: paddler is too tired to continue without assistance.

- *Incapacitated kayaker*: paddler is sick or injured.

- *Inability to stay upright* due to fear or loss of balance.

- *Boat control problems* in strong wind: paddler can't maintain course.

- *Need to keep a group together* in difficult conditions.

Often, towing is an assist to aid a paddler who can't keep up with the group or is having trouble with boat control. In these situations, the towed kayaker continues paddling; the towing kayaker is simply helping. In other cases the towed kayaker cannot paddle at all and the towing kayaker is providing all the power. A paddler who cannot keep his boat upright will need to be stabilized by another kayaker, while a third paddler tows them both. It is sometimes desirable to have two or more kayakers towing in tandem. These configurations are discussed in detail after a discussion of tow systems.

Towline Setup

Numerous towline setups have been devised for kayaks, many of which work well. Personal preference plays a large part in deciding which towline setup to use. The towline can be attached to the kayak with a cleat or to the waist or the back of the paddlers lifejacket. Many kayakers claim that towing with the line attached to the body works fine, but I find the idea somewhat unsettling. I know at least one paddler who suffered back strain after towing a kayak for several miles. In any case, it is important that the tow system be easily deployed and that it has a quick release mechanism. The quick release is especially important if the line is to be attached to your body. Regardless of what setup is used, a good sea-kayak tow system should meet all the following criteria:

- **A strong, floating line that should be at least 30 feet long:** The line should be strong enough to eliminate any possibility of breaking and long enough (roughly two boat lengths) to prevent the towed kayak from colliding with the lead kayak when towing downwind in a following sea. If the line floats, it will be easier to find after it is released.

Exception: A shorter line is preferable when retrieving a kayak (without the paddler aboard) and towing it a short distance. This allows greater control of the loose kayak.

- **A short length (approximately 2 feet) of shock cord should be incorporated to act as a shock absorber:** The shock absorber is very important to prevent sudden, intense jerks that would create considerable discomfort and could pull the line loose. This is especially true when paddling downwind in a steep following sea.

- **Attachment point should be located just aft of the cockpit:** This is the best towing point because it does not affect your boat control. If you attach the line to the end of the stern, you'll have difficulty with directional control because your stern will tend to be anchored by the towed vessel.

- **It should be easy to deploy in rough, windy conditions:** The towline should be kept close at hand, preferably on deck, where it can be deployed without difficulty even while bouncing around in steep waves and howling wind. Ken Howell, an experienced sea-kayak guide and instructor, once capsized in a 30-knot wind on San Francisco Bay as he reached inside the cockpit behind his seat, while searching for his tow line. More often than not, you'll need your tow line when conditions are less than ideal.

- **It should allow for a quick release.** You may need to release the line quickly, especially if it becomes entangled.

My favorite tow system is a *throw rope* (a 30-foot rope, coiled inside a bag, that will play out easily when the bag is opened) with a short length of shock cord attached to one end. The throw rope is easily stowed and can double as a rescue line to toss to a swimmer. I keep one end of the line attached, via a loop in the end of the shock cord, to a cleat just aft of the cockpit. The loop releases easily from the cleat, if

Throw rope attached to kayak, ready for use as a towline.

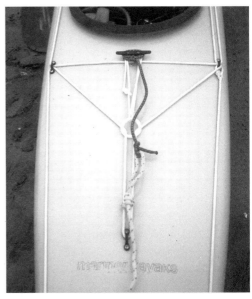

Towline deployed. Note attachment point directly behind cockpit.

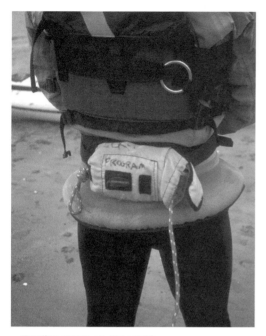

Towline worn on the waist.

necessary. The other end of the line has a carabiner (a strong aluminum ring with a spring clip) attached, which can be clipped to the bow of the kayak to be towed. This setup is simple to deploy and meets all the important criteria.

The waist-attached tow system is popular with many kayakers and seems to work fairly well. The line is kept in a bag attached to a belt around your waist or a belt passed through loops on your lifejacket. The belt has a very efficient quick-release mechanism, activated by pulling a cord. The main advantage to this system is ease of deployment. The tow line is attached to your body, so all you have to do is reach back, pull the bag open, and clip the line onto the kayak to be towed. Be aware that this method could cause back strain. Whatever system you decide to use, be sure to test it thoroughly.

Towing Configurations

Towing configurations depend on the particular situation and number of paddlers available to help with the tow. A different configuration will have to be used for an incapacitated kayaker than for a tired kayaker who can still paddle. The *standard tow, rafted tow, tandem tow, and push tow* are four basic configurations you should become familiar with.

Standard Tow

The standard tow is used for the most common situation, when one kayaker tows another. The main reason for this tow is to help a tired paddler who can't keep up or is having problems controlling his boat. The person being towed needs to be able to remain upright on his own and should continue paddling while being towed. The standard tow can also be used for a sick or injured kayaker who cannot paddle, as long as he can keep from capsizing.

The towing kayaker simply hooks the towline to the bow of the vessel to be towed and paddles forward, periodically turning around to check on the towed kayaker. When paddling downwind, be aware that the towed kayak will tend to surf forward, creating slack in the line. This is not a problem as long as the towed kayak doesn't overrun the lead boat and the towed paddler can maintain control. Otherwise, it may be necessary to slow down.

Tandem Tow

With a tandem tow, two or more paddlers can share the chore of towing the distressed kayaker. This system can be used to paddle into a strong headwind or to keep a group together. It can also be used when towing two paddlers who are rafted up (see "Rafted Tow," below). The towline of the lead kayak is attached to the bow of the next boat in line. All kayaks involved are hooked together in sequence, with the towed boat last in line.

Note that the towing kayaks are hooked in *tandem*, one behind the other, so all kayaks pull in the same direction. Don't be tempted to attach two or three separate tow lines to the bow of one kayak. You would all be pulling in slightly different directions, resulting in difficult boat-control problems.

Rafted Tow

With a rafted tow, one or more kayakers tow two other kayakers who are rafted together. This tow is necessary if a paddler is incapacitated or cannot keep from capsizing. One paddler can come alongside the distressed kayaker and hang onto the boat (*raft up*) to prevent it from capsizing. The tow line should be connected to the bow of the kayaker in trouble.

It is possible for one kayaker to do the towing in a rafted tow. However, it is much easier to pull the rafted kayaks using a *tandem tow* (described above) with two or more paddlers if the group is large enough. This is especially true if you have to tow upwind.

I first "discovered" the rafted tow on a rough, windy day outside the Golden Gate Bridge, while paddling with a group of kayakers who had widely varying skill levels. One less-experienced paddler began capsizing in rough seas off the rocky headlands near Point Bonita. The seas and swell were very large and the nearest protected landing was 2 miles away, at Kirby Cove. We performed several rescues and with each capsize the paddler got colder and less able to stabilize the kayak. We soon realized that we would never get to Kirby Cove without changing our tactics, so one paddler rafted up with the unstable boater, as I hooked my towline up and began towing the raft. This was not too difficult because we were traveling downwind. After a mile or so, someone had the brilliant idea of hooking another line to my bow,

FIGURE 2. Towing Configurations

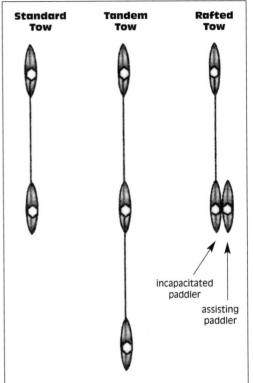

Standard Tow — Tandem Tow — Rafted Tow

incapacitated paddler

assisting paddler

DEBRAH VOLTURNO

MICHAEL POWERS

The push tow.

forming a tandem tow. This made it easy and we landed at Kirby Cove without further incident.

Push Tow

The rafted tow works fine if you have enough paddlers. However, if you are with one other kayaker who is incapacitated, you'll need a different technique, one that allows you to raft up and tow simultaneously. The push tow is a good way to accomplish this seemingly impossible task.

To perform a push tow, you push the other kayak backwards with the paddler hanging onto your bow. The two boats face in opposite directions and the incapacitated paddler either holds onto or drapes himself across your bow, holding the two kayaks together while you paddle forward. This allows greater control than having the towed boat next to your stern, and it is easier to keep the boats from separating while underway. You can tow with the paddler at your stern if you tie the two boats together;

however, this requires a more complicated setup. Pushing from the bow also allows easy communication and you can keep an eye on each other.

The push tow is obviously not the optimal way to kayak. It can create some problems when paddling in rough seas, but it may be your only choice if you need to get an incapacitated paddler to safety.

Retrieving and Towing a Loose Kayak

If a paddler gets separated from her kayak, it may be necessary to retrieve the boat and tow it back to her. In this situation, a shorter tow line of 10 or 12 feet is preferable, to keep the boat fairly close and under control. You can either keep a separate line for this purpose, or tie off a shorter length of your regular tow line. If the boat to be towed is capsized, turn it upright to reduce drag. Then clip onto the bow and tow the kayak back to the swimmer.

Be Ready

You never know when it might be necessary to tow another kayaker. If you spend time guiding or paddling with beginners, you will inevitably need your tow line. If you usually paddle with experienced kayakers, you probably won't need to tow very often, if at all. However, there is a chance that someone could get sick or injured and require assistance. Keep your tow system handy, in good working order.

You never know when it might be necessary to tow another kayaker.

CHAPTER 10.
WEATHER AND SEA CONDITIONS

Sea kayaking is all about freedom: the unfettered freedom to cruise in open water, explore convoluted coastlines and distant islands, ride waves, camp on hidden beaches, and experience all the moods of the sea. To enjoy this freedom to the full, you will occasionally need to paddle several miles from shore or from a reasonable landing site. You may then have to deal with inclement weather; you won't be able to pull over to shore the minute the wind starts blowing.

How you handle changing weather conditions depends on your skill and your experience. As a novice you prepare for deteriorating weather by paddling only in areas where a swift bailout is available (i.e., close to shore with easy landings). This restricts where you can paddle. Eventually, as you gain experience and your skills improve, you will be able to range wider and farther on the sea.

To paddle safely in open water, you must be prepared to deal with a wide range of weather conditions. It is not enough to decide you will paddle only when conditions are benign because the weather can change quickly. It does help, however, to understand the overall weather patterns in the area where you are paddling and to plan accordingly.

Wind and fog are the major weather factors of interest to the sea kayaker. Wind is the main influence on the state of the sea and will affect your ability to control and stabilize your kayak. Fog is primarily a navigational problem. When paddling in fog on inland waters, you have to beware of boat traffic and know how to navigate when visibility is reduced. On the open coast fog presents an additional problem: it can hide hazardous waves and rocks, making it dangerous to paddle in some areas near shore when the swell is up.

Other weather phenomena are less challenging. Heat and cold can be dealt with by dressing appropriately. Rain is not a big issue because you are already dressed to get wet. However, a combination

Be prepared to deal with a wide range of weather conditions.

of wind and rain can result in difficult paddling conditions.

Before venturing out in a sea kayak, get a forecast on the weather radio. Storms and periods of fair weather can be predicted to *some* extent. A period of high pressure means fair weather, but it could also bring wind. Strong winds often occur along a gradient between high-pressure and low-pressure cells. An approaching low-pressure front usually means stormy and windy conditions. If a major storm is predicted, it is probably best to stay out of the water, unless you already have substantial experience paddling in storm seas. And *everyone* who goes with you should also have the appropriate skills and experience.

Treat all weather predictions as possibilities, not certainties. This is especially true for predicted wind speeds. I've found that most wind predictions are conservative: they generally err on the high side. Actual wind speeds reported *at the time they are measured* for a given location are accurate and can be trusted.

Waves

Waves are caused by wind blowing across a distance of water (the *fetch)* over a period of time. The wave size is determined by the fetch, the strength of the wind, and the length of time the wind blows. A *fully developed* sea is the size limit the waves can reach at a given wind speed with unlimited fetch (such as out on the open ocean). In a fully developed sea on open water, a 20-knot wind (1 knot = 1 nautical mile per hour; 1 nautical mile = 1.15 statute miles) will generate waves 4 to 8 feet high. With a 30-knot wind the waves range from 10 to 15 feet high. These wave heights are reached only with a fetch of many miles. With a more limited fetch, such as in a bay or estuary, the waves will not develop to the maximum heights.

Seas tend to be chaotic. This is because winds are turbulent, varying in speed and direction. Hence the waves vary in size, speed, and direction. The waves also interact with one another, sometimes combining to form larger waves, and forming a choppy surface overall. As the wind continues to blow, the waves move predominantly downwind.

Sea kayaks are designed to handle turbulent wave conditions. Because a kayak is narrow, it can be tilted and balanced to compensate for the infinite variety of waves as they pass under the hull. A kayak can also take advantage of the wave energy by surfing the waves when traveling downwind. Of course it is up to the paddler to control and maneuver the kayak. This is covered in more detail below (see "Paddling Techniques in Wind and Rough Water").

Wind

Wind is common on open water just about anywhere. A light breeze is enjoyable and has a minimal effect on paddling. With increasing strength, the wind can begin to create problems for kayakers. There are two wind effects important for paddlers: 1) waves (sea state) and 2) the direct force of the wind acting on your body, paddle, and kayak. The common notion is that the waves are the main problem. However, with practice, you can and should learn to handle steep waves and rough seas. The direct force of the wind is the real culprit; you never really get used to this howling, powerful force, trying to rip the paddle from your hands, push your kayak off course, and sap all the energy from your body. The *combined* effect of wind and waves can be a real challenge.

Although sea kayaks are relatively low to the water, they can get blown around by the wind, making boat control increasingly difficult with increasing wind speed. Also, in strong wind, communication between paddlers can be nearly impossible. Even hand and paddle signals are difficult—it can be perilous to raise a paddle in the air or to remove a hand from the paddle shaft. Rescues become more challenging in wind, and if you let go of the kayak, it will get away from you. The wind can also be demoralizing and a mental challenge. The best way to overcome all the problems of paddling in wind is to get plenty of practice and experience doing so.

The Beaufort Wind Scale

The Beaufort Wind Scale (Table 1) correlates wind speed with its effect on sea conditions. Spend some time studying the Beaufort Scale, paying attention to sea state and kayaking conditions at different wind speeds. The listed kayaking conditions take only the wind and waves into account. Other factors, such as strong tidal currents and surf will increase the challenge.

The combined effect of wind and waves can be a real challenge.

TABLE 1. Beaufort Wind Scale

Force	Wind Speed (Knots)	Sea Term	Sea State	Kayaking Conditions
0	0–1	Calm	Mirror-like, smooth surface.	Very easy, flat water paddling; beginners will be at ease.
1	1–3	Light Air	Small, scale-like ripples.	Very easy; still no problem for beginners; good fishing weather.
2	4–6	Light Breeze	Small wavelets; no breaking crests.	Easy, comfortable kayaking for everyone.
3	7–10	Gentle Breeze	Small waves; crests just beginning to break; a few scattered whitecaps.	Fairly easy; good kayaking weather.
4	11–16	Moderate Breeze	Small waves, becoming larger; more whitecaps.	Moderate; invigorating for most; comfortable limit for novices.
5	17–21	Fresh Wind	Moderate waves, getting longer; numerous whitecaps.	Moderately difficult; novices find boat control difficult and feel unstable. No problem for experienced kayakers.
6	22–27	Strong Wind	Large waves, whitecaps everywhere; some spray blowing off wave crests.	Difficult; hard paddling into the wind; wind catches paddle blades; communication difficult. Weather for experienced paddlers only.
7	28–33	Moderate Gale	Moderately high waves; spray and foam flying in streaks off wave crests.	Very difficult; even experienced paddlers may begin to curse; little or no progress into the wind.
8	34–40	Fresh Gale	High waves; dense streaking spray and foam.	Extremely difficult; no progress into the wind; boat control is a real problem; communication and rescues very difficult. You'll be on your own!
9	41–47	Strong Gale	Very high waves beginning to tumble; dense spray reduces visibility.	Dangerous; constant fight to maintain control; rescues and communication almost impossible.
10	48–55	Storm	Huge waves with overhanging, breaking crests; sea is white with spray and foam.	Very dangerous; survival situation; only real option is to run with the wind or possibly deploy a sea anchor.

Notes on the Beaufort Wind Scale:

Force 0—2

Very easy, benign conditions,* suitable for beginners and pleasant for everyone.

Force 3—4

Easy to moderate conditions with small, choppy seas, manageable for novice to intermediate kayakers. It is fairly easy to communicate and keep a group together. This is ideal kayaking weather.

Force 5—6

Once the wind increases to the 20 knot range, conditions become more challenging. Moderate to large seas form and the wind gets pushy. Novice paddlers will have difficulty controlling a kayak and may get into trouble. Communication is more difficult and keeping a group together may be a challenge. Experienced paddlers will have no real problem with boat control and will probably enjoy themselves, especially if travelling downwind, surfing the waves. Paddling upwind requires some work, but a strong paddler can make reasonable progress.

Force 7—8

When the wind approaches 30 knots and more, conditions become extremely challenging, even for highly experienced boaters. For most paddlers, the fun is over and the whole thing becomes a fight to get ashore. Paddling downwind might be entertaining if you can hang onto your paddle. It is best to avoid these conditions, especially if the wind is offshore.

Force 9—10

These are full gale to storm conditions and for most paddlers it will be a fight for survival.

All of the above relates only to the wind and resulting sea state; it assumes no complicating challenges such as surf, rocks, or strong current.

Using the Beaufort Wind Scale

When I first started sea kayaking, I found the Beaufort Wind Scale very useful in helping me understand wind speed and how it would affect me on the water. The Beaufort Wind Scale is helpful in several ways. It allows you to:

- **Estimate wind speed based on sea conditions:** By observing the surface of the water and average wave size in a given area, you can get an idea about how hard the wind is blowing and how difficult the paddling conditions will be there. For example, if you see numerous whitecaps out in a channel you want to cross, you can assume the wind is blowing *at least* 15 to 20 knots (Force 5).

- **Predict kayaking and sea conditions based on reported wind speed:** If the weather radio reports wind speeds of 10 to 15 knots, with gusts to 20 knots in the area you want to paddle, the Beaufort Scale will tell you what to expect. If there is a prediction of winds increasing to 25 knots (small craft warning), you should be prepared to paddle in Force 6 conditions, although the prediction might not materialize.

- **Correlate wind speed with actual conditions on the water and determine how those conditions will affect you in the kayak:** If you pay attention to what is happening whenever you're on the water, you'll quickly learn to estimate wind speed and how the conditions at a given wind speed affect you. When you see a few scattered whitecaps, you know that the wind is blowing about 10 knots. As the wind increases, larger waves begin forming, whitecaps become numerous, and you know it is approaching 20 knots (Force 5). You can try to verify this with a weather radio report. For future reference, note how these winds and sea states affect you in the kayak.

- **Define your comfort limit:** Once you have some experience paddling in windy conditions and can estimate the wind speed or the Beaufort Force, you'll know where your comfort limit is. This limit will change with time as your skills increase, but it is very useful to

Note how these winds and sea states affect you in the kayak.

know what you are getting into if the wind and seas indicate a Force 6 or 7 situation.

By combining experience on the water with reference to the Beaufort Scale, you will discover some useful indicators. When a few whitecaps begin to appear, the wind speed is approximately 10 knots (Force 3). This is still fairly easy paddling regardless of what direction you are heading. At 20 knots (Force 5), whitecaps will be numerous and the waves will get larger, depending on the fetch. Conditions begin to get a bit more challenging, directional control can be difficult, and paddling into a 20-knot headwind is tiring and will slow you down. When the wind reaches 30 knots, you'll see spray flying through the air and it will be difficult to make any progress into the wind. Unless you have gained experience kayaking in such conditions, paddling in a 30-knot wind out on open water should be considered dangerous.

Wind Gusts and Squalls

It's a rare wind that is steady and has no variation. On a windy day, it is common to encounter short, sudden gusts of greater strength than the average wind. For example, the wind might be blowing mostly at a steady 25 knots, but with occasional gusts to 30 or even 40 knots. This is very common in Baja California, when northerly winter winds blow down the axis of the Sea of Cortez. The wind blows in gusty sheets of energy that seem to arise out of nowhere. When some of the stronger gusts hit, all you can do is hunker down and brace until the gust passes. Usually these gusts will pass by quickly and it is possible to continue paddling between them. However, if strong gusts become frequent, it may be time to get off the water.

Squalls with strong downdrafts can be a problem in some regions during unsettled weather. They approach suddenly with intense wind and rain, then depart just as quickly. As with strong wind gusts, the best way to handle a squall is to stay low and wait it out. Most squalls last only a few minutes, unless you are dealing with a major storm.

Navigating in Wind

Wind can have a significant affect on your paddling speed, which you should consider when planning the travel time to your destination. A headwind will slow you down and a tailwind will increase your speed. The change in velocity will depend on the strength of the wind. If you normally paddle at 3 knots (find out your paddling speed by timing yourself over a given distance), a 20-knot headwind might cut your speed in half, to only 1.5 knots. This means it will take you twice as long to get to your destination. It won't usually be necessary to know your *exact* speed, but it is important to know how much progress you are making. With experience, you'll be able to factor the wind into your paddling speed. You can help the process by wearing a watch and periodically checking how long it takes to cover a specific distance in different wind conditions.

A beam wind can push you off course. To hold a course across the wind, you'll need to set a *ferry angle*—paddle into the wind at an angle that will carry you directly across the wind. In clear weather, you can find the ferry angle by using a *range*—line up two stationary points (i.e., a buoy and a point of land) along your course and keep them aligned as you paddle, or look over your shoulder at the receding shoreline and take note of the ferry angle needed to stay on course. Make sure you are angling *across* the wind and not just paddling on a treadmill *into* the wind. You may not be able to hold a course directly across a strong wind (25+ knots); in this case, expect to lose some ground in a downwind direction.

Paddling Techniques in Wind and Rough Water

If you plan on kayaking anywhere beyond the most protected waterways, it is important to be able to handle wind and rough water. Direct experience is the only way to learn how to paddle in wind and waves. The safest way to gain such experience is to practice in an area with onshore wind where you can easily get ashore if the conditions become too difficult. Start by paddling in moderate winds of 10–15 knots (Force 4-some whitecaps), then work your way up to winds in the 20–25 knot range (Force 5 to 6). Your goal is to be able to paddle comfortably in Force 6 wind in any direction. Only when you can do this will you be able to kayak safely in the *open water* or the *open ocean domain* (see Chapter 2).

The easiest direction to paddle, in terms of boat control, is directly into the wind (a *headwind*). Unfortunately, this is also the most difficult direction to go in terms of effort, because you have to fight the full force of the wind. You'll take spray directly into your face and your paddling speed will be less than normal. Your main task will be to continue paddling forward with determination. In a strong wind, you'll need a good forward stroke and the endurance to keep paddling. You don't have the luxury of stopping to rest; if you stop paddling, you lose ground, and regaining what you lost takes more energy than you saved by resting. The best way to "rest" is to paddle more slowly, without stopping altogether. Sometimes you can hold your position and take a break by paddling gently, without expending much energy. Ultimately you have to continue paddling until you reach your destination, unless you alter course and paddle to another destination. Strength, endurance, and a good forward stroke technique, are the most important factors when paddling into a headwind.

A *beam* (side) wind offers far less resistance than a headwind, but creates some boat-control problems. Many sea kayaks tend to *weathervane*—turn into a beam wind. There are a couple of reasons for this, but essentially the stern is blown downwind. Some kayaks are more prone to weathervaning than others and require a rudder or a skeg to solve the problem. However, it is also possible to control the kayak by using sweep strokes and boat lean to correct your course. Tilt the kayak into the wind and perform an occasional sweep stroke on the windward side to maintain course. A well-designed sea kayak will weathervane only slightly, if at all, and will require only minor corrective strokes.

In some cases you may experience the opposite problem—difficulty turning *into* the wind. In this situation you'll need to use a strong sweep stroke (or a series of sweep strokes) on the downwind side, while maintaining forward momentum to help induce a weathervaning effect. It will also help enhance weathervaning if you lean forward to lighten the stern. When you try to turn into the wind in this fashion, it is important to maintain forward speed. Don't be tempted to use a stern rudder stroke; it will slow you down. Your sweep stroke should be a full sweep, with a powerful stern draw component.

You may have trouble dealing with steep seas in a beam wind; the waves will be hitting you from the side, threatening to throw you off balance. Lean the kayak slightly into the waves. Most of the time, you'll simply let the boat rise up and over each passing wave, occasionally bracing into larger and steeper waves. Whenever you sense a wave is going

Strength, endurance, and a good forward stroke technique, are the most important factors when paddling into a headwind.

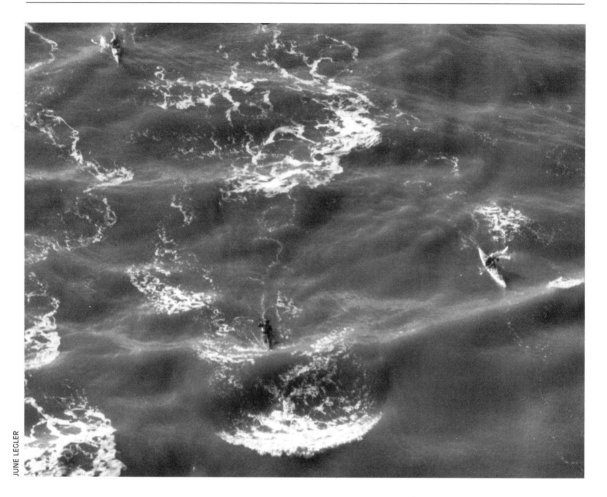

JUNE LEGLER

When paddling downwind, you can take advantage of the waves. This takes good boat control and surfing skill.

to break on the kayak, tilt the boat into the wave and time your stroke so that you plant the paddle blade on the wave side, just as the wave hits. Your stroke will function as a brace. With experience, you'll do this automatically, without even thinking about it.

Paddling downwind in steep following seas can be a nightmare or a thrilling pleasure. It all depends on your experience and level of skill. Unless you prefer terror to pleasure, it is well worth gaining the skills to handle following seas. It is also essential to your safety. In really strong wind, your only choice may be to paddle downwind. A kayak can be difficult to control when traveling downwind because the waves tend to push the stern forward while the bow is somewhat locked in as it plows forward though the water. As a result, the boat wants to pivot on the bow and turn broadside to the waves. With practice, you can compensate by using boat lean and corrective sweep strokes. As you sense the boat turning off course, use a sweep stroke to correct. Tilt the boat toward the stroke side, *away* from the direction you want to turn. In really rough conditions, you can introduce a bracing component to the sweep stroke, by flattening your blade to the water. If your kayak has a rudder or a skeg, it can be used to hold your course. This can save you considerable effort, especially when paddling downwind in a kayak that doesn't track well.

If the waves are steep enough, you can surf them when traveling downwind. This is exhilarating and will increase your speed considerably. Surfing ability pays huge dividends here. If you have practiced in the surf zone, riding the waves downwind will come naturally. To surf the waves, paddle forward perpendicular to the waves. Aim directly for the wave trough as it opens in front of you. Each time a wave trough passes under your bow, lean forward and paddle hard directly down the face of the next wave rising up behind you. You'll feel the stern lift, and if you catch the wave, you'll shoot forward. You may have to lean back to keep the bow from plowing into the wave in front of you. Once you are riding a wave, you can steer with a stern rudder stroke. Try to remain perpendicular to the wave. If you start to turn parallel to the wave, lean the boat toward the wave and use a powerful sweep stroke on the wave side to straighten out. If you are moving fast enough, you can use a stern rudder stroke on the down-wave side while leaning into the wave. However, if you are getting fast rides and making good progress, don't worry about moving in a perfectly straight line; let the boat yaw back and forth a bit, relax, and enjoy the ride. Surfing downwind is a real joy, once you get comfortable with it.

Boat lean (see "Backup Strategy," Chapter 8) is the key to controlling your kayak in wind and rough seas. Use the lean to maintain a relatively even keel in steep waves. You can also use boat lean to help carve turns and, as described above, correct course when surfing downwind. Ultimately you need to be relaxed, comfortable, and balanced while the wind and seas rage around you. Stay loose and allow the kayak to dance with the waves. This is one of the joys of sea kayaking. The ability to paddle in rough, windy conditions is also important to your safety. If you

Boat lean is the key to controlling your kayak in wind and rough seas.

Fog is very common in the marine environment.

spend much time in open water, you will certainly encounter such conditions.

Fog

Fog can seriously impair visibility on the water, creating a navigational challenge. Dense fog may be particularly dangerous if there are nearby hazards, such as boat traffic, breaking waves, or rocks. If you listen closely, you can usually hear oncoming boat traffic and breaking waves. In the fog it can be difficult to determine the distance or direction of various sounds. However, the sound will put you on the alert, and you can then spot the hazard in time to avoid it. On the open coast, the main problem is trying to see far enough ahead to plan your route through waves and rocks. This will be discussed below.

Navigating in Fog

When paddling in fog close to shore, you can use visual references to navigate as long as you can identify surf and shoreline features. Watch for anything you can use to locate your position, including buoys, major headlands, peninsulas, islets, or prominent rock formations. This is much easier to do if you are paddling in a familiar area; otherwise, you'll need to correlate what little you can see with your chart. On the ocean, you can often use the swell direction to maintain a course parallel to the shoreline. If the swell gets steeper, you may be getting close to shallow water and should either move a bit offshore or stay alert for breaking waves.

Using a Compass

If you are paddling offshore or cannot see any shoreline features due to fog, you'll need to rely on your compass, for which are two general techniques. When paddling toward a specific destination that you can still see, such as an island or a point of land, which is soon to be obscured by fog, simply take a bearing on your destination and hold that course with your compass after the fog rolls in. This can work even if you are already compensating for wind or current, using a range or a specific ferry angle (see below); just maintain your compass heading after the fog obscures your visual references.

A second technique for using a compass in fog is called *dead reckoning* (navigation using a compass course, time underway, and paddling speed). Use a chart to determine the course and the distance to your destination. You may have to account for current or wind (as described below) when determining your actual compass heading. Then paddle on course for the length of time necessary to reach your destination at your paddling speed.

For example, if you want to paddle to an island that, according to the chart, is 3 nautical miles offshore (1 minute of latitude = 1 nautical mile), plot the course by drawing a line from your launch point to the island. Then, using the compass rose (use *magnetic north*, which is what the compass will read) on the chart, and a parallel rule, determine the bearing to the island. You'll have to plot the course ahead of time, on shore or at home. Let's assume the course is 270 (i.e., west) and that you have already determined that a comfortable cruising speed for you is 3 knots. This means you should cover the distance (3 nautical miles) in one hour. Assuming little or no wind or current, all you have to do is launch and follow a compass heading of 270 for an hour to reach the island.

I did this with a friend during a kayak camping excursion along the west coast of Vancouver Island. We wanted to paddle out the next morning and fish for ling cod near a small island that we had spotted offshore the previous evening. Using my compass, I took a bearing to the island and wrote it down. The following morning we set out in a blanket of fog. My partner couldn't believe it when the island emerged from the mist after an hour of paddling in a foggy sensory deprivation chamber. But it was very simple; I just watched my compass and stayed on course. There was no wind, and current was not a factor in this case.

Compensating for Current and Wind

If you are crossing a channel with current, the situation is more complex. In order to go directly across and stay on course, you have to set a ferry angle to compensate for the current. This will work only if the current is somewhat less than your paddling speed. If the current approaches your paddling speed, you either have to paddle faster or expect to get *set* (pushed off course) down current. If you are crossing a current in the fog, you will need to know what the current is in order to estimate the ferry angle (see "Crossing Currents," Chapter 11, for information on estimating a ferry angle). In many areas, the current can be determined using a tide and current table.

When paddling across the wind in dense fog, you'll have no accurate way to determine a ferry angle, except from previous experience. In clear weather, take note of your ferry angle when crossing the wind. For example, in light wind of about 10 knots, you might find that a small ferry angle (5–10°) is sufficient to stay on course directly across the wind. In stronger wind of about 20 knots, you may need a 30–40° angle, depending on your paddling speed (faster paddling speed requires less ferry angle). Then apply this knowledge to estimate your ferry angle when paddling across the wind in fog.

If you have to paddle in heavy fog on open water with both wind and current, you can't navigate with much accuracy. Choose a large target area for your destination (e.g., a mile-long beach or a large island) with plenty of margin for error, and have a way to determine your location once you reach shore. One way is to purposely aim a bit to one side of your destination, so you know which way to paddle along the shoreline once you get there. Or you can use a chart to identify prominent features when you get close enough to see them.

Fog on the Open Coast

Paddling along an open coastline exposed to large breaking waves can be treacherous in heavy fog. If you can find a relatively protected passage inside a reef or in rock gardens, you can use shoreline features to navigate. In many cases you need to be offshore to avoid breaking waves. As long as you stay well offshore and use a compass to navigate, you are not in danger of getting caught in the breakers. However, at some point you need to get back to shore, or close enough to figure out where you are. This can be dangerous, because you can't see what lies ahead in order to pick a route through breaking waves and rocks. About all you can do is to proceed carefully and keep searching until you locate a relatively safe route into shore.

I don't like to paddle in thick fog on an unfamiliar coast when the swell is large enough to create dangerous breaking waves. It is too difficult to find a safe passage near shore when visibility is less than about 30 feet. If you stay offshore, you must rely on dead reckoning until you eventually have to pick

Paddling along an open coastline exposed to large breaking waves can be treacherous in heavy fog.

your way back in through waves and rocks, into an area where nothing is recognizable. However, on a familiar coastline, paddling in fog is not nearly so hazardous. If you already know a safe route, you can navigate using key features, such as headlands, rocks, and islands. Of course you have to know where these features are and where safe passages exist.

Weather Predictions and Local Knowledge

Whenever you head out on the water in a kayak, it is crucial to take note of weather conditions and to anticipate changes in the weather. Use a combination of weather forecasts and knowledge of local weather patterns in the area where you are kayaking. A forecast will give you specific information on what *might* happen over the next several hours or days. If it calls for an extreme situation, such as a major storm or huge surf, you should be prepared for the worst—or stay home. If the forecast calls for fair and calm weather, take this as a good sign, but don't assume it will always be correct. Look for ideal conditions, yet prepare yourself for the likely extreme. By "likely extreme", I mean difficult conditions that can and do arise on occasion, not the freak storm that happens once in a hundred years.

Use shoreline features whenever possible to navigate in heavy fog.

Learn to read the signs for bad weather. Clouds such as these herald an approaching storm with strong wind.

The only way to know the usual conditions and what the likely extreme may be in any area is through knowledge of local weather patterns and sea conditions. As an example, I describe the typical year-round pattern for San Francisco Bay in Table 2. This is the sort of information that you should research and compile for any area where you choose to sea kayak.

Conclusion

No matter where you kayak, do some research to find out what the typical weather patterns are for the area. Pay close attention to the possibility of wind and storms. Listen to the weather forecast, but don't be surprised if it isn't accurate. Most importantly, prepare yourself to face the most extreme conditions you are likely to encounter.

While the profile of weather on San Francisco Bay is only a general overview, it provides some useful limits for the kayaker on probable weather conditions in the area. For example, you know that when paddling in summer on the open bay, you must be

TABLE 2. Weather Conditions on San Francisco Bay

Time of Year	Weather Conditions	Likely Extreme
November through February	In between storms, expect generally clear skies or high overcast, cool temperatures, and calm conditions or mild variable winds up to about 15 knots. Occasional storms move in with moderate to heavy rain and southerly winds ranging from 15 knots to gale force (30–40 knots). Strong winds will kick up seas to 4 or 5 feet high. When the wind runs against a strong tidal current the waves will steepen and break. Between storms, paddling conditions are relatively mild and enjoyable.	Powerful winter storm with rain and gale-force winds. However, this type of storm is usually easy to predict.
March through May	Conditions are highly variable in the spring. Northwesterly winds begin to funnel through the Golden Gate, but with no discernible pattern. Some days are calm, others windy. The wind rarely exceeds 25 knots, but stronger gusts can occur. Moderate storms are possible, especially in March, but generally are not as powerful as the winter storms.	Wind to 25 knots or a late storm.
June through August	The main weather feature during summer months on San Francisco Bay is a strong westerly afternoon wind (sea breeze) that blows in through the Golden Gate in response to high temperature, and rising hot air in the Central Valley located beyond a small coastal mountain range east of the bay. After funneling through the Golden Gate, the wind blows directly across the bay toward Berkeley and follows the axis of the bay north and south. These winds occur frequently during the summer and should be expected on any given day. The wind usually starts around 10 or 11 a.m. and continues throughout the afternoon. Wind speed on the open bay commonly reaches 20–25 knots, with stronger gusts locally. Fog is also common this time of year; it typically moves in with the wind late in the day and remains into the morning hours.	Strong westerly wind 25–30 knots.
September through October	This is the warmest time of year. The westerly winds of summer have diminished, and calm conditions prevail, with occasional light to moderate wind. Warm offshore (easterly) winds sometimes blow and, though rare, they can be intense, reaching 30 knots or more. Heavy, low fog often forms, especially in early September. Storms are rare but not impossible.	Moderate to strong winds from the east or west, or early season storm.

prepared to deal with winds up to 25 knots. In winter, you can be fairly confident that conditions will be calm, unless a storm is moving in.

With some research, you can develop a similar profile for any area where you choose to kayak. In the Sea of Cortez (Baja), strong northerly winds ("El Norte") up to 30 knots or more can blow for several days at a time during the winter. Anyone planning a kayaking trip in Baja during winter months should be prepared for this phenomenon and plan accordingly. During late spring in Baja, the winds calm down and conditions are fairly mild. When planning a multi-day kayak trip, it is best to choose a time when weather conditions are not likely to be at their worst. For example, you might not choose to paddle the Oregon coast during winter because you would encounter huge surf. In late summer and early fall, the Sea of Cortez is subject to hurricane-force winds ("chubascos") as well as extremely hot temperatures; this wouldn't be the best time to plan a kayaking trip in Baja.

Finally, be prepared to wait out serious weather conditions. If you are on a trip in the Aleutian Islands of Alaska and a major storm blows in, don't be tempted to get on the water just so you don't miss your plane flight home, or to get a hot shower a day sooner. In wilderness areas, always carry more food and water than you think you need so that you can stay ashore for a few extra days during a period of dangerous weather.

Find out what the typical weather patterns are.

CHAPTER 11.
TIDES AND CURRENTS

You need a thorough understanding of tides and currents if you want to paddle safely in the marine environment. This is especially true in inland marine waterways where currents are a major factor. In some cases tidal current will exceed your paddling speed; you won't be able to paddle directly against such a current. If you are paddling into a strong current at some distance from shore, you might not even realize you are making little or no headway or are even being pushed backwards! Although the phenomena of tides and currents can be complex, a general understanding of them, along with time on the water, will help you resolve any problems involving navigating or kayaking in current.

Tides are changes in sea level which result from the gravitational force between the earth, sun, and moon. Tides are more extreme during periods of the full and new moon; at these times the sun, the

earth, and the moon are aligned, creating a strong gravitational force. At quarter moon, the sun and the moon exert gravitational pulls at right angles, which dilutes the overall effect. In most parts of the world, high and low tides occur twice daily, resulting in approximately a 12-hour tidal cycle for the rise and fall of the tide. Depending on the configuration of the local ocean basin and adjacent land masses, tides are more extreme in some parts of the world than others.

Tidal currents occur in constricted areas between islands, and in inland waterways. They result from the rise and fall of the tide. These currents form because of a difference between the oceanic sea level and the level of local inland bays and estuaries. In other words, as a tide rises on the ocean, the water level is temporarily higher than the level in the bay. Water rushes into the bay to reestablish balance. The movement of water inland in response to a rising tide is called the *flood*. When the tide falls, the opposite situation occurs, and water rushes out to sea. This is termed the *ebb* tide.

Tide *height* is not the same as tidal *current*. Most tide books have separate tables giving times of high and low tide and times of maximum flood and ebb current. You'll want information on the *height* of the tide in order to know when you might get stranded on a mud flat, whether a pocket beach where you want to camp will be fully submerged, or how to predict the surf conditions across a rocky reef. You need to consult the *current* predictions in order to ascertain the direction and strength of the current in the area where you will be paddling at the time you'll be there. Be aware that the times of maximum current and of the highest and lowest tides do not usually coincide. For example, high tide might occur an hour or more before maximum flood.

Use tide and current tables with caution. Although predictions are fairly accurate, they are only estimates and can be off by as much as an hour. Predictions of current strength can be off due to the influence of unusual runoff, wind, or atmospheric pressure conditions. In general, you can trust the tide book as long as you allow for a margin of error.

Understanding Tidal Currents

The first step toward dealing with tidal current is to figure out what the current is doing. If you have a current table for the area you will be paddling, use it to determine times of maximum current and of *slack* current (period during which the current is changing from flood to ebb or vice versa). Also note the strength of the maximum currents. These figures will be given for a particular location, so you will need to correct for other locations. The current tables will give the correction factors, or you can correct using a *current chart*, which gives current speeds and directions over a wide area on an hourly basis throughout the tidal cycle. The best way to learn how to use these predictions is to get a tide and current table and read it thoroughly. These tables generally include an excellent user's guide; you just have to read it carefully.

Figure out what the current is doing.

Tidal Cycles

In most parts of the world, the high-low tidal cycle lasts approximately 12 hours (it is actually closer to 12½ hours): the tide will rise for 6 hours, then fall for 6 hours, resulting in 2 high and 2 low tides in a 24-hour period. Currents correspond to this cycle also; the current will flood for 6 hours, then reverse and ebb for 6 hours. The 6-hour figure is an approximation; during extreme tides, the time difference between high and low tides (and maximum ebb and flood) can be 7 hours. If so, there will also be a correspondingly small difference between the "high" low tide and the "low" high tide, and the time between these tides will be about 5 hours. A careful reading of the tide table will reveal this.

During a tidal cycle, the current will build to a maximum speed, then drop off. Take, for example, the case of an ebb current with a maximum of 4 knots. Approximately 3 hours prior to the maximum ebb, there will be little or no current (slack current). Two hours before maximum ebb, the current may be 1.5 knots, and 1 hour before maximum ebb the current may be 3.5 knots. Notice that the current speed increases quickly as it approaches maximum. The current will decrease for the 3 hours after maximum ebb, then reverse direction and begin to flood. The flood will last 6 hours, completing the 12-hour cycle.

Knowing the strength of the current and where you are in the tidal cycle can have a major influence on your decisions. If you know the current is slacking off, you may decide to cross a channel or paddle in a direction that would otherwise be problematic if the current were gaining strength. If the current is just starting to flood, you know you'll have an easy paddle if you go in the flood direction.

Observing Tides and Currents on the Water

Even if you don't have a tide book (or you forgot to consult it), you can gain a lot of information once on the water. Use ranges and shoreline features to monitor your progress or to determine your *drift* (the direction and speed the current or wind is pushing you). For example, pick out a range, *to one side* of the direction you are paddling, such as a bridge abutment with an island in the background, and watch these two features as you paddle forward. If you see no apparent movement between the bridge and the island over a period of time, you are not moving forward and are probably fighting a current (assuming no headwind). If the two objects appear to move apart, you are moving forward or backward, depending on the direction of this apparent separation. Watch the more distant object; this can be termed the *background*. You will be moving the same direction as the background is appearing to move, relative to the near object. So if the island appears to move forward with you, relative to the bridge abutment, you are making progress forward. If this all sounds confusing, don't worry; once you start using ranges on the water, it will be very clear what is going on. The important thing is to look around and use whatever ranges you can find.

To determine whether you are being set off course, look for a *front range*: line up two stationary points in front of you and watch to see if they stay in line. If they don't, you are being pushed off course by wind or a side current (assuming you can paddle in a straight line). Another method is to read your compass as you paddle. Watch your heading as you paddle toward a feature up ahead, such as an island or a point of land; if this heading changes over time, you are being pushed off course. The way to compensate for a side current or wind is to set a ferry angle (see "Crossing Current," below).

On a multi-day trip, you can tune into the tides and currents by simply observing what is going on as each day passes. Once you have determined the general times of high and low tide and of maximum currents, you can extrapolate for coming days. Each day parts of the tidal cycle will occur approximately one hour later. This is because the tidal cycle is actually about 12½ hours long. So if the maximum flood

Use ranges and shoreline features to monitor your progress or to determine your drift.

current occurs at noon today, it will occur at about 1:00 p.m. tomorrow. Also, be aware that currents and tides are more extreme around the time of new and full moons.

Paddling in Current

As a general rule, when paddling in current, you want to *go with the flow*. Try to plan your trips with this rule in mind. Suppose, for example, that you want to paddle out the Golden Gate and return later in the day. Time your trip so that you launch during the ebb; you will enjoy a free ride out the Gate, and return later in the day with the flood current, after your picnic lunch on the beach. Be sure to also consider wind direction and strength. If the wind is strong and the current is weak, the wind may be a more significant factor.

There will be situations where you won't have the luxury of paddling with the current: you may not be able to plan your trip to coincide with the current direction, your timing might be off, you might find yourself fighting a current that you didn't anticipate, or your destination could be across the current. Also, some currents are not caused by tides. In certain areas along the open coast, you may encounter a *longshore current* (an oceanic current that moves parallel to shore). Although longshore currents are usually weak (less than 1 knot), they can reach 3 knots or more. You need a strategy to deal with all these situations.

Paddling Against the Current

If you have to fight the current (whether it is a tidal current or a longshore current), your best bet is to *hug the shore*. Unless the shoreline is a sheer drop-off, the current will be weaker close to shore. You should also look for *eddies* (areas where the current reverses direction) in coves or embayments, and on the downstream side of headlands, islands, or peninsulas. When paddling in an eddy, you'll get a push from the countercurrent. Watch the surface of the water; eddies will sometimes appear smoother on the surface than the water moving in the main current.

In situations where you have to fight directly against the current, you can continue as long as you are making reasonable headway. This is similar to paddling into a headwind. You'll need a strong forward stroke and have to keep paddling. In some cases you need only make a short sprint into the current as

Go with the flow.

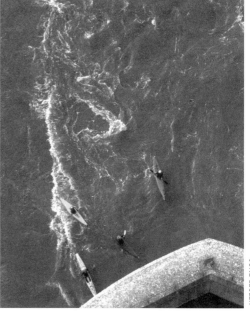

Large eddy on the downstream side of a major bridge abutment at the south tower of the Golden Gate Bridge. Note the sharply-defined eddyline on the left side of the photo. Main current is moving toward the top of the photo. Current in the eddy is moving in the opposite direction, toward the abutment.

It is vital to realize when, in fact, you are fighting a current.

it accelerates around a headland or a point of land. Paddle hard, maintaining a quick cadence (take fast, short, powerful forward strokes). Obviously, it is not desirable to paddle for a long distance into a strong current. If the option exists, you may want to land and wait for the current to diminish (assuming you are fighting a tidal current). If you are not making headway or are getting exhausted, *ferry toward shore* and look for an eddy, where you can paddle with the counter current, or find a place to land.

It is vital to realize when, in fact, you are fighting a current. On one occasion, I was paddling from Angel Island toward the Golden Gate with my partner, June Legler. Although we had checked the tide table and knew a strong flood current was predicted, we thought we were launching soon enough to paddle the 2 miles to Horseshoe Cove (just inside the Golden Gate) before the current got too strong. After paddling for about 30 minutes, I noticed a green buoy up ahead. It didn't look very far away. Twenty minutes later the buoy didn't look much closer and I began to suspect that we were fighting a current. So I started paddling as hard as I could. Eventually, the buoy crept closer, and when I finally reached it, I noticed the buoy was bent over toward me, with water rushing past on both sides. I stopped paddling and turned around to look for June, who had fallen behind during my sprint for the buoy. When I looked forward again, a few seconds later, the buoy was about 20 feet away; I was rushing backwards with the current! June and I decided to ferry across the current toward the shoreline. From there we were able to paddle to our destination, staying in the eddies and the weaker currents closer to shore.

This tale illustrates several key points:

- **Don't cut it too close when using current predictions, especially if you might end up fighting the current.** Allow a margin of error of an hour or more. In this case, we launched just as the flood was starting; we should have launched a couple of hours earlier.

- **Always look for indications about what the current is doing while on the water.** Look for side ranges and pay attention to elapsed time to monitor your progress. On the journey above, far too much time and energy was lost fighting the current before we realized what was happening. The buoy, which was only one mile from Angel Island, should have been reached in about 20 minutes; instead, it took over an hour of hard paddling to get there.

- **Once you discover you are fighting a strong current, look for a way out of the situation.** In most cases, you can ferry across the current and get close to shore, where you can land or look for eddies.

Crossing Current

When paddling across a current, you will have to use a ferry angle if you don't want to get set downstream. The *ferry angle* is the angle between the course you want and the *heading* (the direction you point your kayak) you need in order to maintain that course. When ferrying, your heading will always be at some angle into the current. The larger this angle is, the more you'll have to fight the current, and the slower you'll go.

You can use a range to determine your ferry angle or you can calculate the angle, using paddling speed and current speed (see below). The best way to determine and maintain a ferry angle is by using a front range, keeping two stationary points (e.g., the end of a peninsula and a distant island) aligned as you paddle toward them. You can also use a *back range* (a range behind you), looking over your shoulder occasionally, as you paddle away from shore.

You can't always depend on finding a range, especially on a long crossing or in fog. In this case, you can calculate the ferry angle using a vector solution (see Figure 3), or you can estimate it using an algebraic formula: when crossing the current at right angles, *Ferry angle = current speed ÷ paddling speed × 60*; with current and paddling speeds in knots. When crossing a current "on the quarter" (with the current at approximately 45° to your desired course), *Ferry angle = current speed ÷ paddling speed × 40*. These formulae are approximations of the vector solution and are not accurate at current speeds approaching your paddling speed. For further information on calculating ferry angles, see *Fundamentals of Kayak Navigation* by David Burch. Once on the water, try to verify the calculated ferry angle using ranges.

Table 3 shows calculated ferry angles for various current speeds, assuming a beam current (perpendicular to your course). Note how your *speed made*

FIGURE 3. Calculating a Ferry Angle Using a Vector Solution

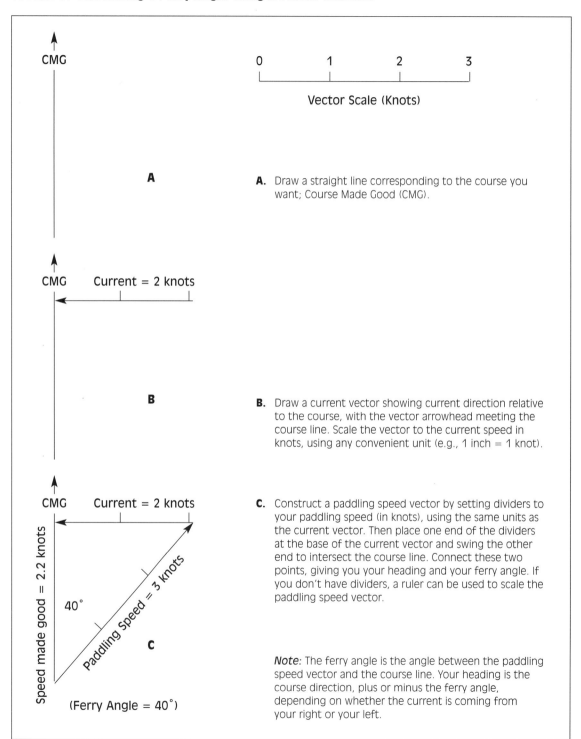

A. Draw a straight line corresponding to the course you want; Course Made Good (CMG).

B. Draw a current vector showing current direction relative to the course, with the vector arrowhead meeting the course line. Scale the vector to the current speed in knots, using any convenient unit (e.g., 1 inch = 1 knot).

C. Construct a paddling speed vector by setting dividers to your paddling speed (in knots), using the same units as the current vector. Then place one end of the dividers at the base of the current vector and swing the other end to intersect the course line. Connect these two points, giving you your heading and your ferry angle. If you don't have dividers, a ruler can be used to scale the paddling speed vector.

Note: The ferry angle is the angle between the paddling speed vector and the course line. Your heading is the course direction, plus or minus the ferry angle, depending on whether the current is coming from your right or your left.

TABLE 3. Paddling Speed and Ferry Angle

Current	PS = 3 Knots		PS = 4 Knots	
	Ferry Angle	SMG	Ferry Angle	SMG
1.0 k	20°	2.8 k	15°	3.8 k
1.5 k	30°	2.6 k	22°	3.6 k
2.0 k	40°	2.2 k	30°	3.5 k
2.5 k	55°	1.6 k	40°	3.1 k
3.0 k	—	—	50°	2.6 k
3.5 k	—	—	60°	2.0 k

Ferry angles and speed made good (SMG) when ferrying across a beam current with a paddling speed (PS) = 3 knots and PS = 4 knots; derived from vector solutions.

good (your actual speed, resulting from the combination of paddling speed and current speed) decreases with increasing current speed and larger ferry angles. Also note the difference in ferry angle and speed made good (SMG) when you increase your paddling speed from 3 to 4 knots. There is a major payoff in your speed made good if you are capable of maintaining a 4-knot cruising speed. This is a good argument for developing a strong forward stroke and working on your paddling endurance.

Calculated ferry angles must be treated as estimates. Their accuracy depends on maintaining a constant paddling speed and on the accuracy of tidal current predictions. The current generally changes across a channel and over time. Therefore, you will have to use an *average* current for the ferry-angle calculation. In spite of limitations in the calculation, ferry angles can work amazingly well. I've managed to find a buoy in dense fog after paddling two miles out in San Francisco Bay across a 2-knot current, using a calculated ferry angle.

Beware of large ferry angles. As the current approaches your paddling speed, the ferry angle increases significantly. If the ferry angle is much larger than about 40 degrees with a beam current, you'll be heading well into the current and progress will be slow (see Table 3). You can reduce the ferry angle by increasing your paddling speed, assuming you can maintain the faster speed.

If the current is strong enough to require a large ferry angle, you may be better off paddling with a smaller ferry angle and accepting some downstream movement. This is a good strategy if the current is slacking off, allowing you to make up the downstream loss at slack current, after crossing. Another way to deal with a strong current is to paddle upstream along the near shoreline, putting your destination across the channel downstream. Now you can cross with a smaller ferry angle. Because your destination is downstream, the current will be on your stern quarter and will help your progress rather than hinder it.

Practical experience crossing currents is the only way to learn how to use ferry angles effectively. Also pay attention to how the current affects your paddling speed. If you don't know your paddling speed, figure it out by paddling a known distance (e.g., 1 nautical mile) and timing yourself in an area without current.

Changes in Current Direction

The general direction of tidal currents can be easily predicted. A flood current flows *inland* and an ebb current flows *out toward the ocean*. However, in its journey to and from the ocean, the current can change course considerably as it flows through inland channels and around islands. A current table uses arrows to indicate current direction at various locations. The arrows are *generalizations,* so you will have to be prepared for subtle but important variations in current direction, especially near islands and in convoluted waterways.

The current may not always do what you expect. The best way to anticipate unexpected changes is to use ranges to monitor your progress. When you detect a change in motion, especially a lack of forward progress, figure out what is happening and adjust your heading accordingly. This is especially important when you are using a ferry angle to cross the current. If there is a significant change in current direction, you need to adjust your ferry angle.

A classic case of a change in current direction can be found near Alcatraz Island in San Francisco Bay. I first discovered this while crossing from Angel Island to Alcatraz on a group trip. A strong ebb current was running across our course and we had to set a ferry angle as we began the crossing. We were making good progress until, about three-fourths of the way across, some of us noticed that Alcatraz Island was no longer getting any closer. By using a side range on one end of the island against the backdrop of the city buildings, we verified that we were essentially on a treadmill, paddling forward and going nowhere. Instead of ferrying *across* the current, we were now paddling directly *into* the current. Our heading hadn't changed—the current direction had. We adjusted by changing our heading until the range indicated we were once again moving toward the island; or, at least, going *somewhere*! In the process, we fell off to the west (the current direction), but were still able to ferry into the large eddy on the west side of Alcatraz.

Meanwhile, the rest of our group had not made the ferry-angle adjustment. We sat in the eddy and watched as they paddled forward valiantly, but fruitlessly, as if on a treadmill. From our vantage point it was easy to see they were making no progress. In time, they realized the situation, changed course, and eventually made it into the eddy, but not until they had nearly exhausted themselves fighting the current.

Why did the current shift direction? Alcatraz Island sits in an area where currents from the South Bay and the North Bay converge during the ebb (Figure 4). The current that flows out of the North Bay swings around Angel Island and heads west out through the Golden Gate. This is the current that we were ferrying across most of the way. Current flowing out of the South Bay flows directly into and around Alcatraz Island. On the south side of the island, the current turns and flows west. On the east side it flows to the northwest along the island. This is the current that we ran into as we approached Alcatraz. At that point, we had to change our heading to compensate for the change in current direction.

These changes in current direction are typical, especially in the vicinity of islands. Sometimes you can predict everything ahead of time. More often, you'll have to react based on what is happening to you on the water. In the example above, we didn't predict the situation; we had to adjust to it. Keep a sharp eye on the shoreline and watch for ranges to give you an indication of what is happening, then decide how to proceed.

Handling Tide Rips

When the current flows over underwater obstacles, or accelerates around headlands and between islands, traps waves, or flows against other forces such as wind or cross currents, *tide rips* (not to

FIGURE 4. Ebb Currents on San Francisco Bay

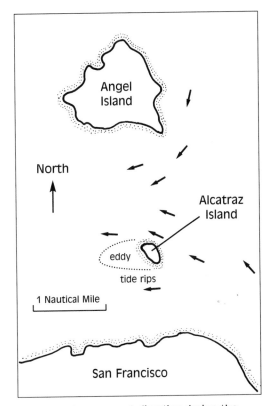

Arrows show current direction during the ebb tide. Note change in current direction between Angel Island and Alcatraz Island. In the area northeast of Alcatraz Island, current flowing out of the north bay meets current flowing from the south bay. Currents in the vicinity of Alcatraz Island can reach speeds of 3 to 4 knots during a strong ebb.

Tide rips are areas of rough water that can present a challenge to kayakers.

be confused with *"rips" or "rip tides,"* which occur in the surf zone) form. In a general sense the term tide rip includes all rough water phenomena related to tidal current; other terms for tide rips include *overfalls, tide races,* and *tidal rapids.* Places to watch for tide rips include shoals or underwater shelves, areas off points of land that jut into the current, the mouths of constricted channels, bottlenecks that drain large volumes of water, and areas of colliding currents. Also, whenever a strong wind blows against the current, the waves slow down and steepen, creating chaotic, choppy seas.

Tide rips can be hazardous to unwary or inexperienced kayakers. If you plan on paddling in marine waterways that are subject to currents, develop the ability to handle tide rips; don't just assume you'll be able to avoid them. The skills needed include balance and boat lean, bracing ability, an Eskimo roll, and comfort kayaking in rough conditions. Paddling in tide rips will help refine these skills. Surf zone and whitewater river kayaking skills are also useful for learning to handle tide rips.

Your goal is to be able to control your kayak in current and rough water. Of all the skills listed in the paragraph above, boat lean (see "Backup Strategies," Chapter 8) is the single most important one needed to stay balanced, relaxed, and in control while being bounced around in a chaotic tide rip. This is especially true whenever you are at an angle or broadside to the waves: keep your boat on a planing angle by tilting it slightly downstream into the waves, thus preventing you from catching an edge on the upstream side (which could result in a capsize). With practice, you'll do this naturally, without thinking about it too much. The trick is to stay balanced as you lean so you can paddle or maneuver the kayak; don't think of it as bracing or leaning on the paddle. Of course, if you start to capsize and need to brace, by all means do so. Be ready to shift your lean from one side to the other, if necessary. This is often necessary when surfing into the current or changing the direction of your ferry (see below).

In addition to balance and bracing skills, there are four tactics which you should master in order to become proficient at handling your kayak in swift current and tide rips:

- **Crossing eddylines**
- **Paddling with the current**

- Ferry gliding across the current
- Surfing waves into the current

Crossing Eddylines

Whenever you paddle into a swift current from an eddy or vice versa, you have to cross an *eddyline*. This is a shear zone between the main current and the reverse current in the eddy. An eddyline can be sharp and fairly obvious, usually near the top (upstream end) of the eddy, or a broad zone of swirling water. The main thing to remember when approaching an eddyline is to paddle hard and to continue paddling all the way across, so you don't stall or spin out. Be sure to approach the eddyline at a fairly high angle to enable you to get across. Stalling on the eddyline is a common mistake for beginners who don't paddle hard enough to punch through. Broad eddylines are often full of whirlpools and currents diverging and converging in several directions. It is best to paddle hard through such a zone unless you want to spin around in circles.

There are three possible scenarios for crossing an eddyline:

- **Entering an eddy:** When entering an eddy, approach the eddyline at an angle of approximately 60°. Set this angle *before* you reach the eddyline, then paddle hard across. The current will give you momentum, but you still need to paddle to pierce the eddyline. The boat will start to turn into the countercurrent as you enter the eddy. You can continue to paddle deep into the eddy, or you can plant your paddle blade in the water on the inside of the turn to sharpen it. As you cross the eddyline, keep your boat flat or tilt it slightly *into* the turn to avoid catching an edge. Sea kayaks won't turn as sharply as whitewater boats.

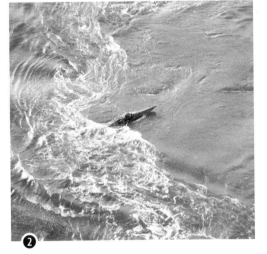

PHOTO SEQUENCE: JUNE LEGLER

❶ Approach the eddyline at an angle of 45–60°. Paddle hard to maintain speed and forward momentum.

❷ Paddle clear across the eddyline, leaning slightly into your turn as you enter the eddy.

❸ Keep paddling well into the eddy.

- **Peeling out of an Eddy:** This maneuver is performed in much the same way as entering an eddy. Paddle hard to accelerate across the eddyline. Your angle should be approximately 60° to the eddyline, angling upstream, into the main current. As you enter the current, keep the boat flat or tilt it slightly *downstream* to keep the upstream edge clear. Keep paddling well beyond the eddyline into the current. The bow will start to turn downstream with the current. Perform a powerful sweep stroke on the upstream side to help turn the kayak downstream. Advanced kayakers can experiment with leaning *upstream* toward the sweep stroke to sharpen the turn. Do this with care; it is easy to catch an edge and capsize when leaning upstream.

- **Leaving the Eddy and Setting a Ferry Angle:** If you want to ferry across the current, paddle across the eddyline at a smaller angle than you would use to turn downstream (head more upstream, into the main current). The stronger the current, the smaller the angle will have to be to keep your bow from being swept downstream. As you cross the eddyline, perform a sweep stroke or a stern draw on the *downstream* side to hold your bow into the current. Continue to paddle *well out into the current* and set your ferry angle (see "Ferry Gliding Across the Current," below).

Paddling with the Current

If your destination is downstream, enter the tide rip, point your kayak downstream, and paddle forward. The current will carry you swiftly along as you punch through the waves. Lean forward slightly as you bounce through and over the steep seas. If there is a large eddy nearby, you can catch the eddy by turning toward the eddyline and punching across, as described above. Once in the eddy, paddle back upstream and reenter the tide rip by peeling out near the top (upstream end) of the eddy; then run the tide rip and turn back into the eddy again farther downstream. This is a good way to practice crossing eddylines and running tide rips.

Ferry Gliding Across the Current

The best way to gain directional control in a current is to ferry back and forth across the current. To ferry across, either enter the current from the eddy (as described above) or, if you are already moving downstream, turn upstream by using forward and reverse sweep strokes. Once you face upstream, paddle forward and angle your bow left or right with a forward sweep stroke. Keep paddling forward so you don't get swept downstream. If you set an angle to the right, you will move to the right across the current as you paddle. Watch the shoreline to observe your direction of movement and adjust your ferry angle to increase your speed across the current.

In strong tide rips with waves, the only way to ferry without losing ground is to *ferry glide*: surf the upstream face of a wave while ferrying. As you paddle forward, set a ferry angle, then catch a wave. With the optimum angle, you'll shoot swiftly across the current on the face of the wave. Keep your boat tilted slightly into the wave to maintain stability. As long as you are on the wave, you can use a stern rudder stroke on the upstream side to hold your trajectory. Ferry gliding is an efficient and fun way to cross a tide rip. Eventually, you'll lose the wave. Paddle forward until you catch another wave. Keep adjusting your ferry angle as necessary to continue moving across the current.

Use a ferry glide whenever you want to move laterally in a tide rip. This maneuver is especially useful when you need to move toward shore or toward an eddy without getting set downstream. It is essential if you are trying to avoid a downstream hazard or need to get ashore quickly. If you have trouble holding a ferry glide and find yourself going nowhere while fighting the current, don't panic. Point more toward shore, paddle hard, and you'll begin to move shoreward. In a strong current, you may have to accept some downstream drift in order to make good progress toward the eddy or the shoreline.

Surfing Waves into the Current

Ability to surf waves in a tide rip will allow you to ferry glide across the current, hold position, and make progress upstream. Most of all, if you can surf the waves, you'll be able to maintain control when you have to maneuver in a tide rip, thus increasing your margin of safety.

DEBRAH VOLTURNO

Ferry gliding across a wave in a tide rip. Kayaker is facing upstream at an angle to the current.

DEBRAH VOLTURNO

Surfing in a tide rip.

Tide rips tend to trap waves: As wind waves, ocean swell, or boat wakes flow against the current, they slow down and steepen. Most of these waves continue to move through the tide rip. However, in some cases, standing waves can form where the current flows over underwater obstacles, such as rock ledges. Standing waves remain in place, just as they do on rivers. You can surf a standing wave, but cannot move upstream on it.

When surfing in current, you are riding the upstream face of a wave. To catch a wave, paddle upstream and ferry back and forth until a wave lifts your stern. As you feel the stern lift, lean forward and paddle hard. Once on the wave face, use stern rudder strokes to steer. Lean back if your bow starts to dig in. When you lose the wave be ready to catch the next one. One trick to catching waves in tide rips is to watch for wave troughs under your bow as you paddle upstream. Whenever a wave trough appears under your bow, paddle hard into it. While surfing, steer and paddle into consecutive wave troughs to keep the ride going.

Surfing can be used as a way to hold position or make progress upstream. To hold position and "rest" in a tide rip, ease up on your paddling while on a wave face, paddling just hard enough between waves to avoid drifting downstream. Thus, you can maintain position in current that is stronger than your top paddling speed because the waves are providing the additional push you need. Since the waves are usually moving through the tide rip (unless they are standing waves), you can make gradual progress upstream if you continue surfing.

Rescues in Tide Rips

Due to the rough seas in a tide rip, there is a chance someone will capsize and end up swimming. You'll always have to be prepared to perform a rescue. A tide rip is also a great place to practice rough water rescues, as long as there is a safe run out, with no hazards downstream. For this purpose, it is best to have a large eddy nearby, where you can escape the tide rip and rest. When doing an assisted rescue, such as the T-rescue, be careful not to catch your hand or fingers between the boats as they bang together in the waves. You'll need to time all your movements with the movement of the waves as you bounce up and down. If you do this carefully, the waves can help you lift and drain water from the capsized boat. Be sure to tilt your kayak toward the bow of the capsized boat, use both hands to grab the bow, and have the swimmer push on the stern (see "T-Rescue," Chapter 4). You will want to time it so that you don't scoop water from the crest of a wave when righting the kayak. Practice reentry rolls or paddlefloat rescues in tide rips to make sure you can perform them in rough water. Have a partner standing by in case you need assistance.

If you are performing a rescue in a tide rip and are having real difficulty or are in danger of being swept into a hazardous area, you may want to do a side-rescue, getting the swimmer into the kayak quickly. Then use a push tow (see "Towing," Chapter 9) to get the paddler and the swamped kayak into an eddy where you can pump out the water. This will work best if the eddy is close by and the eddyline is not too wide. In any case, you'll have to paddle very hard to break through into the eddy. You may spend some time stalled on the eddyline in the process. Once you make it into the eddy, it will be easy to complete the rescue.

Paddling in tide rips is a great way to improve your rough-water skills and to prepare for kayaking in areas subject to strong currents. As always, start with less challenging conditions and work up gradually to stronger current and rougher water. Find a tide rip with a large eddy nearby or a safe run out with no hazards downstream, so you can practice all the maneuvers safely. Once you master kayaking in tide rips, you'll be safer paddling in currents anywhere.

Paddling in tide rips is a great way to improve your rough-water skills.

Key Points for Dealing with Tides and Currents

The information presented in this chapter is very important. I've noticed that quite a few sea kayakers know very little about currents and how to handle them. Of course, the only way to really learn how to deal with tides and current is through experience on the water. Learn all you can about tidal currents in the area you kayak by spending time navigating and paddling in the currents. Pay close attention to how the currents affect you. Use the following key points as a guide.

- Get a tide and current table; study it and know how to use it.

- Times of high and low tide do not usually coincide with times of maximum current.

- In most parts of the world, a tidal cycle covering high and low tide lasts 12½ hours, resulting in two high and two low tides each day. The same is true for the cycle of flood and ebb currents.

- Tides and currents are more extreme during the periods just before, during, and after the full moon and new moon.

- Flood current flows inland; ebb current flows out to the ocean.

- Tidal currents range from less than 1 knot up to 8 knots or more (6 to 8 knots would be considered a very strong current).

- When paddling with the current, stay out in the channel where you can take advantage of the free ride.

- When paddling against the current, hug the shore and use eddies wherever possible.

- Look for eddies in embayments and on the downstream side of points, peninsulas, headlands, and islands.

- When crossing current, use a front or back range to set your ferry angle and hold course. On open crossings or in reduced visibility, calculate a ferry angle beforehand, using a vector solution.

- To calculate a ferry angle you need to know: average current speed, paddling speed, current direction relative to your course.

- Use side ranges to monitor progress across or into current. Don't get stuck "paddling on a treadmill." A minor change in your heading can make a major difference.

- If you are fighting a current and making no headway, turn toward shore and paddle across the current until you get out of the main channel, find an eddy, or reach shore.

- Look for tide rips (current with rough water) wherever the current encounters obstacles: shoals, submerged rocks, converging currents, wind against the tide.

- To gain maximum control of your kayak in current and rough water, learn to ferry glide and surf in tide rips.

- When crossing an eddyline, set an angle of approximately 60°, paddle hard to punch the eddyline, and keep paddling until you are well across the eddyline. Tilt the kayak slightly into your turn for stability.

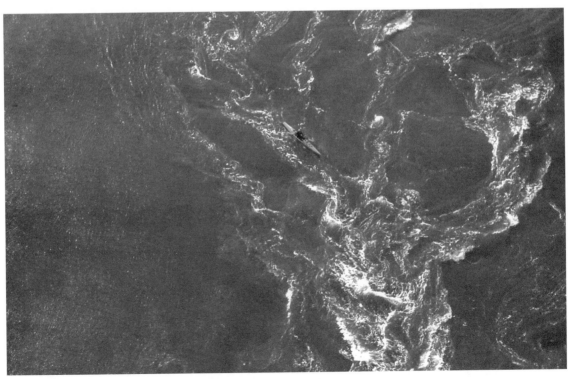

CHAPTER 12.
DEALING WITH BOAT TRAFFIC

If you paddle in busy ports, marinas, or waterways in populated areas, you will encounter boat traffic. Because almost all other vessels on the water are considerably larger and faster than a kayak, they pose a definite hazard to the kayaker. Whenever paddling in boat traffic, you must be constantly on the lookout for other craft. Monitor the course of all nearby traffic periodically, and be ready to take evasive action if you determine you are on a collision course with another vessel. This is not as difficult as it might seem; the main requirement is that you stay alert and respond appropriately to any situation. Knowing how to use the bow-angle method (described in this chapter) to judge whether you are on a collision course, is invaluable—especially when dealing with ships and other large vessels.

In areas with shipping traffic, make sure you know where the shipping lanes are. Shipping lanes are shown on charts and are also marked with buoys. You have to worry about ships only when you are in these lanes. However, other commercial traffic, such as ferries and fishing boats, are not restricted to the shipping lanes.

Be constantly on the lookout for other craft.

Rules of the Road

The "Rules of the Road," published by the Coast Guard under *Navigation Rules*, are a set of laws that govern the interaction of vessels on all waterways. Familiarize yourself with these rules because they are important to your safety. The basic rules apply to all vessels, including kayaks, and you need to understand what rules other vessels (ships, sailboats, etc.) are operating under. In this section I discuss some of the rules that apply to kayakers.

The primary purpose of the Rules of the Road is to prevent collisions. In fact, these rules can be encapsulated by stating that you must always act to avoid collision. To this end, some of the rules involve right-of-way for both specified (e.g., sailing vessel) and unspecified vessels (e.g., a kayak). In general, more maneuverable vessels must yield to less maneuverable vessels. For example, ships always have the right-of-way because they are restricted to a specific channel and cannot maneuver easily. In a kayak, you should always be prepared to yield the right-of-way, especially since you would take the worst of it in a collision! There are, however, situations where you do have the right-of-way (see "Overtaking Vessel," below). You need to be aware of who has the right-of-way so that your actions don't confuse other boaters, although you certainly wouldn't insist on your right-of-way at the risk of a collision.

The following procedures are paraphrased from the more specific rules; for the sake of simplicity I've combined some of them.

Avoid Collision

All boaters must continually assess the risk of collision and take action to avoid it. In practical terms, this means that whenever approaching another vessel, you should choose a course that will allow you to pass well clear of it. A general convention to remember when approaching "head-on" is to alter course to starboard (as should the other vessel) so that you pass "port-to-port," as you would when passing a car coming from the opposite direction on the road in the United States. As you approach the other vessel, make your course change to starboard *clear and deliberate*, so it is obvious to the other boater. Watch for the other vessel to do the same.

Bow-Angle Method

The *bow-angle method* is a powerful technique for determining whether you are on a collision course with an approaching vessel. You are required by law to know this technique.

When you see a ship or boat heading in your general direction, point your paddle (or your arm) toward it and note the angle between your paddle shaft and your bow. Continue checking this angle every few minutes as you paddle, while *maintaining course and speed*. If the angle gets smaller (the paddle shaft moves closer to the bow), the vessel will pass in front of you. If the angle gets larger, the vessel will pass behind you. When the angle doesn't change, you are on a collision course. If on a collision course, you should alter your course to avoid any chance of collision.

Keep checking the bow angle in case the approaching vessel changes course. This is crucial; if you stop checking the angle after determining that a ship will pass in front of you, and the ship changes course, it may be heading right toward you and you won't know it.

The bow-angle method is very effective and useful. I've used this method many times while paddling in shipping lanes on San Francisco Bay to avoid ships, freighters, and huge container vessels. It even works well with smaller craft, such as sailboats and ferries, although you have to be diligent about checking the angle, because smaller vessels tend to change course a lot.

The bow-angle method is most useful when the approaching vessel is some distance off (as much as 2 or 3 miles for large ships). When a large vessel gets close (less than 1 mile away), you can watch its bow to see whether you are in danger of colliding, although it is best not to get this close. If you can see an equal amount of the ship on each side of the centerline of the bow, you are on a collision course; when the bow centerline is pointed right at you, the ship will run you down if you don't take immediate evasive action. If one side of the bow is becoming more prominent than the other, the ship will pass by you.

Overtaking Vessels

When one vessel is overtaking another from behind, the overtaken vessel (*stand-on* vessel) has the right-of-way (except in shipping lanes, where ships always have the right-of-way). If a boat is approaching you from behind, you have the right-of-way. The overtaking boat is obligated to take action to stay well clear as it passes you. You, in turn, are obligated to maintain course and speed until the overtaking vessel has passed. Note that if you make a sudden change in course to try to get out of the way, you might actually cause a collision because the overtaking vessel is assuming that you will not change course. This is one exception to the oft-stated theme that kayakers should never assume the right-of-way. As the stand-on vessel, you are usually safer if you maintain course and speed. Of course, anytime you think you are going to be run down, you should move out of the way.

Keep checking the bow angle in case the approaching vessel changes course.

Shipping Lanes

Shipping lanes and traffic lanes are designated for ships and other large commercial craft. Small craft, including kayaks, have no right-of-way and must not impede vessels in designated traffic lanes. These traffic lanes are clearly marked on charts, so you should always know when you are in them. Spend as little time as possible paddling in traffic and shipping lanes. However, in some areas you cannot avoid them. Be especially vigilant and watch carefully whenever you paddle in these lanes.

The Rules of the Road are based on common sense and are designed primarily to avoid collisions. If you learn and use the bow-angle method and keep a close watch for all approaching vessels, you will be acting in accordance with these rules, and, more importantly, will not risk collision.

General Procedures in Boat Traffic

Besides knowing the "rules of the road" and the "bow-angle method" of avoiding collision, there are some basic precautions and procedures that will help keep you out of trouble when paddling in boat traffic. These precautions mostly involve your ability to see and be seen on the water.

Awareness

Awareness may be the single most important tool you have when dealing with boat traffic. Pay attention to what other vessels are doing so that you can make decisions and plan ahead, rather than reacting at the last minute to a potential collision. Be aware of what is going on in all directions, not just directly in front of you. Look to both sides and behind you, especially when paddling in dense traffic.

Be aware of any sea conditions that might affect your course or your ability to maneuver. Wind and current will affect both you and most other vessels. Be aware of what the current is doing; if you try to get out of the way of a ship by paddling directly into a 4-knot current, you won't get far. Conversely, if you are in strong current and want to let a vessel pass, you'll have to face into the tidal stream and paddle to hold your position. Also, keep in mind that the sailboat headed your way is subject to the same current you are.

Awareness may be your single most important tool.

Visibility

Kayaks are difficult to see on the water, especially from a distance or in rough conditions. If you paddle regularly in boat traffic, use bright colors to enhance your visibility. Yellow and red are the two most visible colors on the water. The three items that will attract the most attention if brightly colored are your paddle blades, kayak, and lifejacket. You can also use reflective tape for greater visibility.

Even with color enhancement, assume you are *nearly invisible* to other boaters, especially large commercial vessels and ships. When close to smaller craft, such as sailboats and powerboats, I always try to establish eye contact with the pilot of the other craft. If you look someone right in the eye, they will usually notice you and will register that you see them and are paying attention. Then, if you make a definite course change the other vessel can respond appropriately.

Predictability

Behaving predictably in the face of oncoming boat traffic is a close corollary to visibility. Once you have made yourself visible to another boater, it is important to either maintain course or make a very clear change in course, so that the other boater knows what you are doing. Don't just paddle around in a haphazard fashion. When paddling in a group, this is very important. If everyone paddles off in different directions, an approaching craft will have to thread its way through an obstacle course, assuming the skipper even manages to spot every kayak. By paddling close together on the same course, a group of paddlers will be more visible and more easily avoided by other boats.

Night Paddling

When paddling at night carry a waterproof light. If you tape *light sticks* (chemically activated lights, used for diving) on your paddle shaft, you will be visible to your paddling partners and, as you paddle, the moving lights may be visible to other watercraft. The best thing about light sticks is they don't interfere too much with your night vision. However, when paddling in any kind of boat traffic, you should also carry a powerful flashlight or headlamp. A headlamp can be shined directly ahead or at your bow to

Kayaks are difficult to see on the water, especially from a distance or in rough conditions.

illuminate the kayak. This helps other vessels see and identify your boat.

I don't like paddling with a bright light on all the time because it destroys my night vision. Instead, I turn on the flashlight whenever another vessel is in the vicinity and keep it off otherwise. Of course, if you are paddling in a congested area, you may need to keep the light on constantly.

Sailboats, powerboats, and larger vessels all carry colored sidelights and a white stern light. The starboard (right) light is green and the port (left) light is red. Boats under power also carry a top white light, and ships carry two white range lights, one above the other. By watching the configuration of lights on a vessel, you can determine where it is heading. This is very simple: If you see both a red and green light, the boat is moving toward you; a single green light means you are looking at the starboard side of a boat, moving to your right (if it is moving); a single red light means you are looking at the port side of a boat moving to your left; a single white light indicates the stern of a boat moving away from you. With range lights on a ship, you can accurately gauge the direction of the ship. If the two white top lights are aligned one above the other, the ship is moving directly towards you. Change your course and proceed until you see the two lights separate.

When paddling at night, be aware of the fact that you can't easily judge distances, especially the distance of a light. On one occasion, I paddled for over an hour to reach some lights on shore that I initially thought were only about 100 yards away. It turned out the distance to shore was over 3 miles.

Dealing with Different Types of Boat Traffic

Your strategy for avoiding collision will vary depending on the type of boat traffic in the area. Predicting what a ship will do, and staying out of its way, is a somewhat different matter than avoiding collision with a jet ski. Some basic strategies for dealing with each type of vessel are described below.

Ships, Freighters, and Large Commercial Vessels

Ships and freighters often move at speeds up to 20 knots. Because of their size, they appear to be moving much more slowly. So if you see a huge ship off in the distance, it is important to realize that it may be moving at a relatively high speed. The best technique to use for gauging a potential collision course with a ship is the bow-angle method. You should start checking the bow angle as soon as you see the ship, even if it's 2 or 3 miles away. A ship traveling 20 knots will eat up 2 miles in only 6 minutes.

The bow-angle method works great for ships because they generally maintain a steady course and speed. However, shipping channels often have *turning points*, where a ship will make a significant course change. You can identify these turning points on the chart. In any case, don't assume a ship will never turn; be alert for a change in course.

Ferries and Commercial Fishing Boats

Ferries and commercial fishing boats are not restricted to shipping lanes and are far more maneuverable than ships. They generally keep a lookout for smaller vessels and other obstacles, but you can't assume that they will always see your kayak. Use the bow-angle method to determine relative course and watch for sudden course changes.

Ferries are faster than they appear. Watch and plan ahead when you see one heading in your direction. Also be careful near the entrance to ferry terminals and marinas, where ferries and fishing boats can suddenly emerge. When you approach such an entrance, look both ways before entering or crossing, just as you would before crossing a busy street.

Sailing Craft: Sailboats and Board Sailors

Sailboats and board sailors (wind surfers) are highly maneuverable. They usually can see your kayak, and can maneuver around you if necessary. However, they don't often like to give way or change course, especially when they are flying along with their sails full. This is especially true if they are competing in a race. Then, you are mainly perceived as an unwelcome obstacle if you get in the way. The best strategy is to use your sense of distance, timing, and direction to avoid getting directly in the path of any sailing craft. This doesn't mean you have to stop paddling and wait for a sailboat that is 2 miles away to pass in front of you. Use the bow-angle method to estimate which way a distant sailboat is moving, then make adjustments as it gets close. With good timing, you will rarely have to stop paddling, although you might adjust your course and speed up or slow down as the sailboat gets closer.

Try to establish eye contact. This will ensure that the other boater sees you and will make it clear that you are paying attention to them. The sail can impede vision, so position yourself where you can be seen. Make any course change decisive so that the sailor knows what you are doing.

Board sailors zip along at high speed and you don't have much time to maneuver if they are heading your way. They sometimes make sudden course changes, but generally will speed along in a straight line with a favorable wind. As you paddle, make a quick estimate of where the board sailor is headed, then stay out of that path. This is not too difficult—it just requires attentiveness.

Powerboats and Jet Skis

Power boaters and jet skiers are often unpredictable and are usually trying to get somewhere (or nowhere) in a hurry. Sport fishermen might be an exception; they are usually heading on a straight course to a specific fishing area or are trolling at slow-to-moderate speed. In any case, you have to be alert and stay out of the way, just as you do with all other vessels.

When a powerboat or a jet ski is bearing down, there may not be time to gain eye contact. You have to use timing and judgment to paddle out of the way. Stay alert and watch to see whether the other craft is moving predominately in a straight line or weaving. In the former case, you can easily avoid collision; in the latter, your best course of action is to move out of the area as soon as you can. In the meantime, keep you eyes open and maneuver as necessary.

Jet skis are a special case. They may be obnoxious, but jet skiers do not want to collide with a kayak. Most jet skiers will be on the lookout for logs, rocks, and other obstacles, including your kayak. You can take advantage of this. Make yourself as visible as possible, gain eye contact, and be predictable in your movements; if you do this, the jet skier will tend to maneuver around you. If not, your paddle makes a good spear. Perhaps the best way to deal with the whole problem is to avoid paddling in areas that are congested with jet skis.

If you employ the strategies outlined in this chapter, you'll have no problems paddling in boat

Try to establish eye contact.

traffic. I have paddled many times on San Francisco Bay when it appeared to be packed with sailboats. I'm always amazed at how much space there is to paddle in this situation, and at how easy it is to maneuver through such a maze of boats. Just constantly watch all nearby vessels and make course adjustments as needed. Once you get used to it, you might even find paddling in such traffic enjoyable and stimulating.

Boat Traffic At-a-Glance

Boat traffic is a hazard to kayakers in heavily traveled waterways. Your main concern is to avoid collision with other water craft. To accomplish this, do the following:

- Use a chart to identify shipping lanes; know when you are paddling in shipping lanes, and paddle in them only as necessary.

- Familiarize yourself with the Rules of the Road, especially where they apply to kayaks and other small craft.

- Stay alert and maintain a constant watch in all directions for other vessels.

- Learn and use the "bow-angle method" of detecting possible collision.

- Make yourself as visible as possible.

- Act in a predictable way; stay close together when paddling in a group.

- Know what the current is doing and how it affects you and other craft.

- Always carry a bright light when paddling at night.

- Adjust your collision-avoidance strategy for different types of water craft.

To paddle in ocean rock gardens and surf, you must be prepared to deal with breaking waves.

CHAPTER 13.

SAFETY IN SURF AND OCEAN ROCK GARDENS

Anyone who has spent time watching majestic waves crash onto the rocks and beaches along a jagged ocean shoreline has sensed the powerful forces at work in this environment. Kayakers who paddle in the realm of ocean whitewater experience these forces directly, and quickly learn to respect the power of the sea. Surf and ocean rock gardens are demanding and challenging paddling domains. Kayaking in these areas requires special skill, sound judgment, and careful attention to some specific safety issues.

If you have no desire to seek out the surf zone or rock gardens, yet still intend to paddle in the ocean, learn something about paddling in surf and rocks. Some kayakers paddle on the open ocean and stay in deep water, well clear of the shore. This is fine as long as they can find protected launching and landing sites. However, if you plan on paddling any distance along an exposed coast, you are limiting your options if you cannot land in surf or navigate through rocks to get ashore.

Surf and rock gardens share one essential characteristic: they are both exposed to breaking and surging waves. The primary strategy for paddling in surf and rock gardens involves reading and handling these waves. Most of the safety issues revolve around dealing with such waves; knowing how to judge them, when to avoid them, and how to handle them when necessary.

Wave conditions and the size of the swell are constantly *changing*. The swell can change considerably from one day to the next. This is very important on a multi-day trip on the open coast. The gentle 2-foot waves lapping the beach where you camp could easily turn into 6-foot crashing surf overnight.

You are limiting your options if you cannot land in surf or navigate through rocks to get ashore.

Wave Dynamics

To kayak in waves you must first understand the forces involved. A thorough understanding of wave dynamics can be achieved only through direct experience. However, it does help to have a basic idea about the various types of waves you may encounter and how to recognize them. This is especially important because some waves are "friendlier" than others.

Two factors will determine how friendly or unfriendly a wave is: 1) the *shape* of the wave, or *wave type,* and 2) the *size* of the wave. Both factors have to be considered. For example, a 6-foot *spilling* wave (see below) will be more challenging than a 3-foot spilling wave, but *less* challenging than a 3-foot *plunging* wave.

Wave Type

As ocean swell moves into shallow water, the waves begin to "feel" the bottom. A wave will break when the water depth is approximately 1.3 times the wave height. In practical terms, this means that larger waves will break in deeper water, and breaking waves can be expected in near-shore areas wherever the water is shallow enough. This includes beaches, reefs, and rock gardens. The *type* of wave is determined by the bottom profile, as described below. There are three basic types of surf: *Spilling* waves, *plunging* waves, and *surging* waves. All three, and *every gradation in between*, can be found in surf zones and rock gardens. A fourth type, the *dumping* wave, is an extreme type of plunging wave that forms along very steep shorelines.

Spilling waves form over a gently sloping bottom. The waves steepen and break over a relatively long distance. These waves lose energy gradually and, if not too large, are relatively easy to surf and to punch through. They can be recognized by their gently spilling crests; the whitewater tumbles softly down the wave face as it moves toward shore. Spilling waves generally form on wide, gently-sloped beaches and on relatively flat wave-cut terraces inside rocky reefs.

Plunging waves form where the bottom slopes steeply away from shore. As a wave suddenly encounters shallow water, it steepens dramatically and breaks as the crest of the wave is thrown forward and plunges into the wave trough, sometimes forming a tube. Because plunging waves expend most of

GRACE IANNOTTI

Spilling wave: Spilling waves break gradually and are relatively easy to handle.

their energy suddenly, they are far more powerful than spilling waves, and are more difficult to handle in a kayak. Plunging waves higher than 4 feet are difficult to punch through. When surfing a plunging wave, you have to be ready for the impact when it breaks. Plunging waves occur on steep beaches, along sandbars off any kind of beach, at point breaks where there is a sudden change in slope, and on steep, rocky reefs.

A *dumping wave* is a kayaker's term for a plunging wave that breaks right at the shoreline. This is common on very steep beaches, where the waves move in through deep water, suddenly rise up, and break right on the sand or cobbles. Dumping surf is characterized by the *lack* of a soup zone. The *soup zone* is an area of white water inshore of the main breaking waves (see Figure 6, "Surf Zone Anatomy," page 190). A soup zone acts as a buffer between the breakers and the shoreline. In an area of dumping waves, this buffer zone does not exist, making it difficult to launch and land safely. Dumping waves cannot be surfed in the usual fashion; the only way to land is on top of the wave or, in rare cases, between waves (see "Surf Technique," later in this chapter). Large dumping waves, higher than 4 or 5 feet, should be avoided if at all possible.

Surging waves also form off steep beaches; the waves steepen and surge up onto the beach without breaking. On some beaches, surging waves alternate with dumping waves; the smaller waves surge and the larger waves break. Surging waves provide a safe transport to and from shore, but good timing is required to ride the surge efficiently. In rock gardens, surging waves are very common, especially where the swell is squeezed into narrow slots between rocks. Where waves enter a squeezed area and the water is relatively deep, they will surge instead of break. Because the wave energy is released gradually, surge is more friendly than breaking waves. However, the surge can be very powerful when forced through tight passageways in rock gardens. You'll need all your strokes and excellent boat control to handle your kayak in these powerful surging waves.

Actually, a complete gradation exists among all of the wave types outlined above. In some cases, the crest of a wave will plunge, then spill down the lower part of the wave face. Such a wave would be excellent for surfing. It also is very common to find more than one wave type at any given location. For

Large plunging surf: Plunging waves release most of their energy in one large explosion and are much more difficult to handle than spilling waves.

Dumping waves plunge right on the shoreline. The best way to land in dumping shorebreak is to ride the top of the wave. Note the lack of a soup zone.

Surging wave. Stay high on the surge to ride it in.

MICHAEL POWERS

In rock gardens, be prepared to handle surging whitewater.

There is a world of difference between a large, but gentle, spilling wave . . . and a steep plunging wave that can drive you into a cliff.

example, a beach with offshore sandbars can have steep plunging waves over the sandbar and spilling waves closer to shore. Sometimes the larger waves plunge and the smaller waves spill. Some beaches have spilling surf at one end of the beach and plunging surf at the other end. In a rock garden, large plunging waves might be crashing on the outer reef, while surging and spilling waves form between the rocks and inside the reef.

You can increase your safety margin considerably by knowing how to identify the various wave types and understanding how they can affect you. There is a world of difference between a large, but gentle, spilling wave that you can punch right through and a steep plunging wave that can drive you into a cliff. To the inexperienced eye, both of these waves might look equally dangerous (or equally "safe"). A friend of mine once got pummeled in a 3-foot dumping wave at Navarro Beach in northern California. Although he is a relatively experienced kayak surfer, he had never tried to ride the face of a dumping wave before. It was quite a shock when he found himself torn from his kayak as both footbraces popped out, finally emerging with sand filling his eyes, ears, and mouth, after tumbling around helplessly for a couple of minutes. Since I had done the same thing on a previous occasion, I tried to explain what had happened, but he didn't seem to grasp the problem. If he had recognized the wave for what it was, he could have saved himself a lot of trouble by landing on the crest of the wave, instead of trying to surf the wave face.

To gain a better understanding of wave dynamics, always stay alert and watch the waves closely when you are paddling on the open coast. The ocean will teach you everything you need to know, if you pay attention. Even onshore, sitting on a beach or watching from a bluff over the rocks, you can learn a lot about what is going on. Once you can gauge wave size and shape and understand the consequences of each wave type, you can develop techniques for dealing with, or avoiding, any wave you may encounter.

Wave Size

As a general rule, larger waves of a given type are considerably more powerful than smaller waves. A wave that is twice the height of another wave will be *more than twice* as powerful; it will be several times as powerful. As wave size increases, the force of the breaking wave increases dramatically. You must understand this when making a judgment about the wave energy you can expect to encounter from a breaking wave. Your goal is to formulate a couple of benchmarks regarding wave size. Develop a feel for the following size limits.

- **The point at which you can no longer punch through a breaking wave:** There is some gradation between breakers that you can easily paddle through and breakers that will stop you cold. However, with experience, you can spot breakers that you know you can get through by paddling hard into them. You can also spot breakers that you know will shove you violently backwards, no matter how hard you paddle. It may be too dangerous to launch in such waves, unless you are sure you can time it to get through during a window (a break in the larger wave sets).

- **Waves that are too large to surf:** When the waves are so large that you don't think you can surf them without taking a beating, it is best to look for a more protected landing site, or a different route through a rock garden. Your wave size limit will depend mostly on your experience and your surfing skill, but everyone has their limit. Interestingly enough, a good kayak surfer can land in surf that is too large to punch through during a launch. This is because when surfing in, you are going with the wave energy, instead of fighting it head-on. For this reason, I would much rather land than launch in large surf.

The only way to determine the wave limits you can handle is to spend time in the surf. Of course, you need to learn and practice basic surfing skills in small surf before pushing your limits.

Whenever making decisions regarding wave size, it is important to look at the *largest* wave sets. Waves *vary considerably in size,* so you must watch for at least several minutes to see most of the size spectrum, keeping in mind the possibility for an even larger *sneaker wave.* When assessing the conditions, you should base your decisions on the larger wave sets. If you determine that these larger sets will give you no problem, then you can proceed into the surf or the rock garden. If the largest waves look like trouble, the

With experience, you will discover which waves you can punch through.

Beware of waves that are too large and powerful to punch through.

Judging the actual size of a wave is less important than knowing how the wave will affect you.

When learning to surf, start in a surf zone with small, easy waves.

When paddling on the open coast, seek out protected landing sites whenever possible.

next step is to determine how frequently they arrive and whether you can time it to get through safely. If not, back off and choose another route.

Judging the actual size of a wave is less important than knowing how the wave will affect you. As a general guide, surf in the 1–3 foot range is easy to handle, 3–6 foot surf is moderately difficult, and surf larger than 6 feet can be very difficult, depending on the type of waves. Keep in mind that the crest of a 3-foot wave will be over your head when you are sitting in a kayak.

Basic Safety in Surf

Whether you are playing in the surf in a whitewater kayak or landing in a sea kayak full of camping gear, some general safety guidelines are necessary. These include choosing an appropriate site, avoiding collision with other kayaks or surfers, surf etiquette, and protecting yourself from shoulder and wrist injuries. Knowing how to swim in the surf and deal with rip currents is also very important—this has been covered in Chapter 6, "Rescues in Surf and Ocean Rock Gardens."

Site Selection

Site selection is the first consideration. If you are going out to practice or play in the surf, you should look for waves that are within your skill level. When you arrive at the beach, watch the waves before paddling out. For ideal surfing, you'll want spilling or moderately plunging waves where the breaking section peels along the wave crest to the right or left. Watch out for *closeout* plunging waves; such a wave tends to break all at once along a significant section of the wave. A large closeout wave will punish you at the end of your ride.

You need to choose your launching and landing sites carefully. If your main goal is to get through the surf with the least amount of trouble, look for the most protected site you can find. Find a beach or a cove that is protected by offshore rocks, a reef, or a major headland. If the predominant swell direction is from the northwest, look for protected beaches on the south side of points and headlands (see Figure 5). However, waves *refract* (bend) around headlands as they approach shore. The refraction results in wave trains that advance parallel to the shoreline. The waves can refract around a headland and move onto

FIGURE 5. Landing Site Selection

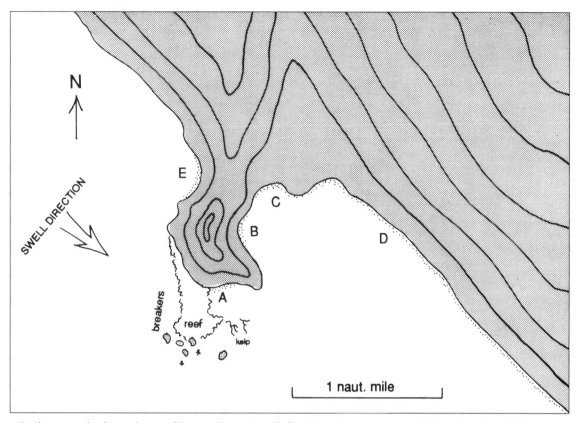

In the example shown here, with a northwest swell direction, the most protected landing sites will be inside the reef (**A**), and on the southeast side of the point (**B** and **C**). Location **A** will be more protected at low tide, when the reef is exposed and acting as a barrier to the waves; at high tide, waves may be able to move across the reef and into the cove. Moving south along the beach (**D**), the surf will increase in size as protection provided by the point is lost. Areas north of the point (**E**) are directly exposed to the swell and may have large surf.

a beach that might appear on your chart to be protected. Nevertheless, if the beach is well-tucked into the headland, with a few offshore rocks to absorb wave energy, the waves will be smaller than on beaches more directly exposed to the swell. In many cases, one end of a beach will have smaller waves than the other.

If you can't find a completely protected beach, find a surf zone that you can launch or land in safely. Check out the size and type of waves. Ideally, you'll find spilling or moderately plunging waves that are not too big. To avoid dealing with dumping surf, find a beach with a soup zone if at all possible. If you have to launch or land in a steep shorebreak,

Waves refract (bend) around headlands as they approach shore.

MICHAEL POWERS

To prevent collision, avoid crowded situations when surfing.

Never follow directly behind anyone when paddling in surf.

avoid dumping waves larger than about 3 feet, unless you have had lots of practice and know what you are doing. Also, watch for and avoid obstacles such as partly submerged rocks and floating logs.

Avoiding Collision

Collision between kayaks is probably the most dangerous hazard in the surf zone. There are several things you can do to prevent spearing another paddler or getting speared yourself. Stay well clear of other paddlers whenever you are in the surf. If you are launching or landing with a group, paddle through the surf one at a time or spread out *parallel* to the beach. Be aware you can move some distance laterally when surfing a wave. Before taking off on a wave, always scan ahead and make sure no one is in your way.

Never follow directly behind anyone when paddling in surf. This is a sure formula for disaster. I was speared in the back on one occasion when another kayaker followed me while I paddled out through a point break. I didn't know anyone was there until a large wave smashed into me head-on, pushing me violently backwards. A sudden and severe pain shot through my lower back as I was impaled on the bow of the sea kayak behind me. All I could do was brace and try to stay upright until the wave finally released me. I didn't think I could roll or swim with the pain I was experiencing. When the wave action finally calmed down, I wiggled my toes to make sure my back wasn't broken, then carefully paddled into shore. Luckily, my vertebrae were spared, but I sustained deep bruising and contusions to muscles and tissue. It took three months to recover fully. *Don't let this happen to you!* Avoid collisions at all costs.

Any time you see a kayak hurtling down a wave in your direction, paddle quickly out of the way. If collision is imminent, *immediately roll over toward shore*, away from the oncoming kayak. The kayak will pass harmlessly over your hull, after which you can roll up or bail out. Even if you end up swimming, this is far preferable to getting speared. If you are surfing on a wave and notice someone in your way, do whatever it takes to maneuver around the other paddler. If the wave hasn't broken yet, you may be able to turn back up the wave face and off the wave. If the wave has broken and you can't maneuver, turn sideways and lean well into the wave. This *may* slow you down a bit and it would be preferable to hit someone sideways rather than to spear them. In general it is the responsibility of other paddlers to stay out of the way of anyone who is riding a wave.

Surf Etiquette

Surf etiquette is designed mainly to prevent collision between surfers, whether they are kayak surfing or board surfing. Good etiquette also allows a surfer to get the most out of a ride. The key postulate of surf etiquette is this: *The surfer who takes the drop first has the wave; all others should yield to this surfer and stay out of the way. If two or more surfers take off simultaneously, the surfer closest to the peak of the wave has possession.* The peak of the wave is the steepest part of the wave and the place where it first begins to break. If you see someone off to your left paddling forward onto the steeper part of the wave, don't jump in on the shoulder; you will be in the way. Wait for the next wave. Even if you can't read waves well enough to catch them in the steepest section, you can practice surf etiquette by taking turns catching waves. If you are out with a few friends, line up and let everyone have a chance to catch a wave individually. Another important part of surf etiquette applies when you are paddling back out through the waves: *Paddle out away from the primary surfing area.* After taking a ride in, paddle parallel to shore, then head out beyond where anyone is surfing in to shore. Finally, stay alert and watch for other kayakers, surfers, and swimmers at all times.

It is the responsibility of other paddlers to stay out of the way of anyone who is riding a wave.

Surf etiquette: Paddler to the right side of the photo is closest to the wave peak and has possession of the wave. The paddler on the left should peel off the wave.

GRACE IANNOTTI

Avoiding Shoulder and Wrist Injuries

When caught in a breaking wave, your kayak may be tossed violently. In the process, your paddle can catch the water and stress your wrist or shoulder. This is especially likely when you are getting *worked* (tossed around) by a wave after capsizing. You'll be yanked around like a rag doll, all the while trying to hang onto your paddle, which is in danger of being ripped out of your hands. The best solution is to immediately tuck into the roll set-up position (see "The Eskimo Roll," Chapter 7) with the paddle held close alongside the kayak. If you can't tuck immediately and the wave really gets a grip on your paddle, release one hand. This will remove all the stress on your shoulders, and you can easily hang onto the paddle with your other hand until things settle down.

Shoulder and wrist injury is also a risk when *broaching* (when you are pushed sideways to the wave; see "Side Surfing," below). In the broached position, you are leaning the kayak into the wave on a high or a low brace to prevent capsizing toward shore. In this position, you must keep your arms and paddle low to prevent shoulder injury.

In the high brace position (bracing with the power face of the paddle blade facing down) *keep the paddle shaft low and horizontal, with elbows tucked in close to your sides.* The paddle shaft should be at chest level or *lower*. If you hold the paddle at eye level or higher, you are in real danger of dislocating your shoulder. Also, there is absolutely no need to reach with your arms in an attempt to extend the paddle blade out away from the kayak while bracing; this will not improve your brace and will only serve to place your shoulder at risk. Stay relaxed; the object is not to lean onto the paddle. When broached on a wave, the most important part of the brace is a controlled boat lean.

The low brace (with the back of the paddle blade facing down) can be just as effective as a high brace when broaching. Remember, it is the boat lean that prevents capsize in the broached position, not the paddle. When low bracing, keep your elbows above the paddle shaft. This will keep your wrist, hand, and arm aligned, protecting your wrist from injury. There is little danger of shoulder dislocation when using a low brace, but you can strain your wrist if you drop your elbow so that the wrist is bent.

If you side-surf onto the beach, maintain your seaward lean, otherwise you can trip on the

It is the boat lean that prevents capsize in the broached position, not the paddle.

sand and tip over. If this happens, just roll with it, do not reach out with your hand or paddle to brace against the sand; this could result in an injury to your wrist or shoulder.

Surf Technique

In the surf zone, your safety largely depends on using the correct technique for the given situation. In the story above about dumping surf, my friend could have been injured when he used the wrong technique for landing in a steep shorebreak. In this section, I describe various techniques to use in the surf zone. Master these techniques in small surf before moving into larger waves.

In spite of the common perception, launching and landing a sea kayak in the surf involve more than simple wave avoidance. Just as with other types of sea kayaking, you have to prepare yourself to deal with all the potential situations you may encounter. If you are paddling on a semi-protected coast where you will be dealing only with local wind waves, you can probably get away with paddling in fast between waves, as is usually prescribed for landing in surf. In such easy conditions, you may even be able to land by backing in, as I've heard more than one kayaker recommend (not my recommendation!). On the other hand, if you are going to be dealing with real surf on an exposed coastline such as the coasts of northern California and Oregon, and many other coastlines throughout the world, *you have to learn how to surf the waves.*

In fact, a sea kayaker who wants to paddle the open coast needs to know a bit more than the average kayak surfer, who uses a specialty surf kayak and seeks out only the best waves. The sea kayaker needs to know how to deal with all types of surf, not just ideal surfing waves. Of course, in a sea kayak, you will not be able to perform all the maneuvers that are possible in a surf kayak. The techniques presented here will benefit any surfer, regardless of the type of kayak used.

Surf Zone Anatomy

Your launching, landing, and other surf techniques will depend largely on the nature of the surf zone, and the size and type of waves. Surf zones vary a great deal, but most can be subdivided into the following (see Figure 6).

Launching and landing a sea kayak in the surf involves more than simple wave avoidance.

FIGURE 6. Surf Zone Anatomy

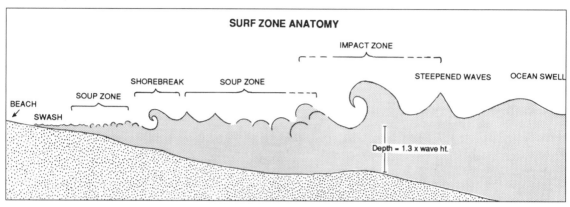

This diagram shows a typical surf zone with a moderately-sloping bottom configuration. The main impact zone is offshore, over the sandbar. A soup zone and small shorebreak occurs inshore of the impact zone. With a steeper beach, the impact zone would move close to the shoreline, creating a dumping shorebreak with no soup zone.

The impact zone is where waves break and expend most of their energy.

The soup zone is an area of whitewater shoreward of the impact zone.

- The *impact zone* is where waves break and expend most of their energy. The impact zone will shift in and out, depending on wave size; larger waves break farther out, in deeper water. If you are approaching a surf zone from offshore, you'll know you are getting close to the impact zone when the waves start getting steep. Another clue will be the thunderous crash and flying spray of breaking waves up ahead. An irregular bottom, usually caused by sandbars, can create two or more impact zones; the waves breaking farther out will be larger and more powerful than those breaking closer to shore.

- The *soup zone* is an area of whitewater shoreward of the impact zone. Waves that have already broken roll in through the soup zone. Small secondary breakers sometimes form in the soup. Although the water there is surging powerfully back and forth, the soup zone is far less intense than the impact zone because the wave energy is diminished. In a sense, the soup zone provides a buffer between the shore and the impact zone. The soup zone varies considerably from one surf zone to another. With a gently-sloping beach and offshore sandbars, the soup can extend out 50 yards or more. On steeper beaches, or beaches with sand bars close in, the soup zone may be only a few yards wide. As mentioned in a previous section, a soup zone may not be present at all off very steep beaches. In this case, the impact zone is right at the shoreline, forming a steep, powerful shore-break (dumping waves), sometimes interspersed with surging waves.

The presence or lack of a soup zone is very important when deciding how to launch and land. It is hard to overemphasize the importance of the soup zone. On a week-long trip along the Lost Coast of northern California, we had to launch and land on several steep beaches with large, 6–8 foot dumping waves. Every launch and every landing was an adventure. Eric Soares broke three rudders while launching his heavily laden Tsunami X-2 (double wash-deck kayak), before finally making it out; I felt fortunate having a single kayak that didn't need a rudder. Toward the end of our journey, we arrived at a beach with large spilling and plunging waves, and a wide soup zone! I gleefully paddled in and surfed the first wave that came my way, knowing I didn't have to worry about getting slam-dunked onto the beach. Even though the surf was big, the sight of a wide soup zone was welcome.

Side-Surfing

One of the first techniques to learn for survival in the surf is how to side-surf when broached sideways on a breaking wave. This is critical to your safety for several reasons.

- In many cases, the wave will push you sideways, especially in a sea kayak. So you will often find yourself in this situation.

- Broaching is the *most common cause of capsize* in the surf, until you know how to deal with it. Because the kayak is being pushed sideways swiftly toward shore, the shoreward edge tends to catch and flip the boat. The kayak rolls over in an instant. This is known as *windowshading*.

- You will sometimes find it necessary to paddle laterally in the soup zone, where you are vulnerable to beam waves.

- Side-surfing is a reasonable landing technique in a sea kayak (see "Surf Landings," below).

Broaching is the most common cause of capsize in the surf.

JUNE LEGLER

Side surfing (broached on the wave): Tilt the kayak into the wave.

If you stay loose and maintain your lean, you'll be able to ride out some very big waves.

Before continuing, be sure you have read the section "Avoiding Shoulder and Wrist Injuries," above.

The way to handle a broach is to tilt the kayak into the wave, using a J-lean (see Chapter 8), while pushing your paddle into the wave on a high or a low brace. Anticipate the wave break and lean a split second *before* the wave breaks on you. Common errors are to flinch away from the wave and to not lean soon enough. If the wave has already broken and is rolling toward you, set your lean *before* the wave hits you.

The amount of lean needed varies depending on wave size. With a smaller wave (less than 3 feet), you won't need too much lean. Tilt the kayak slightly, but keep your body upright and centered over the boat, using a standard J-lean. You should be able to balance the kayak in this position even without any help from the wave or from a paddle brace. When the wave hits, maintain the lean, *keeping your shoreward edge lifted clear* as you are pushed sideways, and place a high or low brace into the wave. Stay relaxed and balanced as the wave pushes you sideways. This is a very stable position, once you get the right amount of lean. If the wave dies out or passes under you, be careful not to get caught leaning too much. Be ready to bring the boat onto an even keel. However, if you have a balanced J-lean, you shouldn't tip over, even if the wave no longer "supports" you.

Larger and more powerful waves require more lean, especially when they first hit you. If the wave is a large plunging breaker, you may need to lean your body with the kayak and nearly capsize into the wave, then sit up and maintain a balanced J-lean after the initial explosion of wave energy. Expect to bounce along rather violently when side-surfing larger waves; if you stay loose and maintain your lean, you'll be able to ride out some very big waves fairly easily.

Side-surfing takes a lot of practice. The only way to get a feel for the right amount of lean is through trial and error. Don't get frustrated; there are no shortcuts. Start in small waves in the soup zone, work on both sides, and gradually work up to larger waves. Before getting into larger waves, make sure you can roll so you don't have to bail every time you capsize. Once you are comfortable side-surfing, you will spend far less time upside down in the surf and will be ready to move on to launching, landing, and other surfing techniques.

Surf Launching

Your primary goal when launching in the surf is to get past the impact zone with the least amount of trouble. If the largest wave sets are 3-foot mushy spilling waves, all you have to do is paddle straight out with good forward momentum and punch right through. With larger, steeper, plunging waves or a dumping shorebreak, you will have to use a different strategy. Time it so you get through the impact zone during a window. In any case, look for the easiest place to launch. Head out where the waves are smallest. Also look for rip currents that will provide a free ride out past the impact zone.

When launching in a typical surf zone with plunging or spilling breakers and an inner soup zone, get a feel for the timing and size of wave sets, then push off the beach directly into the soup. Paddle forward perpendicular to the waves, then slow down and *hold your position* well shoreward of the impact zone. By paddling forward and backward, as necessary, you can wait in the soup zone indefinitely, until you are ready to make your move. Gradually work your way toward the impact zone, getting as close as possible without getting pummeled. Watch the incoming waves out on the horizon. When the sea appears to flatten out, paddle forward fast and hard, just after the last wave of the set breaks. *Keep paddling forward until you are well clear of the impact zone.* If you time it right, you'll make it out through the window between wave sets.

In many cases, your window will be only a short interlude between waves. You may not be able to get all the way through without engaging one or more waves. The best way to handle this is to time it so you either paddle up and over a wave just *before* it breaks, or let the wave break in front of you, then paddle *hard* through the wave *after* it breaks. When punching through the broken wave, you can lean back momentarily to clear the wave with your bow; this is especially effective in whitewater kayaks and surf kayaks. Don't lean back if the wave is just breaking; you may cartwheel on your stern and flip over backwards.

No matter how experienced you are, occasionally you will be faced with a large wave about to crash down on you. Usually the best way to handle

Waiting in the soup zone for a window.

JUNE LEGLER

When confronted with a breaking wave, paddle hard to punch through.

this situation is to keep paddling directly into the wave with as much momentum as possible; *don't slow down or stop paddling.* Just as the wave breaks, lean forward, pierce the wave with your paddle blade, and continue paddling right through. If the wave is too powerful to break through, your forward stroke will convert to a brace and bow rudder as you surf backward; lean well forward into the wave to prevent cartwheeling backwards. Another way to deal with this situation is to capsize just before the wave breaks, tuck into roll set-up position, and hang out until the wave energy diminishes or the wave releases you, then roll back up. The advantage of this method is that you are less likely to be pushed all the way back to the beach; your body tends to anchor the boat when hanging upside down. Nevertheless, unless I know for sure I can't "break the wave barrier," I prefer to remain upright and take my chances punching through the wave.

Launching through a dumping shorebreak can be difficult, especially if the waves are large. Because the impact zone is right at the shoreline and there is no soup zone, you have to wait on the beach for a window. The best method is to have someone give you a vigorous push into the water after the last wave in a set. Once you hit the water, paddle fast to get offshore. The good news is you won't have to go far to clear the impact zone. If you have to launch unassisted, use the steep beach as a ramp to slide into the water during a window. Sometimes you can launch on a surging wave; this is ideal because it will give you a large cushion of water to ride off the beach. Just be sure the wave you choose is surging and not breaking.

Another way to launch in dumping surf is to toss the boat into the water, swim out to it, and climb on. This is the preferred method with a sit-on-top kayak. It is more difficult with a closed-deck kayak, unless you have practiced the *scramble rescue* method of remounting (see "Self-Rescues," Chapter 5).

Surf Landings

The first step to a safe landing in surf is to choose the easiest landing site available. Ideally, you want relatively small waves on a gently sloped beach. However, if you want to paddle on the open coast, you should have the ability to land in a wide range of conditions, using the best technique for the situation at hand. You need to learn a few different techniques, including the ability to surf the waves under control. Below are four landing methods that should cover most situations you may encounter.

Landing during a window, between waves:

Line up just outside the impact zone, wait for a window, then paddle in as fast as you can, well into the soup zone or all the way to shore. *This landing method has very limited application*; it will work only under ideal circumstances. Nevertheless, it is one of the most commonly cited methods for surf landings. The problem is, in even moderate-sized surf you usually won't be able to outrun the waves. Instead, you'll get partway through the impact zone, only to have a wave pound you from behind.

The two situations where you might be able to use this method effectively are when the surf zone is narrow and the waves are small, and in moderate-sized surf on the *rare* occasions when the windows between wave sets last a long time (at least several minutes).

Surf and broach:

This landing technique will apply in many more situations than the one above. Position yourself just outside the impact zone, where the waves are beginning to steepen. As a moderate-sized wave approaches, paddle forward, directly toward shore.

Surf and broach: The paddler is preparing to broach on his right side as the wave breaks.

JIM KAKUK

When you feel the stern lift, lean forward a bit and keep paddling until you are surfing down the face of the wave, angling *slightly* to the right or left. Use a stern rudder on the shoreward side to hold your trajectory. Just before the wave breaks, remove the stern rudder stroke and convert to a high or low brace on the wave side. The boat will pivot sideways to the wave. At the same time, tilt your kayak into the wave as it breaks. Prepare yourself for the initial impact, then relax and hold your boat lean while you side-surf. You are now in the familiar broach position. The wave will push you sideways through the soup zone, close to or onto the beach.

The surf-and-broach method is a good technique for everything except steep, dumping shorebreak (see below). It doesn't require split-second timing, and once you catch the wave the broach is easy to accomplish. You also get through the surf zone quickly, with little effort, because you are using the wave energy. When you catch the wave it is best to already know which way you want to turn; this allows you to prepare for the lean and broach. Broaching on purpose might seem strange to the kayak-surfing purist, but a sea kayak has a strong tendency to broach anyway. Instead of fighting this tendency, you can use it to your advantage. Also, in steep waves, longer sea kayaks will tend to pitch-pole forward if you try to run straight in on the wave. This risks injury to you and damage to the kayak. If you do decide to forgo the broach and to surf straight in, lean well back onto the stern deck to help prevent pitch-poling.

MICHAEL POWERS

If you take off on a steep wave, lean well back to avoid burying the bow and pitch-poling.

Get past the impact zone, then turn and broach:

This is a variation on the two methods above. It is mainly used to deal with large, powerful waves. The idea is to get inside the impact zone to prevent taking a direct hit, then, after the wave breaks behind you, broach and side-surf the foaming steamroller into shore. The problem is getting past the impact zone unscathed. You might be able to sneak past during a window, but if you don't time it well, you'll get hammered.

The best way to proceed is to ride the *top* of a wave through the impact zone, paddle hard into the soup, then turn sideways and prepare to broach on the next wave. Set up as usual just outside the impact zone. Pick the last wave of a set, if possible, then paddle forward. As your stern lifts, let the wave push you on, but don't take the drop. Stay right on top of the wave crest; your bow will extend slightly out over the front of the wave. You may have to back paddle to prevent going *over the falls* (off the front of the wave) when the wave begins to break. If you get too far back, you will slide back off the wave, but this is preferable to plunging off the face. Once the wave breaks, paddle forward as fast as you can to get well into the soup zone. If you do this correctly, the next wave will break well behind you. Prepare to broach and side-surf it in when it catches up to you.

This is a good technique to use if you have to land in large, scary waves, especially in a wide, turbulent surf zone. Riding the top of a wave through and past the impact zone allows you to avoid the powerful outer break. Side-surfing will ensure that you don't pitch-pole out of control and will also take you most of the way into shore.

Practice riding the top of waves in small surf until you get the timing down. This will take a lot of practice but is well worth it. Surfing the wave crest in this fashion is also used when landing in dumping surf (see below), and when riding surge in rock gardens. Note that the object is to ride the *top* of the wave, not the *back* of the wave, as is often suggested in the kayaking literature. If you ride the back of a wave, gravity will ensure that you slide back into the trough of the next wave.

Riding the top of the wave to land in dumping surf:

Riding the top of the wave is the safest way to land in steep dumping shorebreak. Paddle in close to shore, just outside the impact zone of the larger waves. Watch several waves go by to get a handle on the timing of the wave sets. Pick the last wave of a set, then paddle forward, staying right on top of the wave. Be careful not to go over the falls, or fall back off the wave; either could result in disaster. Keep the kayak horizontal, balanced on top of the wave. You may have to use a backstroke or two to slow down, or a forward stroke to stay with the wave. The wave should break just under your bow. As soon as it breaks paddle hard, using powerful forward strokes, to stay with it. If you do everything right, you'll land well up on the beach. Dig your hands into the sand to prevent the kayak from sliding back, release your sprayskirt, and *immediately* leap out of the kayak, grab the bow and pull the boat up the beach. Do this *fast*! Don't waste time or you could get pulled back into

Correct position for riding the top of a plunging or dumping wave. Kayak should remain horizontal and stay on the crest of the wave.

Follow through after the wave breaks by paddling hard to stay high on the surge.

the maw of the next exploding wave. Practice rolling out of your kayak to one side, pulling both feet out at once. Don't try to step out daintily, one foot at a time; it won't be fast enough. You can practice a fast exit anywhere, including your backyard.

This is an excellent technique for landing in dumping waves. You will have to practice to get the timing right. When landing on a steep beach, you'll need to pick at least a medium-sized wave. If you try to get in on a very small wave, it won't take you far up the beach and you risk getting nailed by a larger wave before you get out of the kayak. If possible, pick a surging wave, rather than a breaking wave. Just be sure it is large enough to propel you well up on the beach.

On rare occasions, you might be able to paddle in during a window. This will leave you down low on the beach, in the path of the next wave set, so you have to be very quick exiting the kayak and moving up the beach.

All of the above landing methods work well if used for the appropriate type of surf. You can practice surfing, broaching, and riding the top of a wave in just about any surf zone. The exception is dumping surf, where you can use only the wave-top landing. Once you are proficient with all these techniques, you can paddle and land safely along the open coast. However, use discretion and avoid excessively large surf.

Surfing Large Waves Safely

When paddling on the open coast, you generally want to look for launching and landing sites with the smallest waves, to make the task easy and safe. This is especially true if you are touring in a gear-laden sea kayak. However, the ability to handle larger waves will increase your margin of safety and allow you more choices for landing sites and bailouts. If your main goal is to kayak-surf, you'll seek out waves that provide the best rides. As you get better at surfing, you'll naturally look for larger waves. When discussing large waves, I am speaking mainly of waves in the 6–8 foot range. Even larger waves can be surfed, but they must have a good shape and not be closing out or plunging too steeply.

When surfing for fun, you will be better off in a whitewater kayak or a surf kayak, especially in larger surf. These kayaks are much easier to control and maneuver than a long sea kayak. Even more impor-

GRACE IANNOTTI

The best place to surf a wave is "in the pocket": the steep part of the wave just ahead of the break.

tantly, from a safety standpoint, you will not get near-ly as trashed in the smaller, low-volume kayaks.

Regardless of the kayak, when surfing larger waves you absolutely must know how to read the wave and know where to position yourself on it. This is mostly a matter of knowing where the wave will peak and break. Watch several wave sets to locate the best *take-off* spot (the place to catch the wave). You want to take off in the steeper part of the wave, short of where it breaks. Once you are surfing, stay in the pocket just ahead of the break. In a surf kayak, you will be weaving back and forth, climbing up and down the wave, to stay in the pocket. With the right kayak, there are many tricks you can perform in this part of the wave, but don't get caught in the break if the wave is pitching forward; keep surfing away from the break, especially in a sea kayak. Use stern rudder strokes to control your direction. Sweep strokes and stern draws can also be used if the wave face is large.

As long as you stay ahead of the breaking section, it may be possible to pull off the wave by turning away from the break and pivoting up and over the *shoulder* (the part of the wave crest that has not broken yet). This could be a critical maneuver if you notice an obstacle (a rock or another kayaker) in your path. You also might want to pull out if you sense the wave is going to pitch and throw you over the falls. The more moves you know how to make, the more options you have.

In a sea kayak, your moves are limited, but you do have hull speed on your side. If you time it right, you can rocket across the wave face and pull out, if necessary. You also might be able to get up enough speed to run out in front of the wave, allow-ing it to break behind you, rather than right on top of you. What you can't do in the sea kayak is make a lot of turns. You have to plan ahead and set a trajectory in the direction you want once you are surfing.

Whenever out surfing for fun with a group of other paddlers, be sure to use surf etiquette to avoid collisions. Don't jump on a huge wave with one or more of your buddies; if the wave breaks suddenly, you could be tumbled together like a handful of dice.

The only way to gain competence in surf is to spend time playing around in the waves. As your skills increase, so will your safety, and you'll have more fun. However, don't get complacent when surf-ing larger waves. No matter how skilled you are, you cannot overpower a big breaking wave.

What you can't do in the sea kayak is make a lot of turns.

A rocky reef provides protection from breaking waves.

Basic Safety in Ocean Rock Gardens

In a general sense, you can view an ocean rock garden as a surf zone full of large rocks. The outer rock barrier absorbs much of the wave energy and is analogous to the impact zone; the more protected area inside the rocks is roughly analogous to the soup zone. Because of the presence of breaking and surging waves, most of the same safety issues of the surf zone apply to rock gardens. All the same wave-reading skills apply, and you'll find all the same wave types in and around the rocks as you do in the surf.

There are a few important differences between rock gardens and surf zones. These differences are due mainly to the presence of rocks. Rocks present either a hazard or protection, depending on the situation. If you are surfing a wave through a rocky area, the rocks are obstacles that you must avoid. On the other hand, you can position yourself *behind* a large rock and use it as a barrier to avoid getting slammed by a large wave. In the surf zone, waves move toward the beach and break when they reach shallow water. In a rock garden, waves can be deflected, channeled, refracted, and reflected off of cliffs and between sea stacks. Waves also surge or break over shallow submerged rocks. When waves enter a sea cave or any restricted area walled off by cliffs on two or three sides, they reflect off the cliffs, colliding with other waves and generally creating a chaotic mess of whitewater. This can be either a fun place to play or a very dangerous one, depending on your skill level and the size of the waves. Deeper within many rock gardens are areas of quiet water, entirely protected from the crashing waves farther out.

Navigating ocean rock gardens requires the ability to read the water and make sound judgments regarding where and when to paddle. This requires experience. Such experience can be gained safely by following some basic guidelines and using a sound strategy, described in the following sections. You must also know how to swim and be familiar with rescue techniques in rock gardens. These skills are covered in Chapter 6, "Rescues in Surf Zones and Ocean Rock Gardens."

Time and Place

The best time to paddle in ocean rock gardens is during a period when the swell is small, especially for your initial forays into the rocks. A good rule-of-thumb to follow is: When the waves are too small to go surfing, consider it a good opportunity to paddle in rock gardens. Even when the waves are down, there will be plenty of action in the rocks. Also look for rock gardens that offer a reasonable amount of protection from the waves. An extensive area of emergent rocks and reefs along a convoluted coastline makes an ideal rock garden for kayaking. You can often scout an area from a bluff top onshore. Look for clear channels (where the waves don't break) in and out of the rocks and protected areas inside the rocks.

When you first start paddling in rock gardens, find the easiest route through. Try riding *small* surging waves and washovers where the water surges around and over submerged rocks. Work on your timing and boat control in these surging waves (see "Special Techniques," below). Stay with small, gentle waves until your skills improve. Also be sure that you have an easy bailout if something goes wrong and that you are in an area where you can get back in your boat if you swim, using a self-rescue or an assisted rescue. Of course, rock garden kayakers should have a reliable Eskimo roll.

JIM KAKUK

Hydraulics created by converging waves in the rocks can create a play spot or a danger zone, depending on your skill level and experience.

When the swell is not too large, calm water and protected coves can be found deep within the rocks.

MICHAEL POWERS

Practice paddling though easy channels where the waves surge, rather than break. Choose a day when the waves are small.

Avoid areas between large plunging waves and rocks.

Don't get caught between a powerful breaking wave and a rock.

Hazards

When paddling in rock gardens you must be able to identify hazardous areas, or *danger zones*. As you gain paddling skill and judgment, some danger zones will become *play spots* where you can have fun riding waves and surge; others will always be dangerous, no matter how skilled you are. The main hazards are listed below.

- **Large, powerful breaking waves:** Such waves are always a hazard and should be avoided, especially in areas where they can toss you into a rock or a cliff. Just as in the surf zone, some waves are friendlier than others. Steep plunging waves are more serious than spilling waves. It is important to have an idea of your benchmark wave: the largest breaking wave that you can punch through. You can't ever be completely sure about every wave, but you must develop a general feel for waves you can and waves you cannot handle.

- **Sneaker waves:** Occasionally, a wave or wave set that is much larger than the norm for the day will arrive. Such waves are called sneaker waves because they tend to catch you off guard. Always be watching and ready for larger-than-average waves.

- **Areas between large breaking waves and rocks or cliffs:** The obvious problem here is that you can be pushed with considerable force by a breaking wave. If a rock lies in your path, it could mean trouble. If caught in this situation, lean well into the wave and *present your hull to the rock*. As long as you hit hull first and don't pitch-pole or land on your head, you can probably avoid injury and boat damage. Often the water will provide a cushioning effect as it caroms off the rock, but don't count on it. The best way to deal with this hazard is to avoid it. Don't get caught between a powerful *breaking* wave and a rock. A *surging* wave is a different matter; you can usually ride a surge into a rock or a cliff and bounce right back with the reflecting surge, never touching the rock.

- **Rocks:** Rocks are hazards in two ways: 1) rocks can be obstacles in your path, and

2) waves (*boomers*) can suddenly break over submerged rocks. The way to deal with both rocks and boomers is to stay alert and paddle around them. When paddling through closely spaced rocks and narrow slots, you'll need good boat control and excellent stroke technique. Draw strokes and precision leaned turns are very useful. If you are surfing a wave through the rocks, make sure you have a clear route before catching the wave. You can also ride the top of a wave or surge over rocks and through shallow areas.

When surfing through rocks, plan your route carefully and take a clear trajectory.

- **Narrow slots and sea caves:** When paddling though a narrow slot in the rocks, or into a narrow sea cave, keep your kayak parallel to the rock walls. If a surge or a wave pushes you sideways, your kayak could get jammed and folded in half.

- **Low ceiling in a sea cave:** Sea caves with low ceilings are very dangerous if exposed to waves that close out against the ceiling. You could be crushed between your kayak and the rock if caught in such a cave when a wave rolls in. If you do get pushed close to the ceiling of a cave, immediately capsize to prevent major injury. An even better strategy is to avoid any cave where you see waves rising close to the ceiling.

Narrow slots and sea caves can be deceptive. Don t allow your kayak to get jammed sideways.

- **Powerful surging waves:** Surging waves in rock gardens and sea caves can set up very strong currents as they wash around and over rocks. The surge often comes from two or more directions, creating conflicting and unpredictable currents that cascade over ledges and wash back and forth through a rocky sieve. Although surge does not have the impact of a breaking wave, it can pick you and your kayak up and toss you into a foaming rock-garden pinball game. Once you are out of control in a powerful surge, about all you can do is brace and keep your hull to the rocks until the surge finally releases you. Practice paddling in milder surge and avoid the more powerful surging waves until you know what you can handle.

Surging water is often more powerful than it looks. Good boat control and bracing technique is mandatory for paddling in surging waves.

Rock Garden Strategies

To kayak safely in rock gardens you need a strategy. It is dangerous to paddle blindly into a rocky area along the exposed coast, even when the waves are small. Look ahead and plan your course through the waves and rocks, while constantly staying on the lookout for optional routes. The basic strategy is to look for a *sneak route* through and around breaking waves and rocks, while avoiding any hazards. Sometimes the route is straightforward and obvious; in other cases it is more subtle and convoluted. The best routes are completely free of large breaking waves. However, you'll often have to use timing and make subtle course changes to avoid the breakers.

Safe Zones

One useful tactic is to paddle from one *safe zone* to the next. A *safe zone* is an area that is protected from breaking waves and excessive surge, where you can rest and look around without being in any danger. This is analogous to an eddy on a whitewater river.

Safe zones in ocean rock gardens exist on the shoreward side of most large rocks. The wave energy is absorbed by the rock on the seaward side, leaving a protected area just behind the rock. There may still be some surge created by residual wave energy, but if you position yourself correctly, the rock will shield

A safe zone is an area that is protected from breaking waves and excessive surge.

Safe zones can be found on the shoreward side of emergent rocks.

MICHAEL POWERS

you from the main impact of the wave. If you are paddling through the rocks and spot a large wave set advancing, duck behind the closest large rock, where you can wait out the onslaught of the waves. Then paddle on to the next rock during an interlude between wave sets. Larger rocks offer the most protection, but even small rocks can act as shields from the waves as long as they *stand well out of the water*. Rocks that are mostly submerged will not offer protection; instead, the waves will break over them.

Safe zones also exist wherever the water is too deep for the largest waves to break. These deep-water zones exist where there are channels or basins within the rocks. You can spot them by observing the larger wave sets and watching for areas where the waves pass through without breaking. Other safe zones can be found deep in the rocks, close to shore, where most of the wave energy can't penetrate. This zone could change, however, with rising tide or larger waves. Many areas that are protected at low tide can be inundated with waves at higher tide, especially if the wave size increases.

Transition Zones

Sometimes the most difficult and dangerous tasks are entering and exiting a rock garden. Wave energy is concentrated along the outer margins of the rocks, where the largest waves break. Inside the rocks, there are often protected areas to paddle. To enter or exit a rock garden, look for a safe route. This is a *transition zone*; a passage that is navigable though subject to surge and wave energy. Ideally, you'll find a deep channel that leads directly into a protected section of the rocks. If you see powerful surging whitewater in the channel, you can paddle through during a window, between the larger wave sets. In many cases, when entering the rocks, you can surf in on a wave or a surge. If you do this, make sure you have a clear path all the way through.

Wait and Watch

One crucial tactic to employ at all times when paddling in rock gardens is to *wait and watch*. Before paddling into the rocks, a sea cave, or a transition zone, *wait for the largest wave set* to see what kind of havoc the larger waves create in the area where you want to paddle. Rock gardens and sea caves can be very deceptive; for a while, all is calm and placid,

Safe zones also exist wherever the water is too deep for the largest waves to break.

MICHAEL POWERS

Riding the surge through a transition zone into a rock garden.

MICHAEL POWERS

Always wait and watch the wave sets before making your move.

**A monster wave
was moving in.**

until a large wave set moves in. Then the calm is suddenly shattered as the waves explode and ricochet through the rocks, demolishing the peaceful scene that existed only seconds earlier. If this violent interplay looks too difficult for you to handle, stay out of that section of the rocks, or don't enter that cave. On the other hand, if you see the larger waves advance through without breaking or they induce only a mild surging action, you know you are looking at a safe route.

If you violate the wait-and-watch policy, you are risking serious consequences. I once had a very close call when kayaking along a stretch of coastline north of Santa Cruz, California, with a small group of paddlers. The swell was large and we had to stay offshore, due to powerful breaking waves. After paddling for a few miles, while searching for some excitement, I spotted a place where the waves were surging and reflecting off a steep cliff face.

Without waiting, I paddled right over, intending to ride the reflecting waves, under the mistaken assumption that the water was too deep for the waves to break in front of the cliff. When I got within a few feet of the cliff, I turned around to face the sea. In one horrifying instant, I realized my mistake. A monster wave was moving in. The crest was already starting to pitch forward and I knew there would be no escape. I also knew this wave was way beyond anything I could punch through. And, to top it all off, there was a sheer cliff only 3 feet behind me; no escape there! In fact, there was nowhere to swim or get ashore, if I ended up in the water. My paddling partners were wisely waiting 300 yards out and not about to come any closer.

I did the only thing I could. I paddled hard right into the wave. When the wave hit, it was like running head-on into a freight train. I tucked forward and waited for the crushing impact of the cliff behind me. I capsized and felt like I was being pummeled at the bottom of Niagara Falls, but to my surprise, I never touched the rock. Evidently, by paddling forward, I managed to bury myself deep into the wave which protected me from the cliff face.

Finally, I decided it was time to roll up. After setting up and rolling, I found myself still underwater. This was not working out very well. I set up and performed another unsuccessful roll. I was nearly out of breath and was running out of time. The thought went through my mind that swimming was a poor option, not to mention the possibility of being trashed by the next wave. As a last resort, I rolled up using an extended paddle roll. It worked! Luckily I was able to paddle out before the next big wave set arrived.

My paddling partners told me I was trying to roll while sliding down the cliff face. That's as good an excuse as any for missing two rolls. I never would have been in this situation if I had simply watched the waves for a few minutes. Always *wait and watch*.

Positioning and Timing

In rock gardens, if you spend some time watching and waiting, you can figure out *where* to go and *when* to go there. This is accomplished by positioning and timing. For example, suppose you want to paddle through a slot in the rocks to reach a protected area behind a large sea stack. First, watch the waves as they wash through the slot, then time it so you paddle through on a moderate surge between larger wave sets. You need to position your kayak close to the slot in such a way that you can catch the surge and shoot through the rocks on a clear trajectory (see "Riding Surge," below). Finally, you take up position in the safe zone behind the sea stack. This may sound fairly obvious when reading it while you sit in your easy chair. However, on the water it takes practice to read the situation and figure out the best tactic. On your initial trips into rock gardens, be conservative. Watch the waves and don't take a route that requires split-second timing to make it between large plunging breakers.

If you observe what is going on around you, it is usually clear how to position yourself. When stationed in a safe zone behind a rock, don't let the surge push you out from behind the rock into the path of a breaking wave. Watch your bow in relation to oncoming waves. Point into the waves for easier boat control and to avoid being pushed broadside. You have to keep paddling, using various strokes, to hold position in the surging currents.

Watch Ahead

Another important tactic is to watch ahead as you thread your way through rocks and waves. In particular, keep an eye on where the waves are breaking, then stay clear of the impact zone. If you aren't paying attention, or misjudge your route, you could get in serious trouble. The difference between getting

On your initial trips into rock gardens, be conservative.

MICHAEL POWERS

When holding position in the rocks, keep your kayak pointed into oncoming waves and surge.

demolished by a large wave and moving through unscathed could be literally a matter of inches.

To illustrate this point, I'll relate an incident that took place while kayaking around Pillar Point, north of Half Moon Bay, California, near the famous Maverick's surf break. I was paddling with Penny Wells and Bonnie Brill on a big day (big waves). As we headed out of the protected waters of the inner reef, Penny was just to my left and Bonnie to my right. We could see the point break off to our right, wrapping around Pillar Point, where 10–15 foot waves were crashing down. Bonnie was paddling just left of the breakers and flirting with disaster, while Penny and I headed a bit farther out to sea.

Just as we rounded the point and began to turn north, a huge wave set advanced. All three of us paddled hard to clear the waves, but Bonnie's route took her into the maw of a plunging wave. Penny and I turned around just in time to see the bow of Bonnie's boat pointing skyward, then cartwheeling backward in the wave like a missile that had gone astray. Two seconds later the boat was lost to sight as another wave barreled through. We spotted Bonnie bobbing around between the breakers, then she too was lost in the welter of crashing waves.

Penny and I had a brief discussion about what to do next. It was clear that all the wave energy was pushing through the rocky reef that we had paddled around. We decided that Bonnie and her boat could be recovered on the other side of the reef, for better or for worse. Sure enough, after paddling around to the inside of the reef, we spotted Bonnie standing on a rock with her kayak. She was a bit dazed, but unharmed. Her kayak sustained minor damage. Bonnie's first words to us were: "Ah thought Ah's gone die," uttered in her striking southern accent.

Bonnie's brush with death resulted from trying to cut it too close and not watching exactly where the waves were breaking. In truth, all three of us were nearly caught by an unexpectedly large wave set. Always be watching for those sneaker waves.

Specific Rock Garden Techniques

There are several techniques that will allow you to control your kayak and stay out of trouble in rock gardens. These techniques will also help you implement the basic strategies outlined above. Good

The difference between getting demolished by a large wave and moving through unscathed could be literally a matter of inches.

stroke technique is the first requirement. Without excellent boat control, you will be at the mercy of the waves. Work on mastering all your strokes, especially the *corrective strokes*: sweep and draw strokes. Boat lean (J-lean), discussed throughout much of this book, is no less important in rock gardens than it is in the surf, tide rips, and wind waves. The lean will help you stay balanced in rough water and allow you to carve precise turns when maneuvering through rocks. With the J-lean, good stroke technique, and a sense of timing, you'll be able to master the following skills.

Surfing

Surfing skills are fundamental and essential for paddling in rock gardens. The ability to read, ride, and handle breaking waves and surge will allow you to paddle in many areas that would otherwise be inaccessible to you. Obviously, you need to have good control on the wave if you are going to surf through a minefield of rocks. Wave-reading skill is needed to determine which waves you can surf and which ones you should avoid. Often, the safest way to get through a transition zone, or passage in the rocks, is to *surf* through swiftly, high on a wave. Otherwise, you could find yourself wallowing in a wave trough, being sucked back into the impact zone of the following wave.

Surfing is an essential skill for paddling in rock gardens.

MICHAEL POWERS

MICHAEL POWERS

Surging waves can provide a cushion for paddling over and through the rocks.

Watch out for powerful hydraulics or suck holes that form when the surge drops over a steep ledge.

MICHAEL POWERS

A suck hole can grab the unwary boater.

MICHAEL POWERS

When riding surge, pick the best route and time it carefully or you will be temporarily stranded on the rocks.

You can learn most of the necessary surfing skills by paddling in the surf zone, but will have to make some adjustments when in rock gardens. Wave selection is more critical in the rocks because you don't want to jump on a wave that will carry you into a rock pile. It is best to avoid large waves in the rocks, unless you have a very clear path inshore. Before you catch a wave, set a trajectory that will take you through, clear of any rocks.

Staying high on a wave and riding the crest has an important application in rock gardens. This is the best way to ride surge (see below) and will allow you to stay clear of submerged rocks.

Riding Surge

When waves break on an outer reef and wash into the rocks, residual wave energy is translated into surging current that moves back and forth through narrow channels and over rocks. You can take advantage of the surging current to get a push through and over the rocks or to make a *seal landing* (land on a rock or ledge—see below). The surge can also create problems. If you don't pay attention, you might get left high and dry (temporarily) or pulled into a *suck hole*. A suck hole forms where the surge drops over a ledge, creating a temporary hole, or where the waves surge around a rock, forming a powerful whirlpool.

Riding surge is similar to riding the top of a wave in the surf zone. To practice riding surge, look for an easy *washover* (where the waves surge over a rock) or a channel where the waves surge through, but don't break. Make sure the surge will carry you into protected water, so you can easily recover if you capsize. Line up on the outside of the rock or channel, catch a wave, and ride it through. Time it so you are paddling forward as the wave moves under you, then stay right on top of the wave as it surges through or over the rocks. Timing is everything: Don't take off too soon or you'll slide down in front of the surge, where you are likely to collide with the rock. On the other hand, if you take off too late, the wave will surge through, leaving you wallowing in the trough.

If you are riding the surge through a narrow passage, be careful not to get jammed sideways between rock walls. This could cause serious damage to the kayak and might injure you as well. Use a stern rudder stroke or a bow draw to keep the kayak headed straight through the passageway.

Practice riding surge until you can tune into the waves instinctively. Just be sure to pick small waves and gentle surge, so the consequences of any mistake will be minor. As your timing gets better, you can ride more powerful surge. From a safety standpoint, you are trying to acquire the following abilities:

- **The ability to judge the size and power of various surging waves and how they will effect you.**

- **The ability to control your kayak in surge and use the surge to your advantage.**

The ability to ride the surge under control will allow you to navigate passages and to surf over rocks that might otherwise present difficulties. Finally, riding and playing in the surge can be great fun. Just be sure to practice all the appropriate skills first. Important skills include balance, boat lean, bracing, the Eskimo roll, and surfing. All your strokes come into play, especially corrective stokes such as bow and stern draws, stern rudder, and sweep strokes.

Seal Landings

If you need to get ashore in a rock garden, your only choice may be to land on top of a rock, using a seal landing. If you have practiced riding surge, a seal landing will be easy. Choose a rock with a relatively flat surface, that is periodically awash with surging waves. Ideally it will be covered with seaweed for cushioning, but that is not essential. If you need to land and get out of the kayak, make sure there is a higher ledge where you can pull the boat up above the reach of the waves after you land.

Riding an easy washover. Note the kayaker is riding high on the surge.

With a larger wave, the small washover (in previous photo) is transformed into a raging cascade.

To control direction when riding surge or surfing, use a stern rudder stroke.

Once you have chosen your landing site, line up facing the rock and wait for a surge that is large enough to carry you well up on the rock. It is best to pick the last wave of a set, so that you have time to scramble out of the boat and pull it to higher ground. Paddle forward on top of the surge until you are deposited on the rock. Then quickly exit the kayak and pull it farther up out of reach of the next wave.

To launch, reverse the process. Place your kayak on the wash rock and wait for a wave to pick you up. Then paddle off the rock with the wave. This is a bit trickier than landing, because the initial force of the surge tends to push you farther up on the rock. It may be necessary to push off with your hands when the wave first hits. Be ready to do a balancing act if you don't quite make it off the rock. A seaweed-covered rock is easy to slide off, even without a wave.

An alternative to the seal launch is to toss the kayak into the water, jump in, and enter using a scramble rescue (if you have a closed cockpit-kayak; if a sit-on-top, just climb on). The scramble rescue is described in Chapter 5.

To practice seal landing and launching, find a smooth wash rock with gentle surging waves. Ride the surge back and forth, on and off the rock. Do this over and over, until you can time it perfectly. Then practice some more on a rock or ledge that is higher out of the water, with slightly larger waves washing up. Once you master this technique, you can land almost anywhere in rock gardens.

Piercing Waves

You may find yourself in a situation where you have to cross an area in the rocks that is exposed to breaking waves. The first decision to make is whether you can handle the waves. If you judge them to be too powerful to punch through, seek another route. However, if the waves aren't too large, there is a technique you can use to paddle efficiently across the surf.

The problem you are faced with is that you will be paddling sideways to the waves, so that when a wave hits you on the beam, it can push you toward shore or into a rock. The solution is to pierce each wave at an angle as it hits you. This means you will have to make a slight course adjustment as each wave arrives, *then resume your original course.* Do this as follows: Begin paddling on course with good forward momentum, keeping an eye on the waves. Just before

1 – **3** Seal launch.

a wave hits you, perform a powerful sweep stroke on the *shoreward* side, turning the bow into the wave. Continue paddling as you pierce the wave, then perform a sweep stroke on the *seaward* side to bring the kayak back on course. Continue paddling forward. The net result is a zigzag course; you "zig" to pierce the wave, then "zag" back on course.

The single most important part of this tactic is to hit the wave with plenty of forward momentum; *don't stop paddling.* The sweep stroke is incorporated into your forward strokes without pause. Be sure to turn the boat right back on course after piercing the wave; otherwise you will be heading out to sea, instead of where you want to go. Heading out too far may put you into the impact zone of larger waves.

You can practice piercing waves in the surf zone. Paddle along shore in the soup, parallel to the waves. As you move along, turn slightly into each wave to prevent being side-surfed, then continue on course. Try to remain the same distance from shore. Once you can do this, you'll have a lot more control when paddling across the waves in rock gardens.

Side-Slipping

When riding surge or paddling through a rock passage or a sea cave, it is often necessary to move a short distance sideways to avoid hitting a rock or scraping along a rock wall where the passage narrows. This can be accomplished with a side-slip maneuver, using a *static draw* stroke. Because this stroke is rarely taught, I'll describe it here.

Paddle forward until you have gained some speed, then twist your torso slightly to one side and place your paddle in the water next to your hip, holding it vertically with the working blade (the one in the water) *parallel* to the kayak and the power face toward the boat; the paddle blade should be knifing through the water with little resistance as the boat moves forward. This is the standard draw stroke position; the shaft is nearly vertical, with both hands out over the water. Now twist the shaft to open the blade (turn the leading edge of the blade outward with power face forward) *slightly*, about 2–3°. The blade will grab some water and pull the kayak sideways toward it. If you place the paddle on your right, you'll side-slip to your right. Hold the paddle in position until you have side-slipped the desired amount.

This stroke is extremely useful for making fine course adjustments when paddling in areas

JIM KAKUK

Always be ready to pierce waves when paddling in rock gardens.

Boat control is second only to good judgment to help insure your safety when paddling in rock gardens and sea caves.

Key Points for Paddling in Surf

- Learn in small surf, working up gradually to larger waves.

- Learn to recognize and handle different wave types: Spilling, plunging, surging, dumping.

- Beware of large, steep dumping shorebreak with no soup zone.

- Look for relatively protected beaches to launch and land.

- Watch the waves closely before paddling into the surf.

- When launching, time it to avoid the impact zone.

- If you do encounter a large breaker while launching, paddle hard with lots of forward momentum to punch through.

- Tilt your kayak *into* the wave when side-surfing.

- Keep all brace strokes low, with a horizontal paddle shaft.

- Learn to surf and to ride the top of a wave under control.

- The "surf and broach" technique is a very useful landing method for sea kayaks in most surf zones, except for dumping shorebreak.

- The "top of the wave" landing is used for dumping surf.

- Use surf etiquette to avoid collisions; always be aware of other surfers.

- Your surfing skills are not adequate until you are having fun in the surf.

where you have to maneuver through and around rocks. It can mean the difference between smashing into a rock and moving freely through the water. Once you have mastered the stroke, you'll find yourself using it all the time. By moving the blade toward your bow or stern, you can convert the side-slip to a bow or stern draw. Because this is a static stroke (the paddle is held in one position), the kayak has to be in motion for it to work.

Back-Paddling

There are a number of situations where you need to back-paddle in the rocks. Sometimes it is necessary to back off a wave at the last second, using backstrokes. You may need one or two backstrokes to stay on top of a wave or a surge when riding over rocks. If you paddle down a narrow corridor and don't have room to turn around, you must back out. Whenever you anticipate this situation, it may be better to back in, so you are facing the oncoming waves when you want to paddle back out.

The most common situation where back-paddling is necessary is when paddling into a narrow sea cave. By backing in, you can keep an eye on incoming waves and stay in better control when a wave set washes in. Backing in also allows you to paddle out quickly, if necessary. Even if you judge it safe to paddle in forward, it will be necessary to back-paddle in order to hold position when waves surge in.

You can practice back-paddling anywhere. Strive for an efficient back stroke and good directional control.

All of the techniques described above are essential skills that will help you paddle in rock gardens under control. Boat control is second only to good judgment to help insure your safety when paddling in rock gardens and sea caves. The greater the wave action, the more important boat control becomes. Practice these techniques and you'll be well on your way to mastering ocean rock-garden kayaking with a high degree of safety.

Summary

Once you have gained some experience and skill at handling surf and paddling in rock gardens, a whole new world of sea kayaking will be open to you. There are many thousands of miles of relatively untouched open coastline around the world. Rocky, uplifted coasts with extensive rock gardens contain uncounted hidden coves, caves, and other treasures awaiting your exploration. Prepare yourself to kayak in these areas safely.

Surf and rock gardens produce powerful ocean whitewater. The presence of breaking waves, surge, and rocks create potentially hazardous situations. The ability to judge waves and read the water is essential for your safety. The full range of sea-kayaking skills comes into play when paddling in surf or rock gardens. Important skills include *precise boat control, surfing skill, and a reliable Eskimo roll,* as well as the more specialized skills discussed in this chapter.

Your ability to paddle safely in surf and rock gardens will increase with experience. To gain such experience, you should start in small surf and relatively protected rock gardens. Then, work up gradually to bigger water. In general, ocean rock-garden paddling is best when the swell is small. Exposed rock gardens are dangerous in a large swell, even for experienced paddlers. Good surfing conditions depend on the type of wave (which is determined by bottom configuration), tide level, and size of the swell. Your skill level will determine the wave-size limit for you. Sea kayakers who want to cruise the open coast need to be able to handle a variety of wave types and to know which waves are too dangerous to deal with.

There are subtleties and tricks to kayak surfing and rock garden paddling beyond what is covered here. This book is focused mainly on safety issues, and the techniques described herein are related to safe procedure and basic survival. These techniques should be mastered first, then you will begin to discover some of the more advanced maneuvers that will further increase your enjoyment in surf and in rock gardens.

Key Points for Paddling in Ocean Rock Gardens

- Rock gardens are best when the swell is small.
- Practice all maneuvers in well-protected rock gardens; work up gradually to areas exposed to more powerful waves.
- Understand the difference between breaking and surging waves.
- Always *wait and watch* to see what the *largest* wave sets are doing.
- Look for sneak routes through the rocks and waves.
- Use *transition zones* (navigable passages) to get in and out of the rocks.
- Identify *safe zones*: areas protected from breaking waves and intense surge, usually behind emergent rocks and in deep water.
- Use positioning and timing to thread your way from one safe zone to another.
- Learn to ride the surge: Stay on top of the surging wave to clear rocks and maintain control.
- Learn to ride the surge onto a flat rock (seal landing) so you can land.
- Learn and use a static draw or *side-slip maneuver* to control trajectory through narrow passages and avoid rocks in your path.
- Beware of sea caves and arches with low ceilings.
- When surfing through rocks, make sure you have a clear path.
- Never get between a *breaking* wave and a rock or cliff.
- If you are pushed by a wave toward a rock, lean your kayak into the wave and present your hull to the rock. (This is not the same as being pinned against a rock by current in a river, in which case you lean into the rock).
- Usually back into narrow sea caves for better control when a wave set comes.
- Always stay alert, watch ahead, and plan your route accordingly.

CHAPTER 14.
RISK ASSESSMENT

Sea kayaking involves a certain amount of risk. The degree of risk varies considerably, depending on the kayaking domain and the conditions. Although risk cannot be entirely eliminated, it can be greatly reduced by knowledge of the kayaking environment, by exercising the judgment and skills outlined in this book, and by learning from your experience on the water. The first step is to be aware of the risks in any given kayaking situation, including the consequences of an error in judgment or a failure in technique. The next step is to stack all the odds in your favor by having as many reliable backups in place as possible (see "Backup Strategy," Chapter 8). Finally, you have to decide for yourself whether a risk is acceptable.

Many of the hazards involved and the skills needed to deal with them have been addressed in previous chapters. The focus here is on how to determine and manage the degree of risk in various sea-kayaking situations.

Stack all the odds in your favor.

Risk Management and Trip Planning

Sea kayaking risk depends on two main factors (assuming the proper equipment is being used).

- **Skill level:** The judgment, skill, and experience of the paddler.
- **Sea Conditions:** Sea state, weather, waves, kayaking domain.

For simplicity, "Skill Level" includes judgment, skill, and experience, "Sea Conditions" includes the entire range of potential hazards found in the kayaking domains defined in Chapter 2. I can now state the obvious:

- **Lower skill level = higher risk.**
- **More extreme conditions = higher risk.**

And the converse:

- **Higher skill level = lower risk.**
- **Milder conditions = lower risk.**

Both factors, skill level and sea conditions, must be considered together to determine the degree of risk. With a higher skill level, you can paddle in more difficult conditions without a significant increase in risk. For example, a skilled and experienced surf kayaker might be taking far less risk paddling in large surf than a novice kayaker paddling in small surf. The main goal in managing risk is to match your skill level to the conditions. To do this, you need to know how to judge the sea state, be able to predict potential changes in weather and sea state, and understand how different conditions will affect you, given your experience and skill level.

You must separate the factors you can control from those you can't. You have control over your training, skills, experience, and choice of equipment. You also have control over when and where you decide to paddle. You don't have any control over the weather and sea state. Since you can't control these factors, you need to learn all you can about the potential conditions you are likely to encounter, then make a decision about whether the risks are acceptable.

Let's take the Sea of Cortez in Baja, Mexico, as an example. This is a very popular sea-kayaking destination, but not all paddlers who go there understand the risks involved (I know I didn't on my first trip there). Most of the Sea of Cortez is protected from ocean swell, so large surf is not a risk factor, although you might encounter a steep shorebreak caused by local wind waves. The main risk is strong wind and, in some regions, tidal currents. During winter and early spring, powerful northerly winds up to 30 knots or more can arise with little warning. Because of the long fetch, large seas build up quickly when the wind blows. Tidal currents can be a major factor also, especially around the Midriff islands, such as Angel La Guarda.

If you plan a sea-kayaking trip to Baja in February, and you understand the risk factors described above, you can make some decisions regarding risk management. First, you need to face the fact that you will have to deal with wind and rough seas, and possibly tidal current. It would be a mistake to assume that you can simply get off the water the minute the

The main goal in managing risk is to match your skill level to the conditions.

wind starts blowing; a ready landing site may not be available, especially if you are paddling around a bluff with steep cliffs. Therefore, you must be sure your wind and rough water skills are in good shape. If you haven't had the opportunity to learn these skills, it would be wise to pick a calmer season to paddle in Baja. Also, you should have some experience dealing with current and tide rips. When the wind blows against the current, the entire sea can resemble one giant tide rip. If you are planning a long crossing out to an island, wind and rough water skills will be absolutely essential. You won't have the option of landing when you are 2 or 3 miles offshore.

Once you have determined the main risks involved, and know you are prepared to meet those risks, you can proceed with the trip, knowing you have reduced the risk factor to a minimum. In the example above, the main risk is getting caught out on open water in strong wind and rough seas, perhaps exacerbated by the wind against the tide. If you know from previous experience that you can handle 25–30 knot winds, you have practiced rescues in such conditions, and have a reliable Eskimo roll, you are ready to deal with the risk. To stack the odds further in your favor, you may decide to forgo any long crossings and plan your trip to go with the prevailing wind. However, you are prepared to handle the situation if the wind changes direction or you decide to do a crossing, after all.

Any time you plan a kayaking trip, whether it is a day trip or a long expedition, you must do enough research to gain a clear understanding of the potential risks. As is evident in the Baja example above, knowledge of the specific hazards involved is essential. This is the critical part of risk assessment. If you are planning a trip on the open coast of northern California, and haven't considered the risk of large surf, you are likely to get into trouble. In the Inland Passage of British Columbia, you need to be aware of tidal currents and weather patterns. Once you know the risks, make sure you have the skills and experience to handle them.

It would be a mistake to assume that you can simply get off the water the minute the wind starts blowing.

Rating the Risk

Several quantitative methods, similar to the class ratings for whitewater rivers, have been attempted to rate sea-kayaking conditions. For those not familiar with whitewater class ratings, *class 1* means easy conditions, *class 3* is moderately difficult, and *class 6* is extremely difficult and very dangerous. When applied to sea kayaking, such systems have shown varying degrees of success. The major problem is the fact that conditions on the open sea are subject to a wide range of variables and tend to *change rapidly*. For this reason, it is difficult to rate a certain stretch of water as *class 2* or *class 4* in the same way river rapids are rated. Using the Sea of Cortez as an example once more, when winds are calm, the paddling is *class 1* (very easy). However, the *class 1* conditions can change to *class 4* in a very short time if a powerful wind arises.

Eric Soares (co-founder of the Tsunami Rangers) has solved this problem to a certain extent by rating the *sea conditions*, rather than any particular stretch of coastline or body of water. His *Sea Conditions Rating System* (SCRS, Table 4) is probably the best rating system to date for sea kayakers. Even so, it must be used carefully. Plugging in numbers and coming up with a class rating is only part of the process of risk assessment. You still need to allow for the potential change in conditions and be aware of any specific hazards. Eric has pointed out that the SCRS is to be used as a general guide to the level of risk. It does not replace solid judgment and overall experience. Nor does it take into account freak incidents, such as sneaker waves, or sudden changes in conditions.

One of the strengths of the SCRS is that it highlights the numerous factors that a sea kayaker must take into consideration, especially when paddling in the ocean (the primary kayaking domain for which the SCRS is designed). These include factors that have been discussed throughout this book, including wind, fog, water temperature, wave height, surf, and rocks. Tidal currents aren't included, but can be factored in under *miscellaneous.*

An easy way to use the SCRS is to note that for every 20 points, the class rating increases by 1 (e.g., a total score of 40 = *class 2*). Also note that it is necessary to *include all relevant factors* to get an accurate result; you can't look at any one factor in isolation. For example, a 40 mph gale-force wind might appear to rate only *class 2* (40 points). However, when you add in the other factors that accompany such a wind, the rating increases. A 40 mph wind will create waves, some of which may break. Let's say the waves are 5 feet in height (the waves could be much larger,

One of the strengths of the SCRS is that it highlights the numerous factors that a sea kayaker must take into consideration.

TABLE 4. Sea Conditions Rating System

Factor	Computation	Maximum Points	Score
1. Water temperature	1 point for each degree < 72° F	40	_____
2. Wind speed	1 point per mph wind speed	50+	_____
3. Wave height	2 points per vertical wave foot	40+	_____
4. Swim distance	1 point per 100 meters	20	_____
5. Surf zone	30 points if waves are breaking	30	_____
6. Rock garden	20 points if rocks are present	20	_____
7. Sea cave	20 points if entering a sea cave	20	_____
8. Night	20 points if paddling at night	20	_____
9. Fog	Up to 20 points if fog is dense	20	_____
10. Miscellaneous	10 points or more for danger	10+	_____
		Total Points	_____
	Divide total points by 20 to obtain	**Class Level**	_____

ERIC SOARES

depending on the fetch). That adds 10 points. The waves that break probably won't have the force of breaking surf, so instead of adding 30 points for this factor, make it 10 points. Now add another 20 points for swim distance because you are on open water, well offshore. If the water temperature is 62 degrees, add 10 points. Adding all this up gives a score of 90 points, which means *class 4+* conditions, requiring advanced paddling skills.

When dealing with strong wind, I would also suggest adding in some miscellaneous danger points for difficulties in boat control, communication, rescues, and potential mental and physical exhaustion. This could bump the above example with 40 mph wind up to *class 5*. If you have ever paddled in a gale-force wind on the open sea, you wouldn't find this rating unreasonable.

After using the SCRS for awhile, you'll probably find that you don't have to add up all the

Class Level Explanation

Class 1: Easy, flat water conditions; suitable for beginners close to shore.

Class 2: Moderate conditions; intermediate skills required, including rescues.

Class 3: Difficult conditions; intermediate to advanced skill required. Eskimo roll essential.

Class 4: Very difficult to extreme conditions; advanced skills essential; loss of life possible.

Class 5: Very extreme, demanding conditions; expert skills essential; life-threatening.

Class 6: Nearly impossible conditions; team of experts only; loss of life probable in a mishap.

numbers every time you go paddling; instead, you'll be able to rate the conditions more intuitively. Even if you are not into number crunching, the real merit of this system is that it forces you to assess all the important factors you may face on the sea. For more information on the SCRS, see the book *Extreme Sea Kayaking* by Eric Soares and Michael Powers.

Bailout Potential

Bailout potential is the ability to get off the water, or to a safe place on the water. For example, if there is a beach with an easy landing nearby, or you can get to a protected cove, you have a bailout if conditions get beyond your skill level. If you are on a long open-water crossing, or paddling along a shoreline with steep cliffs and no landing sites, you have no bailouts and will have to deal with whatever conditions confront you.

Depending on the specific risk factors, an easy bailout will reduce your risk considerably. For example, paddling close to shore in a strong onshore wind involves very little risk (assuming the shore provides easy landings). Even if you capsize and lose the kayak, you will be blown ashore, where you can retrieve your boat. Paddling 3 miles offshore in the same wind blowing out to sea would be much more dangerous. This is a critical concept to keep in mind when planning trips or designing training scenarios (Chapter 16). You can push your limits significantly if you have an easy bailout at hand. If you are likely to encounter strong wind or other challenging conditions, the risks will be reduced if there are numerous opportunities to get off the water. When planning a trip of any length, locate all potential bailouts along your route so you know your options if you need to get ashore.

On long crossings, you will not have any bailouts readily available. However, even on a crossing, be prepared to alter course or turn around, if it will help get you out of a bad situation. For example, if there is an island or a peninsula close by and downwind, you should be aware of it as a potential bailout.

Kayaking Domains

A good general approach to risk assessment is to recognize the specific risks associated with a given domain. Although any stretch of water is sub-

> **Depending on the specific risk factors, an easy bailout will reduce your risk considerably.**

ject to changing conditions that can influence the degree of risk, certain domains will be subject to a greater range of hazards than others. For example, a coastline exposed to the open ocean carries more risk factors than a small estuary protected on all sides from wind and waves. Some specific hazards associated with each kayaking domain (also see Chapter 2) are described below, along with ratings based on the SCRS.

Protected waterways, such as lakes and slow-moving rivers, provide the least amount of risk and are reasonably safe for beginning paddlers. They are not entirely hazard-free, however. Some of these waterways are crowded with power boats and jet skis. Moderate to strong wind can create problems, even on a small lake. In cold water, hypothermia is a possibility if you capsize and cannot reenter the kayak. Most of these risks can be managed easily by learning basic kayaking skills, watching the weather, and staying clear of heavy boat traffic. Using the SCRS, conditions in protected waterways are mainly *class 1*, with the potential to range up to *class 2* during foul weather.

Inland marine waterways are subject to the same risks as lakes and large rivers, with the additional hazards of tidal current and tide rips. The combination of wind and current can create difficult conditions for a beginning paddler. Gale-force winds are also a possibility. Although inland marine waterways are protected from ocean swell and landings are easy, the risk is somewhat increased in areas where shoreline access is difficult or impossible. Conditions are mainly *class 1* to *class 2*. *Class 3* conditions are likely when dealing with tide rips and moderate wind. *Class 4* conditions are unlikely, except during storms.

Large bays or inland seas, and open water crossings of 3 miles or more, are subject to strong wind and relatively large, steep seas. Strong tidal currents are also possible. The main risk is a lack of bailouts on a long crossing, especially if conditions become unmanageable. *Class 2* conditions are the norm, with a good possibility of *class 3* when wind, current, and distance from shore are factored in. *Class 4 to 5* conditions are possible when several hazards are present at once. For example, a storm with gale-force winds, coupled with strong tidal current and steep seas, would certainly rate *class 4* or higher.

On the *open ocean*, hazards include strong wind, fog, large waves, steep seas, and, in shallow

When planning a trip of any length, locate all potential bailouts along your route.

areas, breaking waves. Protected landings may be scarce or nonexistent. All these risks can be managed with the appropriate skills and experience. Sea conditions vary greatly on the open ocean, ranging from *class 2* up to *class 6*. On the average, ocean paddlers need to be very comfortable in *class 3* sea conditions. A major storm would result in *class 5* to *class 6* conditions.

The main hazards in *surf and ocean rock gardens* result from breaking waves. Some waves are more dangerous than others, depending on size and type of wave. Reefs, rocks, and sea caves, combined with large waves, can present considerable risk when kayaking in rock gardens. Paddling in surf and rock gardens requires advanced kayaking skills, considerable experience, and good judgment. Almost any surf zone rates at least *class 2*. Medium to large surf is at least *class 3*, and powerful surf with very large waves is usually *class 4* to *5*. Large surf often requires some miscellaneous danger points added in, due to such hazards as powerful rip currents and steep, pitching waves. Most ocean rock gardens rate at least *class 3*, especially if breaking waves are present. Only the most protected rock gardens will rate as low as *class 2*. If the swell is large, most rock gardens rate *class 4* or higher, depending on exposure to the waves.

Some waves are more dangerous than others.

You can make reasonable decisions regarding the risk, based on the sea-kayaking domain. It is important to know the complete range of possible conditions and be prepared to handle the more extreme conditions you are likely to encounter. As a beginner, you can manage risk well by staying in relatively protected waters (*class 1* to *2*) with bailouts close by. As your skills advance, you can start paddling in more exposed waters.

Conclusion

Assessing risk is a major part of sea kayaking. It is essential to understand all the potential risk factors in the kayaking domain in which you are paddling. Until you are certain you understand and can manage the risks in any given area, make sure you have a bailout close by. Also be sure you have the necessary backups, including rescues, before venturing out on the water.

Once you understand the risks, you need the appropriate skills to deal with them. It is not enough to simply identify various risks and try to avoid them.

The most important part of risk management is to be prepared to handle the entire range of potential hazards in any particular kayaking situation.

Assessing risk is a major part of sea kayaking.

MICHAEL POWERS

Assemble a group of trusty companions for your seagoing excursions.

CHAPTER 15.
GROUP SAFETY
THROUGH TEAMWORK

Most kayakers prefer to paddle with other kayakers, for both social and safety reasons. Although paddling with others is usually safer than going solo, there are some safety issues that a group of sea kayakers must confront. One issue is the myth regarding "safety in numbers." Some paddlers tend to push way beyond their skill level in the mistaken belief that the more experienced members of the group can take care of them if something goes wrong. The fact is, each and every kayaker must paddle his own craft. When conditions deteriorate, paddlers tend to get separated and lose communication with one another. When this breakdown reaches an extreme, everyone must look out for themselves.

A kayaker who gets into trouble through lack of skill or experience can compromise the safety of the entire group. For example, if someone wanders into the rocks and gets hammered by a wave, the group may be confronted with a dangerous rescue scenario. If one or more paddlers have problems handling strong wind and rough seas during a crossing, the rest of the group will need to work out a tow system, possibly putting everyone at risk. This is especially true when the entire group is paddling near the limits of their skill and endurance.

Nevertheless, there are ways to increase your safety by paddling in a group. The best method is to use *teamwork*. Just how you apply teamwork depends on the type of group and the skill level of the paddlers. I'll start by describing the ideal situation: How a group of experienced kayakers, who all know one another, apply the team concept when paddling together. Then I will discuss how other types of kayaking groups can apply the team concept.

A kayaker who gets into trouble through lack of skill or experience can compromise the safety of the entire group.

The Team Concept

We were on the third day of a week-long Tsunami Ranger outing on a remote stretch of the Lost Coast in northern California. The beach we wanted to land on was typical for this area—steep, with large dumping surf. Without any discussion we all paddled to the north end of the beach, where the waves were smallest. Dave Whalen volunteered to land first. No one argued with him. We were glad to let him be the probe.

After Dave landed successfully, the rest of us quickly followed, one at a time. We each chose the wave we wanted and rode in high on the crest to avoid getting crushed. As each of us landed, those already on shore helped out, pulling each boat to higher ground. The fully loaded double kayak came in last and we all grabbed it and ran it up the beach to safety. There were 6 of us, and the whole operation took less than 10 minutes. No prior discussion was needed, and we didn't have to tell anyone what to do. We just did it.

The operation just described is an example of kayak teamwork, when everything falls into place.

Using teamwork will increase your safety and promote camaraderie.

Landing loaded kayaks in a steep shorebreak could have had disastrous consequences. We were able to accomplish the landing efficiently because we were all experienced with surf and were able to read the conditions. No discussion was needed because we knew one another's skill level and were aware of what had to be done to get ashore safely. Of course, any team will occasionally suffer failures in communication or make mistakes (e.g., see the story in Chapter 6). However, even when things go wrong, the use of teamwork can usually resolve the situation.

Although any group of kayakers can use teamwork to some extent, a group is not always a team. A kayaking team is two or more competent paddlers who function smoothly together to accomplish a common goal. The goal may be to do an 8-mile crossing to an island, explore a sea cave, go surfing, launch or land through the surf, circumnavigate an island, play in a rock garden, paddle and camp on the coast for several days, or mount a major expedition. Many groups share similar goals; the difference is in how the goals are accomplished. With teamwork, a group of experienced kayakers can function efficiently, with a high degree of safety. Lacking teamwork and experience, a group may fall apart, get into trouble, or wisely abandon the goal if conditions get too difficult. So what does it take to function as a team?

The team concept is firmly anchored to the ideas that each team member is fully competent for the task at hand, is entirely self-sufficient, and knows the strengths and weaknesses of the other members. Each member can also fill any necessary role, but may specialize in one or two roles, such as lead paddler or navigator. There must also be shared awareness, good communication, and a common mission. Each paddler knows where the others are and what the overall plan is. The paddlers might not always be within sight of one another, but they know whether someone is behind or up ahead.

Competence and Self-sufficiency

For a kayaking group to function as a team, each member must have the necessary skills and be able to operate without relying on the other members. This need for self-sufficiency may seem contrary to the idea of a team. However, as has already been pointed out, your safety as a kayaker depends on your ability to handle your own kayak. A group of paddlers with widely varying skill levels cannot

> **A kayaking team is two or more competent paddlers who function smoothly together to accomplish a common goal.**

function well as a unit; it has too many weaknesses. Only when everyone in the group has the appropriate skills for the situation can they work together as a team, taking advantage of the increased safety of paddling with other competent kayakers. If it is necessary to split up or impossible to keep the larger group together, everyone can function individually or in pairs.

Part of teamwork is knowing your teammates. Each paddler should be aware of the skill level and temperament of the other paddlers in the group. This will reduce the need for long discussions on the water and make it easy to be decisive when a change of plans is necessary. For example, if you know everyone is capable of a surf landing, it won't be necessary to wonder who can or cannot land when you arrive at a beach with surf. It will also be easier to stay in communication if everyone has the skills to handle the conditions.

Communication

Communication and awareness are crucial team concepts. Every member of the team needs to know where the others are and how to communicate when necessary. The most effective way to communicate on the water is with hand or paddle signals. These signals should be *simple, easy to use, and clearly understood by everyone*.

There is no official set of signals for kayakers at present.

There is no official set of signals for kayakers at present. However, several signals are conventionally used and understood by most paddlers. A *raised vertical paddle or arm* usually means to gather around the paddler giving the signal. It can also mean "go now" in certain cases. A *raised horizontal paddle or raised fist* means stop and hold position. Holding position does not always mean you stop paddling; in wind or current you'll have to point your bow upwind (or upstream) and paddle just hard enough to stay in one place. A *waving paddle or arm* is usually understood to be a distress signal; use this if you need help. *Patting the top of your head with one hand* means "are you okay?" The same signal is returned if the paddler is okay; otherwise it is assumed there is a problem. For general safety purposes, these are probably the only signals you really need. Many other signals (e.g. "let's land", or "let's eat") and responses ("okay", or "no way") can be used by the team, as long as they are agreed on ahead of time.

Note that both hand and paddle signals are used. It is important to be able to use either the paddle or your hand (arm) for each signal. The paddle works best when signaling from a greater distance. However, in some cases it is easier and more efficient to use a hand signal. In strong wind you may not want to lift your paddle high in the air. Also, if you lose your paddle, you obviously will need to use a hand signal.

These signals are very effective. Don't forget to use them. On many occasions, when conducting instructor workshops, I've watched a kayaker leave the group to chase down a wayward paddler, when a shout, followed by a paddle signal, would have done the job.

An audio signal (shout or whistle) should be used to *gain attention only*, followed by the visual signal. Some groups use a specified number of whistles to communicate (e.g., two blasts mean stop, three blasts mean trouble, etc.). The problem with this system is that it won't work very well in wind, rough seas, or breaking waves. It is too hard to hear exactly how many whistle blasts have been sounded. This is a prime example of a technique that can break down in difficult conditions, just when you need it the most. The combination of an audio signal, followed by a *visual* signal works best in rough conditions.

Awareness is a very important component of communication. If you aren't paying attention, you won't hear or see any kind of signal. Even worse, you can lose all contact with your partners if you just paddle off willy-nilly, without checking to see what the rest of the group is doing. When paddling near the front of the group, be sure to look behind you periodically to see if anyone is being left behind. If you are in the rear of the group and are falling behind, signal those in front to stop or slow down. A good team will tend to stay together naturally because everyone is aware of everyone else.

A team can use communication for specific tasks that enhance the safety of the entire group. For example, when paddling through a rock garden with blind passages, one paddler (the probe) can move ahead while the rest of the team awaits her signal. If the passage appears safe, the probe will then signal for the team to proceed. If she comes back with a look of terror on her face, giving a signal to stop or retreat, the team will know to look for a different route.

If you aren't paying attention, you won't hear or see any kind of signal.

Knowing the Plan

The ideal sea-kayaking team has no followers. Everyone knows where they are going and how to get there. This is in contrast to a guided trip, where the trip guide is responsible for leading the others on a particular route. The team has considerably more flexibility because all members are experienced kayakers and know how to navigate. If a team member does get separated, he will be able to function on his own, and will know where the rest of the group is going. This is an important safety factor that is not available to a guided trip of beginners.

Part of knowing the plan is having the ability to change the plan. Knowledge of potential bailouts (discussed in the previous chapter) and knowing how to find them is needed when the change of plan involves getting off the water quickly. In other cases, the change of plan may be to change the route or to land on a different beach. A good team can make these decisions easily and efficiently. This flexibility is very important in sea kayaking and will increase your safety and your fun. Such flexibility is easy for the solo paddler; it also needs to be incorporated by a group.

Knowing the plan is having the ability to change it.

Structure

Many paddlers will assume that a "kayaking team" implies a highly structured situation. Just the opposite is true: *A good kayaking team needs little or no structure* when paddling in average conditions. This is because all the paddlers are fully capable on their own, yet maintain an awareness of one another, as discussed above. However, when conditions get challenging (e.g., strong wind, paddling at night in large waves), staying in close contact becomes more important, yet more difficult. In these conditions the team will quickly and efficiently structure itself into a formation. Usually a lead and sweep paddler will be selected; hand signals (worked out ahead of time) can be used for this purpose, if necessary. A larger team may also add flanking paddlers. The whole idea is to keep the team together and in range for communication.

When using the "lead-sweep" formation, both lead and sweep paddlers must understand their roles. The sweep paddler remains at the rear of the group and *keeps watch* over the entire group. If a problem occurs, the sweep paddler immediately relays a signal to the lead paddler, via the other paddlers. Then the problem is dealt with. The sweep paddler should also signal the lead to hold up, if the group is getting too spread out. It is the responsibility of the lead paddler, at the head of the group, to *navigate* and to *keep the group together*. The lead paddler must periodically check behind her to make sure the group is not getting too spread out. She can then maintain a pace appropriate for the conditions and the overall strength of the group.

In really extreme conditions, such as a gale-force wind or large surf, a tight formation is likely to fall apart, or may not even be desirable. In this case, *each kayaker will team up with the closest kayaker* and continue paddling until the team can regroup. How the team reassembles depends on the situation. It may be a simple (but not necessarily easy) matter of reaching more protected waters around a rocky point or getting through a major surf zone. In rare cases, the team may not get together again until reaching their destination. They can rendezvous because all the paddlers are experienced enough to handle the situation and know where the destination is. Usually, two or three paddlers can stay together, even when it is difficult to keep a larger group together.

Mentoring

A good team of experienced paddlers can act as a mentor for a less experienced paddler, providing strong support and training. However, *the team will have to tailor its activities to the skill level of the less experienced paddler*. This is a key safety concept. If the experienced paddlers work together to pick suitable conditions, they can help a paddler push his limits and increase his skill level. The main purpose of a mentoring system is to help the learning paddler become part of the team, with the skills and self-sufficiency necessary to paddle safely. This is not the same thing as bringing along, on a trip, one or more less-skilled paddlers, who need to "follow the leader."

Advantages of Teamwork

By now it should be apparent that a kayaking team, as defined above, has many advantages. To highlight these advantages, I have contrasted (Table 5) a kayaking team of experienced paddlers with a less experienced group of paddlers who lack the

**TABLE 5. Contrast Between an Experienced Kayak Team and
A Group of Less Experienced Paddlers**

Experienced Team	Less Experienced Group
All members are self-sufficient; not necessarily equally skilled, but all have adequate skills.	Not all members are self-sufficient; some rely on others for guidance.
Members function in a coordinated fashion to achieve a common goal.	Members have different agendas, different goals.
Rigid structure not necessary due to experience and common understanding among team members.	Requires rigid structure for safety.
Team has a clear, concise method of communication on the water.	Group communication either does not exist or tends to break down when conditions get challenging.
Team members are fully cognizant of each other's strengths and weaknesses; they know each other well.	Group members are not fully aware of each other's strengths and weaknesses; they don't all know each other.
Each member knows what to do in a given situation without extensive discussion.	Everything must be spelled out in detail ahead of time.
Team responds quickly to unforeseen circumstances.	Group tends to fall apart or get into trouble when confronted with unplanned situations.
Team pushes the envelope by functioning together (whole is greater than the sum of its parts).	Group must back off from challenging situations to accommodate weaker paddlers (whole is less than the sum of its parts).
Team operates on a mentor system with training for less experienced paddlers on a one-to-one basis.	Group uses follow-the-leader guide mentality.
Weakest member is well-supported and able to push his or her limits.	Group is only as strong as its weakest member.

collective skills and experience to utilize the team concept fully.

Table 5 deals with two extremes; an ideal team on the one hand, and a group of relative beginners (perhaps led by a guide) on the other. There is plenty of gray area between the two extremes, and almost any group can use teamwork to some extent. You probably won't start out paddling with an ideal team, and most kayakers will find themselves paddling in a variety of groups. The rest of this chapter will discuss different types of groups, how to use certain aspects of teamwork in any group, and how to transform your own group of selected paddlers into a team.

Guided Trips

One purpose of this book is to help you learn how to have your own kayaking adventures, without the need of a trip guide. However, you might choose to get started in sea kayaking by joining a guided trip to get a feel for the sport prior to investing in the necessary equipment and training to paddle on your own. A guided trip is also a way to paddle in an exotic location when you lack the time or resources to plan your own trip.

If you are a beginner and decide to participate in a guided trip, take a basic course covering strokes and rescues before you go. Many outfitters advertise "no experience necessary." *Don't believe this nonsense.* Such statements are made to attract customers. None of these outfitters will tell you that you'll be better off without any experience. The fact is, you'll have much more fun and get more out of the trip if you know some basic paddle strokes and have at least a minimum amount of kayaking experience beforehand.

The guided trip is unique in that the group members are paying for the services of the trip leader. The leader shoulders most of the responsibility for safety and trip organization. This is in stark contrast to every other type of kayaking group, where members of the group are responsible for their own safety. On most guided trips the majority of the paddlers are beginners. This seriously limits where the group can paddle and requires a very rigid structure and good leadership. Trip leaders must be careful and conservative when planning trip routes. Bailouts are essential, and long crossings are too dangerous for beginners.

Using Teamwork on Guided Trips

Although the team concept cannot be utilized fully with inexperienced paddlers, some of the elements of a good team can, and should be, incorporated on a guided trip. This is largely up to the trip leader. A group formation with lead and sweep

One purpose of this book is to help you learn how to have your own kayaking adventures, without the need of a trip guide.

paddlers (as described under "Structure," above) can be set up to keep the group together. This will work as long as conditions are not too challenging. Don't expect to keep a group of beginners together in wind and rough water; it is essential to choose a route that minimizes the chances of having to deal with such conditions. Hand or paddle signals can be established for communication. The trip leader must be ready to make quick decisions for the whole group and must maintain control at all times.

On a guided trip, the group is engaged in a "follow-the-leader" situation, where the leader is responsible for everyone else, many of whom are inexperienced paddlers. This is the least desirable group situation, due to the presence of many weak links in the chain. It can be successful and reasonably safe only if the leader is very conservative about where she takes the group. Most guided trips should be conducted in protected waterways or inland marine waterways. There is no safe way to take a group of beginners out on the open sea in rough conditions.

Club Trips

There are numerous sea-kayaking clubs all over the world. These clubs provide many valuable services for kayakers and are a great asset to the paddling community. Most kayaking clubs are safety-oriented, and most conduct trips at many levels, from beginner to expert. The best clubs also organize training and practice sessions for their less-experienced members.

The group makeup varies considerably on club trips. On more challenging trips, the group may be composed entirely of experienced paddlers, who all know one another. Groups on easy trips may consist of beginners only. However, in most cases, the group will be a mix of paddlers (some of whom may be new to the club) with varying skill levels. This mix of paddling skills will make it impossible to implement all the teamwork concepts. The situation is a bit different from the guided trip, because on club trips many of the paddlers will be experienced, with their own agendas.

Some clubs do set up trips similar to the guided trip, with a clearly designated leader. However, most clubs prefer not to lay the responsibility onto one or two leaders. They recognize the flaws in this system (over-reliance on the leader and a false sense of security) and don't like the liability implications. Instead, most clubs expect trip participants to take responsibility for themselves. This is a move in the right direction because it encourages everyone to develop their kayaking skills, increasing their safety. It also moves the club trip closer to the team concept of self-sufficiency.

Teamwork on Club Trips

Many of the elements that go into making a good kayak team can be adopted on club trips, especially if the trips are tailored to the skill level of the participants. Paddle signals can be standardized, various group formations (e.g., lead-sweep formation, described above) can be used, and group awareness can be fostered. At the same time, over-reliance on the group should be discouraged, especially for new members, who may harbor the illusion that someone will take care of them, no matter what happens. Good teamwork requires the ability to perform rescues and watch out for each other. However, everyone's safety is compromised when the group has to look after several paddlers who are floundering in conditions way beyond their skill level.

Probably the biggest challenge to teamwork on club trips is the mix of paddlers, some of whom may not know one another. Even when all paddlers have the appropriate skill level, they may not share the same agenda. For example, on an open-coast trip, some of the group may want to explore rock gardens while others want to paddle offshore. One free spirit may wander off alone. To help assure the safety of the group, the agenda needs to be defined. In the example above, the group may decide to split into two pods, one to explore rock gardens, the other to take an open-water cruise. The free spirit may be allowed to take off, but he must notify the group and everyone needs to understand he is *no longer part of the group*; he is now a solo paddler. This is the kind of freedom a good team can have. Of course, the group may prefer to define a more rigid agenda that everyone should stick to unless circumstances dictate a change in plans.

The other common problem presented by the mix of paddlers on a club trip is the wide range in skill levels. If the range in skills is known, the trip should be tailored to the lowest skill level. If the range in skills is not clear, the group should proceed

Most clubs expect trip participants to take responsibility for themselves.

cautiously until skills can be assessed. Ideally, on the more challenging trips, everyone's skill level should be known to the group from the start.

Club trips can adopt the buddy system, where two or three paddlers team up when conditions get really difficult. You must understand how this system works. I've been on several trips where paddlers were asked to buddy-up before getting on the water. This will work only if the paddlers who are paired up are of similar strength and are willing to stick together, even when they don't need to. More often than not, the buddies end up separated after a short time on the water. A much more effective method is to *pair up with the nearest paddler* when conditions deteriorate and the group is drifting apart. This works for a couple of reasons. You'll have plenty of incentive to stay together under the challenging conditions and you are probably of similar strength, since you were paddling close together to begin with.

Many club trips are conducted with a large group of a dozen paddlers or more. Groups of this size can be unwieldy, especially in rough conditions. One common solution to this problem is to break a large group into two or more smaller *pods*. It is much easier to use teamwork and stay together in a smaller group. However, when conditions get really tough, it may be desirable to use the buddy system described above.

Paddlers on a club trip can certainly utilize teamwork to a reasonable extent. However, in most cases they will not be able to reach the "experienced team" level referred to in Table 5. The need to accommodate a wide range of skill levels on most trips makes it difficult to fulfill all the requirements of an experienced team. On a club trip, the group will usually require a slightly more rigid structure than the experienced team does; stronger paddlers must be prepared to look after weaker paddlers. However, the more a kayak club uses the team concept and promotes personal responsibility, the safer and more enjoyable its trips will be.

The more a kayak club uses the team concept and promotes personal responsibility, the safer and more enjoyable its trips will be.

Private Groups

Private kayaking trips with two or three friends probably allow the most freedom on the water and provide the optimal opportunity for applying the team concept. This is especially true if you are all at about the same skill level and know one another well.

The higher your skill level and the more experience you have, the more options you have, in terms of where and when to paddle. A small group of skilled sea kayakers can function safely together and have a lot of fun in conditions that might be too dangerous for a larger group of paddlers with varying levels of skill.

Although private groups enjoy a great deal of freedom, problems can occur when they are too loosely organized. Teamwork is effective only if you use it. When you go out with a group of friends on an "unofficial" trip, there is a tendency to toss the kayaks on the water and take off, without any real plan. Most of the time you can get away with this, especially if everyone is an experienced paddler. However, if you all go your separate ways, you are essentially paddling solo. If you want to paddle as a group, everyone should know the general plan and *pay attention* to others in the group. Agree on a set of hand or paddle signals and use them, when necessary. If you paddle together with the same group on a regular basis, you all can begin to function as a team.

Transforming Your Group Into a Team

If you want to increase your paddling skill, gain experience, and push your kayaking limits in the safest possible manner, you'll want to apply the team concept to the fullest extent. There are several steps you can take to achieve this.

First get a few of your paddling friends together and discuss your kayaking goals. Do you all want to push the envelope and start paddling in more challenging conditions? Do you want to start surfing or exploring ocean rock gardens? Would you be interested in an expedition along some enticingly remote coastline? Do you paddle together on a regular basis? Do you want to improve your paddling skills?

Discuss your kayaking goals.

These are all good reasons to consider kayaking as a team. You don't have to impose a rigid, formal structure, or set yourselves up as an elite cadre and never paddle with anyone else. You are simply going to apply some team concepts that will allow you to accomplish your goals with mutual support. This will be easier to do if you keep the team small at first. I suggest you start with three or four paddlers.

Once you have your team-to-be chosen, the first thing to do is get out on the water and work on all your skills. If one of you can roll, he should teach the others how. Give one another honest feedback on stroke technique. Practice rescues, including self-rescues. If necessary, get some expert instruction to address any basic skill deficiencies. Spend time paddling and gaining experience together. Remember, you cannot function well as a team until you are all reasonably competent paddlers. See Chapter 16 for more detailed training suggestions.

Whenever on the water with your team, maintain a high level of awareness. *Stay focused on where everyone in the group is and on how they are doing at all times*. This is probably the single most important ingredient of kayaking teamwork. Without this awareness, you cannot communicate effectively and will lose touch with one another. As always, you need to be aware of conditions on the water and stay sensitive to changes in weather, tide, and waves.

As you progress, work on your communication. Agree on a set of hand and paddle signals and *use them at every opportunity*. This may seem contrived at first, but you need to form a habit of communicating with one another. Then, when the unexpected happens, and you really need to communicate, you will get the message across.

Once you've mastered the basic paddling and communication skills, a good way to practice teamwork is to plan and execute various missions. For example, paddle to a surf zone and practice launching and landing as a group. Or practice exploring a rock garden (in safe conditions) using hand signals to guide one another. Another good exercise is to paddle in a predetermined formation (like a flock of birds) for as long as you can. Set up different rescue scenarios and practice them. The possibilities are endless. These exercises will help you develop paddling skills, awareness, and communication. Don't forget to have a good time. Maintain a sense of humor and enjoy yourselves.

After paddling together for a period of time, you will gain important knowledge about one another. You'll know one another's skill level, endurance, paddling strengths and weaknesses, fear threshold, and kayaking preferences.

The above ideas on forming a kayaking team can be summed up by the acronym **SACK:** Skills, Awareness, Communication, and Knowledge. If you work on these ingredients, you will begin to function as a team.

Use hand signals to guide one another.

Summary

You can increase your safety when paddling in a group if you employ teamwork. To use teamwork fully, the group must be composed of competent paddlers who remain aware of one another and maintain communication. Teamwork can be applied in various ways, depending on the type of group. Less experienced groups need a more rigid structure and have to paddle within the limits of the least-skilled members of the group.

Characteristics of a Good Kayak Team

- Experience and good kayaking skills
- Excellent group awareness
- Solid communication skills on the water in a wide range of conditions
- Knowledge of one another's skill levels and temperament
- Self-sufficiency
- Shared knowledge of the "plan"
- Flexibility: The ability to make quick decisions and change the plan if circumstances dictate
- Unit integrity: Ability to act as a unit, when necessary
- Common goals among team members

CHAPTER 16.
TRAINING

Skill development is the key to safe kayaking. Although experience and good judgment are equally important safety factors, you need to develop the necessary skills to enable you to gain experience, which in turn will allow you to develop good judgment. The only way to develop skills is to get out on the water and practice them. Although your skills will increase to some extent any time you go paddling, training sessions are the fastest way to master specific kayaking techniques. In a training session, you can practice each skill individually, and conduct drills to perfect your technique.

Another reason to train is to test strokes, rescues, and other techniques in a variety of conditions. Treat most of what you hear from "experts" and what you read in books (including this one) as working hypotheses, until you verify them for yourself. Don't *accept or reject* information until you have tested it on the water in more than one situation. For example, you may read somewhere that the way to land in the surf is to paddle in quickly, between waves. The first time you try this in a real surf zone and get overrun and crushed by a large breaker, you may consider another technique. But don't reject a technique before you have learned it well. If your roll fails you in a tide rip, that doesn't mean the roll is a worthless technique; it means you need more roll practice.

Many of the skills needed for paddling in different situations have been discussed throughout this book. In this chapter, I discuss how to go about learning paddling skills and developing them to the highest level. Obviously you must spend considerable time on the water, practicing every skill, from strokes to rescues. There is a logical progression that you can follow, starting with good instruction.

In a training session, you can practice each skill individually, and conduct drills to perfect your technique.

Opposite page: A good instructor will help you learn important basic skills.

Instruction

Many kayak shops offer quality instruction. There are also numerous kayak schools and independent instructors operating in most sea-kayaking areas. If you are just getting started as a sea kayaker, I suggest you take at least one comprehensive beginning class, covering basic strokes and rescues. After spending some time on the water, you can follow up with a couple of intermediate-level courses. If you've been paddling for a while and want to take your skills up a notch, you might consider getting some private instruction tailored to your needs. Here are several good reasons to get some instruction:

- Instruction is a short-cut to learning how to kayak; it would take a long time to discover many of the techniques on your own.

- Most kayaking skills are anti-intuitive; you need someone to help you train your mind and body to do something that doesn't come naturally. The Eskimo roll is a classic example. An efficient forward stroke is another.

- If you get some instruction early-on, you'll form good habits that you can build on; otherwise, you'll form bad habits that will be difficult to break.

- You need some instruction to paddle safely. You especially need to learn rescues.

- You'll have more fun if you learn enough to control the kayak and to paddle efficiently.

Taking Classes

When you take a kayaking class, you'll want to get the most out of it. The only way to do this is to *practice what you're learning*. Taking the class is only the first step in the process. If you don't *follow up and work on the skills* that you are introduced to in the class, you won't learn much. A lot of people do not understand this concept. Any kayak class you take, whether it is a beginning class on strokes or a kayak-surfing class, is just an introduction. A good instructor can show you how to perform some specific techniques, but *you* have to absorb the information and act on it. Taking the class will only give you the tools; you have to work with these tools and learn to use them by doing lots of paddling.

When you are first learning a skill, such as the forward stroke, you have to think about what you

If you don't follow up and work on the skills that you are introduced to in the class, you won't learn much.

are doing. You need to pay attention to each component of the skill. For example, with the forward stroke you need to know where the paddle enters the water, how long the stroke should be, how to end the stroke, how to rotate your torso, and so on. These are actions that an instructor can help you with. Then, over a period of time, if (and only if) you continue to practice the various forward-stroke components, they will coalesce into one smooth movement. Finally, you reach the stage where you can perform the stroke effectively *without thinking about it*. Only then have you learned it.

If you apply this learning process to all the kayaking skills, you will learn them very well. Some skills can be learned quickly, others take more time. Keep this in mind and you'll be less likely to get frustrated. Those who think they can learn a reliable Eskimo roll in one quick lesson will be sadly disappointed. However, if you realize that it takes time to develop the kinesthetic sense to perform a roll without thinking about it, you can persevere and eventually master it. The roll is an obvious example, but even the easiest strokes take time to perfect.

Throughout the learning process, don't lose sight of your true goal: to experience the magic of paddling a kayak. Every time you learn a new kayaking skill, or get better at a specific technique, you are bringing that magic closer. When you can coordinate all your strokes and balance the kayak in the waves, you will be dancing with the sea. This is an indescribable sensation that you have to experience to appreciate. Of course, as your skills develop, you'll also be safer and more relaxed out on the water, increasing your enjoyment.

To summarize, when you take a kayak class, you are embarking on a training program. The class is the initial step, where you learn what to do. Then you have to spend time on the water practicing the skills you were introduced to in the class. This is where the real learning takes place. If you don't follow up and practice, you will get very little out of the instruction.

Important Skills

Every sea kayaker should learn the basic propulsive strokes, corrective strokes, and rescues, both for performance and for safety reasons. Those who choose to paddle anywhere beyond calm, protected waters should also learn rough water skills

Don't lose sight of your true goal: to experience the magic of paddling a kayak.

(e.g., boat lean, bracing, Eskimo roll) and any techniques specific to the waters on which they paddle. For example, if you paddle in areas with tidal currents, you need to know how deal with current (see Chapter 11). If you paddle on the exposed coast, you need surfing skills.

All of the more advanced skills build on the basic strokes. So it makes sense to learn the basic strokes and boat control first. Then progress to paddling in rough water, surf, and other challenging situations. Below is a list of most of the important sea-kayaking skills, covering a wide range of paddling activities.

Basic Strokes

These strokes are described in most basic sea-kayaking texts and, except for the Eskimo roll, are taught in a comprehensive beginning class. To learn them, get some instruction, then practice the strokes every time you get on the water. Various applications for each stroke are listed below.

Propulsive Strokes

- **Forward Stroke:** Used to propel the kayak forward. This is the most-used stroke when cruising on the open sea. Efficiency and good form are important because you will take approximately one thousand forward strokes per mile. A powerful forward stroke is important in surf for quick acceleration and to punch through waves. In a strong headwind, an efficient forward stroke could mean the difference between making progress and going nowhere.

- **Reverse Stroke:** Used to back up or stop. The reverse stroke is not generally used to cover a great distance, but it has some very important applications, especially in surf and ocean rock gardens. In the surf, you will need a strong reverse stroke if you have to back off a wave or quickly back out of the impact zone. When entering a narrow sea cave it is usually safer to back in, so you can watch the oncoming waves. Sometimes it is faster to set up an assisted rescue by backing up than by turning around. Anytime you have to reposition yourself, it might be necessary to back up.

Corrective (Maneuvering) Strokes

- **Forward Sweep and Reverse Sweep Strokes:** Used to turn or correct course; the sweep stroke is most effective when combined with a boat lean (see below). The forward sweep stroke can be used to turn without losing much forward momentum. The sweep stroke is also a very efficient way to make subtle course adjustments in wind and rough seas. Using a combination of reverse sweep and forward sweep strokes, the kayak can be turned in place. In surf, sweep strokes can be used to reposition the kayak or turn on the wave.

- **Draw Strokes:** Used to move the boat sideways. There are several versions, including the static draw (described in Chapter 13). Many sea kayakers neglect the draw stroke because it isn't used much when paddling in open water. However, it is very important for overall boat control. When setting up a rescue, it is often necessary to move sideways. I've watched kayakers paddle around in circles, trying to get to a capsized boat, when all they had to do was move a few inches sideways. In rock gardens, the draw stroke is absolutely essential for positioning the kayak and for directional control in narrow passages.

- **Boat Lean:** This is not exactly a stroke, but is a basic technique used in combination with certain strokes (especially the sweep stroke) to sharpen turns and make course adjustments. It is also very important for balance in surf, rough water, and when bracing (see Chapter 8).

Capsize Prevention and Recovery Strokes

- **High and Low Brace:** Used to halt a capsize. Brace strokes are used in rough water and surf to help stay upright. (See Chapter 8 for a detailed description of brace strokes.)

- **Eskimo Roll:** Used to recover after capsizing. The roll is an important safety backup and is described in detail in Chapter 7.

Every time you get on the water, you'll get plenty of opportunity to work on strokes. If your kayak has a rudder or skeg, learn to paddle without using it. Save the rudder for paddling in strong wind. Even in the wind, practice paddling without the rudder so that you can handle the kayak if the rudder gets damaged. If you have a good boat design and have refined your stroke technique, you may find that you never really need the rudder. (For tips on paddling in wind, see Chapter 10.)

Rescues

The rescues described in Chapters 4–6 should all be learned and practiced. Initially, learn the side-rescue, T-rescue, and paddlefloat self-rescue. Once you can roll, learn the reentry roll. You need to be able to perform a rescue quickly and efficiently in rough water. Be sure to practice the rescues in a variety of conditions. If a rescue fails, you will find yourself in real trouble.

Intermediate to Advanced Paddling Skills

Once you can control your kayak in flat water with good stroke techniques and know the basic rescues, you are prepared to begin paddling in more challenging conditions. You don't have to wait until your strokes are perfect before you can paddle in rough water; just keep working on the strokes whenever you are kayaking. Learn the Eskimo roll; it will make the transition to surf and other rough water situations much easier and safer. However, with solid rescue skills, you can at least begin training with a couple of partners in wind and waves in a *safe location* (see below), even if you haven't mastered the roll yet. Include rescue practice in your rough-water training.

The following skills are valuable for paddling in rough water and poor weather:

- **Ability to handle wind**
- **Skill in current and tide rips**
- **Surf zone skills**

These are all important skills for sea kayakers who want to paddle in a wide range of conditions. It is a good idea to get some instruction, especially for surf kayaking. However, most of your learning will come from repeated training and paddling sessions. Start small, in easier conditions, then work your way up gradually to bigger water.

Training Site Selection

The point of a training session is to allow you to learn skills in a relatively controlled situation, before exposing yourself to a more dangerous environment, where you will have to rely on those skills. For purposes of training, you need to find a site that will provide a challenge with an *easy bailout*. Below are examples of good training sites for learning various skills.

Wind and Rough Water Skills

An area near shore with a prevailing *onshore* wind is the safest place to practice these skills. Ideally, the fetch will be fairly long so that the waves build up to at least 2 or 3 feet. This is a safe situation, because if something goes wrong you will be pushed onshore by the wind. Practice paddling in all directions relative to the wind and waves until you are comfortable kayaking in these conditions. At first, choose a day with relatively mild wind and scattered whitecaps. Later, go out in stronger wind.

Current, Tide Rips, and Rough Water Skills

A tide rip close to shore, with a large eddy nearby, is ideal for practicing eddy turns, ferrying, and surfing (if waves are present). Pick a gentle current of 2 knots or less for the first time out, then advance to stronger currents. Also make sure that there are no hazards downstream. A large river is a good substitute for a tidal stream.

Surf Zone and Rough Water Skills

A gently sloping beach with small waves and a well-defined soup zone is an ideal training situation for the novice. As your skills develop, look for larger waves. An easy swim into shore is the most important factor for surf training. Stay away from beaches with rip currents and large surf, until you have very strong surfing skills. Also beware of beaches with a steep shorebreak. To practice landing in dumping surf, find a beach with *small* dumping waves (about 2 feet high).

Ocean Rock Garden Skills

Look for a relatively protected rock garden, with easy access to shore, on a day when the swell is small. The ideal training site will have some shallowly-submerged rocks with gentle surging waves where you can practice riding surge and seal landings (see Chapter 13). As your skills develop, you can venture into rock gardens with larger waves. Consider it a training site only if you can swim to shore easily.

Rough Water Rescue and Rolling Skills

The best site for practicing rough water rescues is the same as that for "Wind and Rough Water Skills" above. However, rescues can, and should, be practiced in all the training sites described above. Be sure to use the rescue appropriate to the situation (for example, you wouldn't generally use a T-rescue in the surf). Rolling can also be practiced in all the training sites described. The surf zone is a very good place to work on a "combat roll."

If you spend time developing your skills in training situations, you'll be far more prepared when you have to face difficult conditions. This is especially important when such conditions arise with no easy bailout at hand. For example, if you are on a long crossing and the wind starts to blow, you'll be able to handle it, both physically and psychologically, if you have already trained in strong wind. When confronted with a surf landing on the open coast, you'll know what to do if you have spent time training in the surf. Notice that most of the training situations above allow you to work on rough water skills. The more you paddle in rough water, the better you'll be able to control your kayak and deal with whatever situation you encounter on the sea.

These training sessions are not only valuable for skill development; they can also be a lot of fun. Get some friends together and have a good time while you learn. Let yourself make mistakes, then figure out how to resolve them. That's the purpose of a training session.

Have a good time while you learn.

Learning Progression

Throughout this book, I have discussed many different kayaking techniques that are important to your safety and enjoyment on the water. Of course, you cannot learn to kayak by merely reading this, or any other, book. Kayaking is an activity that must be learned by *doing*. Although this book provides guidance and important information, your real learning will take place on the water. You will learn more quickly and efficiently if you use a logical learning progression. The following progression is designed for the sea kayaker who wants to learn to paddle in all sea-kayaking domains safely and with confidence:

1. **Take a beginning sea-kayaking class covering basic strokes and rescues.** Find a reputable kayak school or instructor and make sure the class you take is a *comprehensive* beginning course, offering both strokes and rescues.

2. **Practice strokes and rescues.** Get out and paddle as much as possible, in easy conditions at first. Schedule a couple of practice sessions with friends to work on assisted and self-rescues.

3. **Get a kayak.** In order to accomplish step 2, you need access to a kayak. You can rent one, but eventually you'll need your own kayak. With your own boat, you can go when and where you choose, and you can outfit the boat so that it fits you properly. You'll also get used to a particular kayak and can "grow into it," as you learn more skills.

4. **Learn and practice the boat lean.** Boat lean is used for so many purposes (turns and boat control, balance, bracing, rolling, surfing) that you should learn it as soon as possible (see Chapter 8 for description).

5. **Learn to use a tow line.** This is fairly simple. Go out with a couple of other paddlers and practice towing. Try the systems outlined in Chapter 9. As your kayaking skills increase, practice towing in wind and rough water.

6. **Keep paddling.** Go on as many trips as possible, within your skill level. Find a couple of partners or join the local kayak club.

7. **Learn basic navigation skills.** Take a compass on your trips and practice using it. Also take a chart and practice piloting with it. Look for ranges and use them.

8. **Practice in wind.** Work on strokes and rescues in an *onshore* wind, as described under training sites above.

9. **Learn the Eskimo roll.** The importance of the roll, both for safety and for the confidence

Kayaking is an activity that must be learned by doing.

needed for further skill development, cannot be overemphasized.

10. **Work on brace strokes.** You will probably learn rudimentary high and low braces right from the beginning. However, to be reliable, a brace needs to be automatic. The only way to really learn how to brace is to risk capsize. Once you can roll, it is much easier to work on braces, because you don't care if you capsize.

11. **Learn to surf kayak.** There is a progression to learning kayak surfing. Start with some basic instruction, then work on the surf skills outlined in Chapter 13, starting in small waves. Once you can handle a kayak in moderate surf, your overall skills and ability to handle rough water will soon take a quantum leap. Surf kayaking is the doorway to paddling on the ocean, in rock gardens, and in rough water anywhere.

12. **Practice paddling in current and tide rips.** This practice can be started before learning to surf, but surf skills will make it much easier to handle the rougher water. Surfing ability is especially useful when ferrying and when surfing waves in a tide rip. Practice all the skills outlined in Chapter 11.

13. **Practice paddling in ocean rock gardens.** You'll use almost all the skills above when paddling rock gardens. The two most important foundation skills for rock gardens are boat control and surfing.

The exact ordering of the progression above is somewhat flexible. For example, committed paddlers might learn to roll shortly after taking a beginning class, then immediately start training in wind and rough water or the surf zone. Others will proceed more gradually and remain in flat water for a year or more. If you live on the open coast, you might learn to surf before paddling on open water in the wind. Most paddlers will probably start paddling in rough water before perfecting all the strokes. However, keep working on the basic strokes until you master them. In time, you'll find yourself linking strokes until they merge into a single seamless technique, allowing you to control your kayak in every situation.

Be sure to consider your own goals. If your main goal is to paddle inland waterways and you have no intention of paddling out on the open sea in rough weather, then you can get by without the more advanced skills. On the other hand, if you are adventurous and want to go on long expeditions or play in surf and rock gardens with a reasonable degree of safety, you need to learn all the skills outlined above.

Putting It All Together

Learning to kayak takes time and commitment. Although there is a lot to learn if you want to be a safe and competent paddler, you can have a good time throughout the entire learning process. Don't lose sight of the fun factor; if you are working at learning too hard, or aren't having a good time, back off a bit and take it more slowly, or less seriously. Don't expect to do everything perfectly the first time. A positive mental attitude will help you learn faster. I have fond memories of my first few sessions in the surf and my first rolling attempts. Even though I was making lots of mistakes, the learning process was a joy in itself, especially when I began to have some success.

Pay attention to what is going on at all times, whether on a sightseeing paddle or a training session. When you discover a technique that works for a given situation, incorporate it into your repertoire. If something goes wrong, figure out why. As you gain experience and increase your skill level, you'll be free to explore and pursue your own adventures in a sea kayak. With the appropriate skills, you can do this with a high degree of safety. Once you get the basic skills down, the sea will be your best instructor.

Quick Review for Developing Skills

- Take classes from a competent instructor.
- Practice what you learn from the class.
- Be patient.
- Work on a skill until you can do it naturally, without letting your thought process intervene.
- Remember that basic strokes and boat control are the foundation for all other kayaking skills.
- Test all techniques in a variety of conditions.
- Practice rescues in wind and rough water to find out what really works.
- Look for good training sites where you can make mistakes without dire consequences.
- Learn all the necessary skills for the type of paddling you want to do.
- Set up a reasonable learning progression that allows you to build on your skills.
- Set goals and work toward them.
- Relax and learn at your own pace.
- Get on the water as much as possible, and have fun while you learn.

...the sea will be your best instructor.

GLOSSARY

The terms below are defined according to their usage in the sport of sea kayaking.

Bailout: An opportunity to get out of a difficult or dangerous situation. Examples of bailouts include: any easy landing, a protected cove, any accessible area of protected water.

Beaufort Wind Scale: A scale that describes the sea state at a given range in wind speed.

Boat Lean: A position allowing the kayak to be balanced on edge, tilted to the side; useful for carving turns and balancing in wind, rough water, and surf.

Bombproof Roll: A reliable Eskimo roll that won't fail in difficult conditions.

Boomer: A wave that breaks suddenly as it passes over a submerged rock or shallow area.

Bow: The front of a boat.

Bow Angle Method: Simple and effective technique used to determine the possibility of collision with an oncoming vessel.

Brace Stroke: A support stroke used to halt a potential capsize and right the kayak using the paddle blade as a temporary support combined with a swift lifting motion of the thigh (a hip snap).

Broach: To turn broadside to a wave, usually in surf or steep following seas.

Bulkheads: Interior partitions in the kayak that prevent flooding of the bow and stern when the cockpit is flooded (usually after capsizing and exiting the kayak).

Cascade (ocean): Temporary waterfall created by the rush of water over a rock ledge in response to a large surging wave.

Chart: A map showing coastlines, water depths, and other information of use to marine navigators.

Churn: Area in an ocean rock garden where water and waves surge around and between rocks. Also, any area enclosed on three sides by cliffs where waves reflect and interfere with each other, creating a churning effect.

Closed-Deck Kayak: Decked kayak with a relatively small cockpit opening in which the paddler sits. The cockpit is closed off with a sprayskirt, worn by the paddler.

Closeout Wave: A plunging wave that breaks at one time across a large section of the wave.

Combat Roll: An Eskimo roll that is reliable in a real situation, such as an unexpected capsize in the surf zone.

Course: A specific direction to a given destination. Also, the actual direction a kayak is moving.

C-to-C Roll: A type of Eskimo roll in which the kayaker moves the paddle to a position perpendicular to the axis of the kayak, then rolls up using a hip snap.

Dead Reckoning: Navigational technique in which course, speed, and time underway is used to deduce position.

Draw Stroke: A stroke used to move the kayak sideways.

Drift: Movement of kayak due to outside influences such as wind, waves, and current.

Dumping Surf: Plunging waves that break violently right at the shoreline.

Ebb Current: Current flowing out to sea in response to a falling tide.

Eddy: An area where the current is flowing contrary to the main current. Usually found on the downstream side of islands, rocks, points of land, or other obstructions. Often used by kayakers to rest or as a means to paddle against the main current.

Eddyline: A shear zone separating an eddy from the main current, sometimes marked by swirling countercurrents and whirlpools.

Eskimo Roll: A technique used to right the kayak after capsizing, without having to bail out of the boat.

Extended Paddle Roll: An Eskimo roll using the paddle in an extended position for extra leverage (also known as the Pawlata roll).

Ferry: Method of holding a course across the current by angling upstream.

Ferry Angle: The amount of angle into the current needed to hold a course across the current. The angle is measured between the desired course across the current and the heading needed to hold that course.

Fetch: Unimpeded distance across the water over which the wind can blow; a longer fetch allows the formation of larger waves.

Flood Current: Current moving inland in response to rising tide.

Following Sea: Waves moving from behind when traveling in a downwind direction.

Forward Stroke: Technique used to propel a kayak ahead.

Hatch: Port on deck needed to gain access to area sealed off with a bulkhead.

Heading: Direction the bow is pointed; may or may not correspond to the actual course, depending on influence of wind or current.

High Brace: Support stroke using the power face of the paddle blade.

Hip Snap: Movement of thighs and lower body to snap the kayak from a tilted position to a level position; used while performing an Eskimo roll or brace.

Hypothermia: Dangerous lowering of body temperature; kayakers are at risk of hypothermia when submerged in cold water without adequate clothing.

Impact Zone: Area where waves are breaking.

J-lean: See "Boat Lean."

Knot: A unit of speed; 1 nautical mile per hour.

Lead Paddler: Kayaker who takes the lead or point position in a group.

Low Brace: Support stroke using the back of the paddle blade.

Nautical Mile: 1 nautical mile = 1 minute of latitude = approximately 1.15 statute miles.

Ocean Rock Garden: Rocky coastal area exposed to ocean swell and surf.

Over the Falls: Falling off the front of a breaking wave.

Paddlefloat: Flotation device attached to the end of a paddle to be used as an outrigger for stabilizing the kayak during a self-rescue.

Parallel Rule: Device used to transfer a parallel line from the compass rose on a chart to determine direction.

Pawlata Roll: See "Extended Paddle Roll."

Peel Out: Dynamic turn out of an eddy; performed by paddling across the eddyline, then allowing the main current to turn the kayak downstream.

PFD: Personal flotation device, worn to help keep a swimmer afloat, especially in rough water.

Piloting: Navigation using visual landmarks for reference. The most basic form is navigation by line of sight (e.g., following a shoreline). Piloting can also include the use of ranges, aids to navigation (e.g., buoys), compass, and chart.

Plunging Wave: Steep breaking wave; the crest pitches forward, sometimes creating a tube.

Point Break: Area where waves break as they refract around a point of land or reef, in some cases at a considerable distance from shore.

Power Face: The side of the paddle blade that exerts pressure on the water when performing a forward stroke; the power face is usually concave to achieve a better grip on the water.

Range: Alignment of any 2 stationary objects; used to define a line of position, follow a course (by keeping the two objects in alignment), or determine sense of movement (by watching the relative separation of 2 objects, or of a single object relative to the background). Using ranges is probably the most important navigational technique available to the kayaker.

Reentry Roll: Self-rescue technique performed by reentering the upside-down kayak, then executing an Eskimo roll to right the kayak.

Reverse Stroke: Stroke used to paddle backwards in a kayak.

Rip Current: Seaward current created in a surf zone, especially off beaches with a steep slope or offshore sandbars; sometimes fed by currents moving parallel to the beach.

Rock Garden: See "Ocean Rock Garden."

Rules of the Road: A set of rules primarily designed to prevent collisions between watercraft.

Screw Roll: See "Sweep Roll."

Sculling Brace: Brace stroke performed by sculling (feathering) the paddle blade back and forth on the surface of the water to support the kayak.

Sculling Draw: Draw stroke performed by sculling the paddle back and forth with the blade in a vertical position, resulting in sideways movement of the kayak.

Sea: Closely-spaced, choppy waves created by local winds.

Sea Conditions Rating System (SCRS): Method of rating the sea conditions and relative difficulty for sea kayakers, based on all relevant factors. The SCRS was worked out by Eric Soares of the Tsunami Rangers.

Sea Kayaking: The act of paddling any kayak anywhere in the marine environment, or paddling a sea kayak in any body of water.

Sea Stack: Relatively large rock outcrop jutting up out of the sea; usually an eroded remnant of a former sea cliff.

Seal Landing: Method of landing a kayak on a rock or ledge by riding the surge up onto the rock.

Seal Launch: Method of launching off a rock by sliding into the sea or riding off on a surging wave.

Shipping Lane: Channel through which ships and other large vessels travel; shipping lanes are marked on marine charts.

Shorebreak: Waves that break right at the shoreline; referred to as dumping surf if the waves are plunging.

Side Slip Maneuver: Means of moving the kayak sideways while underway, using a static draw stroke.

Side Surf: Riding the face of a broken wave sideways, with the kayak tilted into the wave to keep the shoreward edge planing across the water.

Sit-On-Top Kayak: Kayak in which the paddler sits in a depression on deck, rather than in a cockpit.

Slack Current: Change in flow direction during the period between ebb and flood tide.

Sneaker Wave: Wave that is considerably larger than the average wave size; tends to take boaters by surprise, unless they are paying attention.

Soup Zone: Area of frothy whitewater in the surf zone, inshore of the main break.

Spilling Wave: Wave that breaks gradually over a gently-shoaling sea floor.

Sprayskirt: Waterproof neoprene or nylon device worn around the waist and used to seal off the cockpit of a closed-cockpit kayak.

Static Draw: Stroke used to shift the kayak in a sideways direction while traveling forward; paddle is held in vertical position, next to the hip with the power face of the blade facing and nearly parallel to the side of the kayak.

Stern: Back end of a boat.

Suck Hole: Area at the base of a rock or ledge where surging waves create a sudden and powerful reversal that can temporarily trap a kayaker.

Surf Zone: Area of relatively shallow water where waves break.

Surge: Waves that steepen and surge forward and back without breaking.

Sweep Paddler: Kayaker who takes the rear position in a group.

Sweep Roll: Eskimo roll performed by sweeping the paddle blade out in an arc along the surface of the water while performing a smooth hip snap to right the boat.

Sweep Stroke: A turning or corrective stroke, performed by sweeping the paddle in an arc from bow to stern; actually, the paddle blade is locked in position while the boat pivots around it.

Swell: Organized sets of smooth waves that move across the ocean after moving out of a storm center.

Throw Rope: A 30–50 foot length of floating line coiled into a bag that allows the rope to play out when tossed to a swimmer in distress; can double as a towline.

Tidal Current: Current created by the rise and fall of the tide; usually restricted to inland waterways or the mouths of lagoons and rivers.

Tide: The rise and fall of sea level in response to gravitational forces between the sun, moon, and earth.

Tide Rip: Rough water created when tidal current flows over shoals, underwater reefs, and through constricted areas.

Towline: 30–50 foot length of rope used to tow a kayak.

Treadmill: Strong wind or current that prevents forward motion when paddling into it.

Tsunami Rangers: Small, tightly-knit group of sea kayakers who surf and explore ocean rock gardens on the northern California coast.

Wash Rock: Partially-submerged rock over which waves surge.

Washover: Ledge or wash rock in the ocean with surging waves that resemble river rapids.

Wavelength: Distance of wave from crest to crest.

Wave Set: Group of 2 or more waves of similar size.

Weathervane: Tendency for some kayaks to turn into a side wind while underway.

Window: Period between larger wave sets when the sea flattens out, allowing a good opportunity to launch through the surf zone.

Windowshading: Capsizing swiftly when sideways in a breaking wave; may be followed by rolling up into the wave.

RESOURCES

Books

Bascom, Willard. *Waves and Beaches*. Garden City, NY: Anchor, 1964 (currently out of print).

Broze, Matt, and George Gronseth. *Sea Kayaker's Deep Trouble: True Stories and Their Lessons from Sea Kayaker Magazine*. Edited by Christopher Cunningham. Camden, ME: Ragged Mountain Press, 1997.

Burch, David. *Fundamentals of Kayak Navigation*. Chester, CT: Globe Pequot Press, 1999.

Diaz, Ralph. *Complete Folding Kayaker*. Camden, ME: Ragged Mountain Press, 1998.

Dowd, John. *Sea Kayaking: A Manual for Long Distance Touring*. Revised ed. Seattle: University of Washington Press, 1997.

Dutky, Paul. *The Bombproof Roll and Beyond*. Menasha Ridge Press, 1993.

Foster, Nigel. *Nigel Foster's Surf Kayaking*. Old Saybrook, CT: Globe Pequot Press, 1998.

Foster, Nigel. *Sea Kayaking*. Old Saybrook, CT: Globe Pequot Press, 1990.

Hutchinson, Derek C. *The Complete Book of Sea Kayaking*. 4th ed. Old Saybrook, CT: Globe Pequot Press, 1995.

————. *Derek C. Hutchinson's Guide to Sea Kayaking*. Old Saybrook, CT: Globe Pequot Press, 1990.

————. *Eskimo Rolling*. Camden, ME: Ragged Mountain Press, 1992.

————. *Guide to Expedition Kayaking on Sea and Open Water*. Old Saybrook, CT: Globe Pequot Press, 1995.

————. *Sea Canoeing*. 3rd ed. London, England: A.&C. Black Ltd., 1984.

Jeneid, Michael. *Adventure Kayaking: Trips from the Russian River to Monterey*. Berkeley, CA: Wilderness Press, 1998.

Johnson, Shelley. *Sea Kayaking: A Women's Guide*. Camden, ME: Ragged Mountain Press, 1998.

Mohle, Robert. *Adventure Kayaking Trips from Big Sur to San Diego*. Berkeley, CA: Wilderness Press, 1998.

Nordby, Will, ed. *Seekers of the Horizon: Sea Kayaking Voyages from around the World*. Old Saybrook, CT: Globe Pequot Press, 1989.

Romano-Lax, Andromeda. *Adventure Kayaking Baja*. 2nd ed. Berkeley, CA: Wilderness Press, 2001.

Schumann, Roger, and Jan Shriner. *Sea Kayak Rescue: The Definitive Guide to Modern Reentry and Recovery Techniques.* Chester, CT: Globe Pequot Press, 2001.

Seidman, David. *The Essential Sea Kayaker: A Complete Course for the Open Water Paddler.* Camden, ME: Ragged Mountain Press, 1992.

Skillman, Don. *Adventure Kayaking Trips in Glacier Bay.* Berkeley, CA: Wilderness Press, 1998.

Soares, Eric, and Michael Powers. *Extreme Sea Kayaking.* Camden, ME: Ragged Mountain Press, 1999.

Washburne, Randel. *The Coastal Kayaker's Manual: The Complete Guide to Skills, Gear, and Sea Sense.* Chester, CT: Globe Pequot Press, 1993.

Weintraub, David. *Adventure Kayaking Cape Cod and Martha's Vineyard.* 2nd ed. Berkeley, CA: Wilderness Press, 2001.

Videos

Ford, Kent. *Performance Sea Kayaking: The Basics and Beyond.* Kent Ford Performance Video and Instruction, 550 Riverbend, Durango, CO 81301.

Holman, Larry. *Sea Kayaking: Getting Started.* Moving Pictures, P.O. Box 566, Corte Madera, CA 94976-0566.

Lull, John, and Eric Soares. *Kayaking Ocean Rock Gardens: A Tsunami Ranger Guide.* John Lull, P.O. Box 564, El Granada, CA 94018.

Lull, John. *Surf Kayaking Fundamentals.* John Lull, P.O. Box 564, El Granada, CA 94018.

Soares, Eric. *Guide to Ocean Adventure Kayaking.* Eric Soares, P.O. Box 339, Moss Beach, CA 94038.

————. *Kayak Magic.* Eric Soares, P.O. Box 339, Moss Beach, CA 94038.

Paddling Organizations

American Canoe Association

7432 Alban Station Blvd., Suite B-226
Springfield, VA 22150-2311
703-451-0141
E-Mail: aca@acanet.org
Website; www.acanet.org

British Canoe Union

John Dudderidge House
Adbolton Lane
West Bridgford, Nottingham NG2 5AS
England

INDEX

ABOUT THE AUTHOR

John Lull has been sea kayaking since 1985 and has paddled extensively on the wild northern California coastline, the coast of British Columbia, and the Sea of Cortez in Baja, Mexico. He also is an avid surf and whitewater kayaker. John is an Instructor Trainer Educator in Coastal Kayaking for the American Canoe Association and a Commander in the Tsunami Rangers (an ocean whitewater kayaking team). He currently teaches for California Canoe and Kayak where he has been instrumental in developing a comprehensive sea kayaking program. John has also published kayaking articles for *Sea Kayaker Magazine*, and produced instructional videos on surf kayaking and paddling ocean rock gardens. John was born and raised in Oakland, California, and now lives in the coastal town of El Granada, 30 miles south of San Francisco.

JIM KAKUK